ROUTLEDGE LIBRARY EDITIONS: LIBRARY AND INFORMATION SCIENCE

Volume 73

THE REFERENCE LIBRARIAN AND IMPLICATIONS OF MEDIATION

THE REFERENCE LIBRARIAN AND IMPLICATIONS OF MEDIATION

Edited by
M. KEITH EWING AND ROBERT HAUPTMAN

LONDON AND NEW YORK

First published in 1992 by The Haworth Press, Inc.

This edition first published in 2020
by Routledge
2 Park Square, Milton Park, Abingdon, Oxon OX14 4RN

and by Routledge
52 Vanderbilt Avenue, New York, NY 10017

Routledge is an imprint of the Taylor & Francis Group, an informa business

© 1992 The Haworth Press, Inc.

All rights reserved. No part of this book may be reprinted or reproduced or utilised in any form or by any electronic, mechanical, or other means, now known or hereafter invented, including photocopying and recording, or in any information storage or retrieval system, without permission in writing from the publishers.

Trademark notice: Product or corporate names may be trademarks or registered trademarks, and are used only for identification and explanation without intent to infringe.

British Library Cataloguing in Publication Data
A catalogue record for this book is available from the British Library

ISBN: 978-0-367-34616-4 (Set)
ISBN: 978-0-429-34352-0 (Set) (ebk)
ISBN: 978-0-367-42514-2 (Volume 73) (hbk)
ISBN: 978-0-367-85320-4 (Volume 73) (ebk)

Publisher's Note
The publisher has gone to great lengths to ensure the quality of this reprint but points out that some imperfections in the original copies may be apparent.

Disclaimer
The publisher has made every effort to trace copyright holders and would welcome correspondence from those they have been unable to trace.

The Reference Librarian and Implications of Mediation

M. Keith Ewing
Robert Hauptman
Editors

The Haworth Press, Inc.
New York • London • Norwood (Australia)

The Reference Librarian and Implications of Mediation has also been published as *The Reference Librarian*, Number 37 1992.

© 1992 by The Haworth Press, Inc. All rights reserved. No part of this work may be reproduced or utilized in any form or by any means, electronic or mechanical, including photocopying, microfilm and recording, or by any information storage and retrieval system, without permission in writing from the publisher. Printed in the United States of America.

The Haworth Press, Inc., 10 Alice Street, Binghamton, NY 13904-1580, USA

Library of Congress Cataloging-in-Publication Data

The Reference librarian and implications of mediation / edited by M. Keith Ewing, Robert Hauptman.
   p. cm.
   Includes bibliographical references.
   ISBN 1-56024-318-X (alk. paper)
   1. Reference services (Libraries) 2. Reference librarians. 3. Mediation I. Ewing , M. Keith (Melvin Keith), 1950- . II. Hauptman, Robert, 1941- .
Z711.R4443 1992
025.5'2–dc20

92-19037
CIP

The Reference Librarian
and Implications of Mediation

CONTENTS

**Introduction: Mediation: The Librarian's Role
in Information Dissemination**   **1**
    M. Keith Ewing
    Robert Hauptman

I. TRADITIONAL MEDIATION

The Librarian as Mediator   **3**
    Arthur W. Hafner
    Valerie M. Camarigg

    I. Introduction   4
    II. Quintessence of Librarianship as Mediation   5
    III. Libraries, Democracy and Mediation   9
    IV. Conclusions   19

**The Reference Librarian as Information Intermediary:
The Correct Approach Is the One That Today's
Client Needs Today**   **23**
    Herbert S. White

**Back to Basics: Recommitment to Patrons'
Information Needs**   **37**
    Claudette S. Hagle

    Scope of the Problem   38
    A Time for Change   41
    Sources of Information   42

New Technology as a Reference Tool	43
Putting New Technology Skills into Practice	43
Elusive or Hidden Sources	45
The Referral Process	46
Conclusion	47

Mediation in Reference Service to Extend Patron Success   **49**
Jack Alan Hicks

Mediation as a Technique	49
Current Potentials	50
Performance Studies Based on Failure	51
Role of the Librarian as Mediator	53
The Service Encounter Business	54
Mediation Based on Success	55
Enduser: A Flawed Concept in a Public Setting	57
Analyzing the Successful Client	57
Elements of Success	59
Librarian Avoidance Tactics	61
Conclusion	62

II. MEDIATION AND THE ELECTRONIC WORLD

Books and Screens, Readers and Reference: Bridging the Video Gap   **65**
John Swan

Electronic Reference Services: Mediation for the 1990s   **75**
Anita K. Evans

CD-ROMs	76
Electronic Information Services and the Private Consumer	77
The Enhanced Super Catalog	79
The Internet and List Servers	81
A Look at Standards	82
Information Literacy Education	82
Back to Square One: Online Vendors	83
In Conclusion	84

Response to Swan and Evans: "Problems
and Opportunities"   **87**
Michael D. Kathman

III. SPECIALIZED MEDIATION

**Information and Research Support Services:
The Reference Librarian and the Information
Paraprofessional**   **91**
Carol Hammond

Library Programs for a New Institution   92
A New Plan for Reference: Information
    and Research Support   94
The Experiment and the Practice   101

Response to Hammond: "Paraprofessionals
at the Reference Desk: The End of the Debate"   **105**
Larry R. Oberg

**Breaking Through: Effective Reference Mediation
for Nontraditional Public Library Users**   **109**
Sally G. Reed

Factors Affecting Successful Reference Transactions
    with Mentally Impaired Patrons   110
Factors Affecting a Successful Reference Transaction
    with Newly Literate or Illiterate Adults   112
Conclusion   115

Response to Reed: "Unequal but Appropriate Service"   **117**
Emmett Davis

**Mediation and Schemata Theory in Meaningful Learning:
The Academic Librarian's Role
in the Educational Process**   **121**
Barbara Doyle-Wilch
Marian I. Miller

**Questions and Answers: The Dialogue
Between Composition Teachers
and Reference Librarians**   **129**
         Sarah R. Marino
         Elin K. Jacob

IV. MEDIATION AND ACCURACY

**The Reference Librarian as Mediator: Predicting
Accuracy Scores from User Impressions**   **143**
         F. W. Lancaster
         Kurt M. Joseph
         Cheryl Elzy

Methodology	148
Results	149
Conclusions	151

V. THE ECONOMY AND ITS INFLUENCE

Mediation in a Shrinking Information Economy   **161**
         Renee Tjoumas

Introduction	161
Economic Factors	162
Libraries and Librarians	171
Recommendations and Conclusions	176

VI. THE MEDIATOR AS GUARDIAN

**Academic Librarians and Mediation in Controversial
Scholarly Communication**   **183**
         Gordon Moran

Introduction:
Mediation:
The Librarian's Role
in Information Dissemination

During the past twenty years, many social and technological developments have had an enormous influence on the varieties of inquiry, the production and dissemination of information and knowledge, and the nature of information mediation. Librarians and others in the information business are, by nature, intermediaries. They form a connecting link between a query and resources that provide a resolution, between an idea and its realization. It has been the responsibility of information professionals to learn and understand the available resources–personal, print, electronic, or otherwise–and know how to use them effectively and efficiently. Such responsibility often may extend beyond what is locally available to resources located at other sites. This knowledge and understanding of resources has often resulted in a gatekeeper role that is beneficial to neither the librarian nor the client. Reference negotiation developed early in the profession to assist the librarian in understanding an inquiry, ferret out what a client *really* needs, and to pursue an appropriate response. Bibliographic instruction developed to provide patrons with basic mediation tools and information literacy, and thereby reduce the librarian's virtual monopoly, and to promote the librarian's role in mediating the information seeking process. On the whole, the interaction of librarians as information intermediaries and clients has been satisfactory and beneficial to both parties. Collegial relationships, where both parties contribute to successful results, come about slowly, yet when they do develop they often result in new ideas that expand the frontiers of knowledge. Today, successful information mediation has gone beyond gatekeeping, from providing an answer or a resource with an answer to attempts to understand the environment, the physical surroundings, the social or educational context, and the ethical, political, and economic climate in which the process takes place.

© 1992 by The Haworth Press, Inc. All rights reserved.

The librarians and scholars who have contributed essays to this volume were encouraged to interpret mediation in the broadest terms. Herbert White and Claudette Hagle discuss mediation in a traditional context, reminding librarians not to forget the fundamentals. John Swan and Anita Evans are interested in the impact of information technologies upon mediation and the intermediary; Michael Kathman provides a response that highlights a need to focus on the human context. Carol Hammond presents a model of paraprofessionals as mediators; Larry Oberg's response emphasizes the necessity for further experimentation. F. W. Lancaster is concerned with the mediator's understanding of an inquiry and knowledge of resources. Sally Reed notes the increasing diversity of library patrons and emphasizes special services to the mentally disturbed and Renee Tjoumas considers the increasingly bleak economic conditions that affect the mediation environment.This diversity allows for a fuller understanding of the mediation process.

M. Keith Ewing
Robert Hauptman

I. TRADITIONAL MEDIATION

The Librarian as Mediator

Arthur W. Hafner
Valerie M. Camarigg

SUMMARY. This paper examines various aspects of librarianship in order to illustrate that the profession is one that requires the techniques of mediation. Both librarianship and mediation are crafts guided by and furthering the interests of democratic society. The concern of librarians with intellectual freedom and literacy is exam-

---

Arthur W. Hafner is Director and Valerie M. Camarigg is Staff Associate at Division of Library and Information Management, American Medical Association, 515 North State Street, Chicago, IL 60610.

The authors wish to express their appreciation to M. Roy Schwarz, MD, Senior Vice President for Medical Education and Science, for his support for the authors to engage in research and publication.

The authors express their thanks to several librarians in the American Medical Association's Division of Library and Information Management, individuals who have provided examples of mediation in their positions and who made a number of constructive suggestions: Marguerite Fallucco, Senior Research Associate and Archivist; Norman Frankel, PhD, Director of Scientific and Socioeconomic Indexing; Anne White-Michalski, Senior Research Associate and Online Search Analyst; Lorri A. Zipperer, Research Associate and Online Search Analyst; and Sandra R. Schefris, Director of Information Systems. Further, the authors acknowledge the technical assistance of division staff members Ashish K. Bajaj, Cheryl M. Steffen, and Jennifer Sterling-Folker. Lastly, the senior author expresses his appreciation to C. Diane Holtz, Rye Free Reading Room, Rye, NY, for her helpful comments in completing this project.

© 1992 by The Haworth Press, Inc. All rights reserved.

ined as it encompasses the challenges of homelessness and multi-culturalism. These issues call upon librarians to mediate, and to do so dynamically because of changes in library theory, methods, and technology.

Librarians mediate between clients and with themselves. Mediation is required in bibliographic selection and for every library policy. It is hoped that readers of this paper will imagine many other aspects of librarianship that are furthered by effective mediation.

I. INTRODUCTION

This paper examines the inherent tensions librarians must face as mediators. Issues such as collection building, homelessness, and technology are examined according to the ways in which librarians and libraries have resolved these issues through mediation. Because libraries are institutions established to serve democracy (e.g., see Hafner, 1987 and Hafner, 1986), they often have been forums for mediation within society. As a result, libraries are found at the forefront on issues such as intellectual freedom and multiculturalism. An examination of these issues as they relate to the library will highlight the importance of mediation. By focusing on the breadth of mediation skills used by librarians, it is hoped that this paper will prove helpful in enriching both the public's and the profession's general perceptions of, and appreciation for, the tasks and services that librarians perform in American society.

The already vast and ever-growing amount of retrievable information increasingly highlights the importance of mediation skills for librarians. Individual librarians serve as mediators in the conflicts arising between the client and almost every other library element including other clients, regulations, the collection, budget restraints, new technology, and so on. Furthermore, these and other library elements are not mutually exclusive and are often found to be parties to mediation among themselves. To cite only a few examples, the librarian is often forced to mediate when budget restraints conflict with collection needs or new library technology, when collection needs conflict with current politics or the interest in future holdings, and when colleagues disagree among themselves.

Despite all these relationships for which librarians are intermediaries, the suggestion that the role of the librarian might be even remotely akin to that of a mediator has caused sufficient skepticism to warrant a definition: A *mediator* is an individual who acts to reconcile differences or as the conveyor of something, such as information. A librarian practices the skill of mediation by objectifying issues so as to remove personalities from the conflict, thereby allowing attention to be focused on the facts of the dispute. This definition is neither outrageous nor innovative, yet stating it clears the way for myriad possibilities of librarians as mediators.

Some readers may have difficulty in viewing the librarian as a mediator. This difficulty may be due, in part, to the reader not having an adequate understanding or appreciation for the span of responsibilities, tasks, and activities that public service librarians perform. The following listing, albeit not exhaustive, provides an overview of the librarian's responsibilities:

1. Librarians are the custodians of public and corporate property;
2. Librarians manage and facilitate the use of collections;
3. Librarians serve as gatekeepers to the educational and recreational needs of their clientele;
4. Librarians regulate collections by buying, classifying, and weeding informational materials; and
5. Librarians act as conservators of the past.

In discharging these and other responsibilities, the role of librarians in developing collections is to achieve a balance that allows them to convey information to their clientele in an outwardly unbiased manner. Conveying information in an unbiased manner equally applies to the acquisition of classical materials as well as to "popular culture" items such as art work, videos, magazines journals, and newspapers.

II. QUINTESSENCE OF LIBRARIANSHIP AS MEDIATION

Any profession can be subjected to review for its use of mediation or any other skill. As librarians, we may be the least likely to view ourselves as mediators, despite the preponderance of ways in which we mediate. The notion of librarians as mediators is not taught in library school, nor is it widely seen in the professional literature. Mediation is not mentioned in job titles, and it is not mentioned in job descriptions. These oversights are due, in part, to the nature of our clientele. No deliberation is required in defining the library's clientele since librarians serve everyone by helping in the search for information.

We tend to think of mediation as an adjunct of hostility, with two angry parties, each feeling wronged in some way. The mediator serves as a third and impartial person, facilitating the discussion of the dispute and thereby allowing the angry parties to air their complaints. When we think of a mediator, we are apt to conjure up the image we receive through the media–a lawyer, or better yet, a court judge. Thus, a trial judge is often and reasonably thought of as the prototypical mediator, due to the saturation of conflict and liability in today's society.

The media image of a judicial mediator is not entirely accurate. This is because court judges arbitrate; they do not mediate. In fact, a recent article in which the authors explore the ways in which judges mediate was entitled "The Judge as a Mediator." This piece points out that it is something of an anomaly for judges to function as mediators (Wall and Rude, 1991). The judge is a litigation rather than a mediation expert. Mediation embodies the process of arriving at a solution. Before a judge hears the prepared case, much of the mediation process has already been carried out by the opposing counsels.

The difference between mediation and legal arbitration is further highlighted by the Pittsburgh Carnegie Libraries Mediation Center Project, which has worked successfully with public agencies, the private sector, and community members in providing mediation services to the community (Albert, 1987 and Pittsburgh, 1989). Litigation often leads to the imposition of penalties and punishment, while the mediation project allows for communication and resolution without the highly adversarial tone of courtroom battle. Volunteer mediators are motivated to serve the community and therefore seek just solutions. Courtroom lawyers, on the other hand, are more likely to be motivated by money and therefore seek highly capital conscious solutions.

It may escape the notice of many librarians, as well as of library users, that the training and experience librarians require to carry out their tasks are the skills of mediation. Effective mediation requires that issues be treated objectively (Karim and Pegnetter, 1983), and such objectivity is expected of librarians. The profession of librarianship has even been accused of carrying this objectivity too far and consequently of not "defin[ing] its values in political terms and cultivat[ing] a sense of social responsibility" (Blanke, 1989). Nevertheless, librarians and mediators continually try to separate personalities from facts in a conflict.

This commonality has been noticed by one of the Pittsburgh Carnegie Project's volunteer mediators, a judge, who considers library mediation appropriate for many cases that typically come to trial (Albert, 1987). The librarian is, after all, called upon to listen to the question or problem (hear the evidence), organize the essentials (present the

Traditional Mediation

case), and convey information (reach a resolution). This means that every act of the librarian, performing services in the capacity of a librarian, is mediation.

A. Information Processing and Retrieval as Mediation

The library is where people go for answers to questions. This means that a client uses the library to obtain information, to relieve the tension between what is knowable and yet still unknown. There is an inherent tension between lack of information and the quest for information. Librarians and libraries serve to resolve this tension and are perennially playing an intermediary role between questions and their answers.

Client requests for information are presented to librarians in varying degrees of clarity. An expressed question is often as much the unknown as the intended question, hence the adage that knowing the right question will yield the right answer. Yet despite a lack of clarity on the part of many clients, the librarian usually manages to meet the needs of clientele. Whenever librarians are interpreting what it is that the client is requesting or which library resources would best meet the client's needs, the librarian is engaged in mediation between the client and the collection.

In determining the needs and interests of the client, librarians use processes that are subjective. They objectify such internal, procedural data as "... where can I find this?" or "... how can I determine that?" Metaphysically speaking, the information stored in librarians' internal libraries is retrieved and then presented to the client in an easy to use form. We tell them their question essentially boils down to X, which can be answered by looking in Y, which will be found on shelf Z. This conveyance from within the librarian to the cognizant being of the librarian and then to the user is really two mediations between three parties, which results in the objectification of what librarians know. Thus, the objectification skill of the librarian may be seen in the very act of informational conveyance.

With printed or otherwise visually perceptible materials, the issues to be conveyed are pre-objectified by writers, artists, publishers, and so on. The library is a storehouse for these objectified issues. Facts and fiction, truisms and opinions, all appear together under one roof as books, paintings, newspapers, magazines, and videos. This is a very large roof, since technology links libraries around the world. Objectification enables librarians to offer users access to ideas that span time and distance.

B. Collection Development Is Essentially Mediation

Mediators ease conflict resolution by suppressing their own feelings on the subject of conflict. Similarly, acting on behalf of their institutions, librarians collect and manage a wide array of literature and other forms of human expression regardless of personal prejudices. Both librarians and mediators consciously check the influence of their personal prejudices as they discharge their duties.

The process of bibliographic selection has been the topic of much analysis and speculation. Quantitative models of book selection try to objectify selection criteria. This objectification necessitates the librarian's mediation as ". . . a trade-off between precision and relevance of selection criteria" (Schwartz, 1989, p.330). An increased reliance on numbers brings a decreased reliance on qualitative factors. The librarian must weigh the values of each type of classification in making selection decisions. In this, one sees how the subjective self is thrust into the public work of the librarian.

Objectification (or quantification) may go so far as to violate the "principle of dominance," which acknowledges that some choices are obvious and dominant. Quantification may occur at the expense of practicality since it treats all books as "tough choices" with no obviously dominant ones (Schwartz, 1989). Thus, the librarian's mediated interplay of the subjective self and restraint is again at work. This time, however, the subjective self that is being used includes the librarian's training and knowledge, rather than solely matters of personal taste. It is the qualitative skill of the librarian that allows the principle of dominance to operate.

Librarians have always faced the reality of selection limitations since virtually all library institutions are operated with limited acquisition budgets. Library administrators must mediate between budget limitations and everything that is needed to operate a library. Librarians may be asked to forego a cost of living increase despite their already meager wages in order to assure adequate moneys to acquire a given year's best sellers for the collection. The problem is exacerbated by the widespread call for consideration of multicultural issues in library collections. This comes at a time when librarians are facing funding reductions on federal, state, and local levels. Library operations and personnel budget cuts constitute a limitation that makes the mediation skills of the librarian even more crucial.

According to the designers of federal cuts, state funding will fill library budget gaps. Some programs will undoubtedly maintain financial support, such as adult literacy, since it is an issue of the 1990s. Indeed, the proposed (and thankfully unrealized) 1992 federal reduction of 75% from the Department of Education library programs left $35 million for activities provided for under the Library Services and Construction Act, all of which was to be used for adult literacy programs. Various individual state financial planners have also proposed reducing or freezing library funding. As collection budgets tighten, programs and services will be reduced and, in fact, may be cut altogether. Each cut in funding requires mediation on the community need and importance of various library activities.

It is not enough for librarians to mediate for the sake of developing a collection. Collections must be responsive to the changing needs of library users and to the fluctuating parameters of possibility. Collections also require maintenance, which involves such mediatables as censorship, preservation techniques, and collection currency. Although maintenance implies a certain amount of stability, it too is subject to change. The boundaries of acceptable speech expand and contract, new technologies are debated, and the interest and value of historical materials are subject to change. Thus, the librarian must engage in a fair amount of juggling just to address the issues of maintenance.

An example of mediation requirements in collection maintenance is occurring at the National Archives and Records Administration (NARA) and the U.S. Department of Energy (DOE). These agencies are pitted against the University of California (UC) over ownership of scientific papers produced from federally funded projects. NARA currently holds cartons of books containing research papers that the DOE believes may contain classified information. In the spirit of mediation, NARA's library personnel have said that they do not mind if the government agency wants to own the books, as long as the library can display them. In the meantime, however, the informational materials are not accessible while the federal agency determines whether or not the books can be declassified (see Rider, 1991).

III. LIBRARIES, DEMOCRACY AND MEDIATION

Just as conflict and its resolution are underlying assumptions of democracy, access to popular culture at the library was made possible through early mediation between the interests of democratically inspired traditionalists and more marketing-minded individuals (Pungitore, 1989). The library marketers won with their argument that providing recreational materials to users would whet their appetites for more serious literature,

"... and thereby serve as a steppingstone to the library's primary objective–education" (Lee, 1966). Yet, while borrowing a videotape from the library, the client is probably not going to consider that the 19th century decision to infuse library collections with items from popular culture was a decision made with considerable debate. Whether access to that videotape has improved education is a question beyond the scope of this paper.

Prominent among the published rationales for the existence of public libraries are such lofty notions as the promise of an informed populace, the subsequent contribution of that promise as a Public Good, and the public library as a haven of peace and enlightenment in the midst of harsh environs (e.g., see Healy, 1990; Pungitore, 1989; Hafner, 1987; Hafner, 1986). In a recent address to the White House Conference on Libraries and Information Services, President George Bush acknowledged the role of librarians as "revolutionaries" in service to democracy (see Gaughan, 1991). In this sense, public libraries operate to provide free use of the library structure and the information it contains for all. Also included as philosophical bases of the library, though less prominent and less lofty, are the presumed benefit to capital interests in having an educated work force and the potential for engaging otherwise mischievous riff-raff.

In his eloquent address to the 1990 New York Library Association Centennial Conference, Timothy Healy, president and chief executive officer of the New York Public Library, maintains that the very existence of the library was its most important service to democracy (Healy, 1990). He argues that through its very "being," the library offers freedom from ignorance and immediacy. "All civilizations are essentially age long and unbroken, although often interrupted, conversations," Healy notes, and libraries offer ". . . the way of contemplation . . ." on this conversation (1990, p.2). This observation reminds one that the library offers itself as something of an island of sanity in a sea of despair: ". . . escape from immediacy, into the past, or into the future, but escape nonetheless," as Healy observes.

The library's very existence allows for inner mediation because, in the library, one can examine several published arguments on a controversial issue or contrast the styles of several artists. These pursuits may be examined against their historical bases and in the contexts of their evolutions. The library is a place for mediation between genres, tastes, and values. It is a place where one can arrange, witness, and judge a debate among opponents living oceans and centuries apart. As an institution conducive to the art and act of mediation, the library serves as a place for unlimited meditations on democracy or any other topic.

One need not stretch the limits of abstraction to find libraries serving as sites for mediation. The Pittsburgh's Carnegie Libraries Project, mentioned earlier, is one such example of libraries providing mediation services to the community. The aura of quiet intelligence referred to by Healy establishes the library environment as neutral ground conducive to mediation.

The freedom that Healy cites as being offered by the public library is not all passive. Freedom gained through empowerment includes "the way of contemplation." It also, however, entails free access to information for all. This implies that librarians must take positive action. Stressing the need to *ensure* access to information implies a force opposed to that access. Stressing access *for all* implies that access to some groups might be jeopardized. By acting to ensure access for all, librarians face a host of mediatable conflicts.

A. Intellectual Freedom

Ensuring access to information establishes the library as a natural opponent of censorial forces. Libraries are often thrust into the forefront of debates on the reaches and limitations of the First Amendment. In 1990, *Library Trends* published a collection of articles dealing with the topic of "Intellectual Freedom." The common thread of the articles is the assumption that librarians have a vested interest in intellectual freedom (see Woodward, 1990). In particular, Molz (1990) identifies several cases of threats to intellectual freedom in libraries today and concludes that the validity of all ideas must be upheld, even those that are not popular or "politically correct." Whether the censors are from the Left or from the Right, librarians are called upon to serve as mediators between the library's collection and censors, since holdings all too easily can become victims of political fallout.

Although mediation requires issue objectification, or an approximation of neutral presentation, it would be unreasonable to assert that the materials within any given collection are not rife with bias. Society often places differential values on "elite" versus "popular" culture. It has been argued that both have a place in the public library (Stevenson, 1977). From this vantage, intellectual freedom can only be achieved if libraries include a wide variety of works in their collections. For most people, restraint would probably cause some self-mediation. This "cognitive dissonance" calls for mediation between opposing cognitive forces.

Ensuring intellectual freedom also implies mediating between censors and the interests of information-seeking clients. Libraries must debate, for example, whether to carry R-rated videotapes. Within this debate, librarians must determine how seriously they should take the rating system. In October 1990, the Motion Picture Association of America revised its system of rating films. It introduced an "NC-17" rating that is intended to distinguish erotic art films from adult sex films. Graphic adult sex films, which inspired the controversy, are often made by independent film makers who have the freedom to show their films unrated. They also can use the publicity of a potential X-rating to boost ticket sales. This is because only films produced by the major studios are obligated to accept the ratings given them. The librarian choosing videotapes for the library's collection must consider these and other nuances in making appropriate selections. This means that the librarian must mediate within a complex matrix made up of all potential films, library rules and guidelines, individual tastes, and the library's acquisition limitations.

B. Multiculturalism and Mediation

The issue of multiculturalism is of great importance to librarians. Multiculturalism refers to the assumption that the influence of non-dominant cultures is overshadowed by over-promotion of the influence of the dominant perspective. In a school setting, multiculturalism's goal is to include equally weighted cultural material in the current curriculum collection. There are those who argue, however, that schools ought to embrace an "Afro-centric" curriculum instead, an instructional program that stresses "... the history and culture of black people" (see Putka, 1991). This approach is more drastic and ambitious than multiculturalism's goal, yet evidence suggests some degree of success for minority students when a more focused approach is used, as measured by improved attendance, enrollment, and reading scores (Putka, 1991).

When building and developing library collections, the debate over the proper degree of attention to give to multiculturalism's proponents places librarians in an awkward position. They risk accusations of not giving enough thought to multiculturalism or of intentionally ignoring the significance of non-prevailing ideologies. If librarians choose not to follow the appointed "politically correct" path, they will be on the defensive against multicultural proponents. If they commit deeply to the cause of developing a "politically correct" collection, they then face the argument that multiculturalism, although perhaps "politically correct," is not necessarily intellectually correct. For example, D'Souza (1991) argues that multiculturalism is often irresponsibly promoted at the expense of scholarship.

Traditional Mediation

When a librarian acknowledges a need to explore multiculturalism, a number of questions still remain. Similarly, a librarian who commits to multiculturalism must be sensitive to the varying needs of the library's clientele (e.g., see Stoffle, 1990 and Dyson, 1989), and must be a person who is amenable to change (Weingand, 1984). This implies a process in need of mediation between the collection and all of its potential changes. Every effort towards building a multicultural collection is subject to continual challenge.

The difficulty of establishing a library collection that meets with multicultural approval is increased by the changing nature by which works are evaluated. In a discussion of the professional dangers of embracing political correctness in literature, Berube (1991) writes as a member of "the new fundamentalist" young faculty–the "Visigoths in Tweed." Berube states that this group is under attack for allegedly undermining the history of Western thought with writings of leftist extremism. He points out that many works now staunchly protected as literary landmarks of Western civilization were not so highly regarded by their contemporary critics.

Delayed appreciation of literature applies as well to disciplines other than civics. Responding to a suggestion that the proliferation of serials publication be curtailed by encouraging universities to stress teaching over publication, ". . . and thus help reduce the quantity of published 'ignorant drivel,'" Boyce and Wallace (1987, p. 652) argue "in defense of 'ignorant drivel.'" They point out that highly valuable scientific discoveries are not always immediately grasped as works of value. Thus, not only must librarians mitigate tensions due to differences in opinion concerning which current materials are suitable companions for the established collection, they must also weigh the value of yesterday's neglected works in the light of the new day. In short, that which is correct for today's collection might be offensive next week.

Sensitivity to the cultural needs of users involves more than attention to the library's holdings. The multicultural issue of library resource access for minorities and women involves attention to the impact of changes in technology and use of library structure (Stoffle, 1990). It is important that ". . . as libraries expand the use of technology in information delivery, (they) must mitigate any consideration of the increased use of fees to pay for that information" (Stoffle, 1990, p. 50). Stoffle suggests that librarians use the physical resources of their libraries to feature regular programs of multicultural interest. These resources include the billboards, lecture rooms, and reading areas.

The challenge of multiculturalism for librarians goes beyond mediation over whether and how many resources to commit to multiculturalism. The controversial nature of multiculturalism imposes a need for librarians to mediate among themselves on a broad range of topics affected by multiculturalism. In an examination of one library's aggressive effort to recruit a multicultural outreach worker, little was said about what such outreach would entail (Dyson, 1989). Similarly, in the American Library Association's (ALA) 1990 Annual Conference report (ALA 1990, J/A), the Association wrote of having speakers on multiculturalism. However, librarians were not given specific advice on how to incorporate multicultural ideals into their work.

Although the United States is currently wrestling with the debate on multiculturalism and although related discussions abound in the media, there is little for the ready and willing librarian to apply in selecting material for a multicultural collection. Occasionally, assorted mini-bibliographies appear in the backs of library trade journals or in conjunction with articles on multiculturalism (e.g., Putka, 1991). What is lacking, however, are guidelines that address the concern with as much complexity as the sum of interested librarians bring to it.

Large doses of creativity and initiative are needed in calling upon librarians to collect and convey multicultural material that may hold little or no meaning for them. In essence, although it is necessary for librarians to invoke the subjective qualities of creativity and innovation, it is also necessary for them to suppress such other subjective qualities as prejudice and personal taste. This is the mediated interplay of subjective involvement and restraint; it is mediation with oneself. In this regard, librarians' mediation skills are perhaps most important in bibliographic selection. By selecting from the global entirety of available works, librarian- bibliographers serve as intermediaries between the interests of the individual library and the offerings of all potential collections.

C. Homelessness: Mediation on All Fronts

Although ensuring access to information implies a source of conflict, ensuring access to information *for all* ensures tension. Public libraries are open to all, and where there is diversity there is bound to be conflict. The democratic underpinning of libraries assumes that not all clients will be satisfied with the same amount, selection, or depth of information. Further, it would be presumptuous for a librarian to believe or assert that all clients are equally capable of using all library services, particularly without librarian assistance. Ensuring democratic access to information assumes a variety of people will be vying for limited resources. In this regard, the individual librarian is caught as an intermediary between these opposing forces.

The legal case of Richard R. Kreimer, plaintiff, and the Free Public Library of Morristown, New Jersey is evidence that homelessness is an important library issue. The case has been a regular feature of library journals and newspaper editorial pages for some time. It has generated so much interest that ALA has compiled an information packet on it. In this case, several library clients had complained that Mr. Kreimer, a homeless man, had a foul odor, and that he had a habit of ogling women patrons. In July 1989, the library trustees responded to client complaints and instituted Patron Rules that forbid "unnecessary staring" and that require that the hygiene of clients conform to the "standard of the community." The enforcement of this policy was carried out by the Morristown Police Department, which ejected Kreimer from the library on various occasions.

The American Civil Liberties Union (ACLU) later reviewed the Patron Rules and warned the librarian and trustees that the rules might be used to discriminate on the basis of homelessness. Following the ACLU's recommendation, the library's trustees modified the language of their policy to state that library users who stared ". . . with the intent to annoy" and whose hygiene was ". . . so offensive as to constitute a nuisance to other persons shall be required to leave the building." In addition, area social service workers and community relations specialists conducted workshops with library personnel in an attempt to sensitize library staff to the problems of homeless people.

The Free Public Library of Morristown trustees' original policy statement was an attempt to mediate a conflict between library clients. The library's trustees and personnel mediated between library users and the recommendation of the ACLU to arrive at its second version of the Patron Rules. These mediations, however, failed since one party to the original mediation, Mr. Kreimer, was dissatisfied with the outcome. The tension thus remained and shifted in focus to a legal conflict between Kreimer and the library's new regulations. Subsequently, Morristown library director Barbara Rice was named a defendant in Kreimer's suit against the library.

On May 22, 1991, a ruling for Kreimer and against the Free Public Library of Morristown was handed down in the U.S. District Court (New Jersey) by Judge H. Lee Sarokin. In his written opinion, he stated that the various provisions of the library's policy,

16 *The Reference Librarian and Implications of Mediation*

> . . . violate the First Amendment to the United States Constitution, . . . [are] not narrowly tailored or reasonable time, place, and manner regulations which serve a significant government interest, . . . [are] unconstitutionally overbroad, . . . [are] unconstitutionally vague; and . . . violate the equal protection and due process clauses of the Fourteenth Amendment in conjunction with the free association guarantee of the First Amendment. (Kreimer v. Morristown, 1991, p. 39)

Thus, the issue ultimately became one of civil rights with Kreimer and the library trustees squarely at odds and far from resolution.

Considerable objection has been raised that the ejection of Richard Kreimer from the library has become a civil rights issue. Indeed, this is the basis of the library trustees' appeal. Opposition to Judge Sarokin's ruling was strong and compelled him to write a "Letter to the Editor" in the August 6, 1991 issue of the *Wall Street Journal*. Such an action is uncustomary for a judge. In part, Judge Sarokin wrote:

> I know that judges are expected to remain silent in the face of criticism of their opinions, but your editorial . . . regarding my decision involving Morristown Library is such a distortion of my opinion and so demeans the judiciary that I must respond. (Sarokin, 1991)

The American Library Association wondered whether to support the library trustees' appeal and decided to follow the recommendation of its Intellectual Freedom Committee, which was that Judge Sarokin's ruling was consistent with ALA goals. However, the New Jersey Library Association decided to support the Free Public Library of Morristown. The ALA's refusal to support the Morristown library highlights a very real tension within the profession. The resolution of this conflict may require mediation through time, unless the parties can come to terms with their differences. One can only speculate on the treatment Mr. Kreimer might have received had he spent his time in state, county, or city government offices instead of at the library.

The dilemma that the case of Richard Kreimer presents for libraries is not unique to the Free Public Library of Morristown, nor to library service continuity in general. Nor are specific issues of homelessness for libraries limited to situations such as Kreimer's, where a particular community and homeless library clients may have a high propensity to clash. Libraries across the country are learning about the problems of homeless-

Traditional Mediation

ness through personal experience. As with other homelessness situations, it appears that Kreimer uses the library as the haven described by Healy (1990), perusing there while waiting for the soup kitchen to open. And, judging from the offense taken by other library clients, Kreimer is likely considered the sort of mischievous riff-raff who, in part, libraries were originally set up to keep occupied!

It is when the service to some clients is compromised due to the actions of others that a problem surfaces. Richard Kreimer in no way represents a unique threat to service continuity. Furthermore, other libraries have Richard Kreimers. Many communities have seen clashes develop between their housed and homeless populations. Some libraries, such as Morristown's, may ponder a change in their Patron Code to limit access to those considered offensive by some community standard, if the offense is determined to interfere with other's enjoyment of library services. But this solution does not appear to have provided an acceptable resolution for anyone.

Other libraries have sought more thoughtful, creative solutions. For example, many libraries have a policy that before they issue a person a library card, the person must provide evidence to show citizenship in that community. Because the homeless have no address, they may find it difficult to meet this requirement. Other alternatives that have been tried across the country include "browsing" libraries. These auxiliary units are located in library "day shelters" or in separate buildings near the main library. Also, reading rooms in homeless centers and shelters are being set up by many municipal libraries (Pearson, 1988).

A question posed in the *American Libraries'* column "Action Exchange," asked whether other librarians have had experience providing literacy services to children who live in shelters. One answer included an explanation of how other librarians might avoid circulation problems:

> We offer deposit collections of books to each shelter. We usually send an average of two to three books per resident. These books do not have to be returned; however, if they are, we rotate new titles into the shelter. The policy of no return is necessary since the shelters are reluctant to accept responsibility for library materials due to the transient nature of the shelter clientele. (Des Enfants, 1991)

Such solutions abrogate the need for a library card and hence the requirement that the client evidence citizenship in the library's community. Such solutions evidence mediation by individual librarians between

18 *The Reference Librarian and Implications of Mediation*

and among administrators and governmental bodies. The results of this mediation may be funds supplied by a grant under the Library Services and Construction Act (LSCA) to set up a peer-educator literacy program, as in Milwaukee, Wisconsin, or perhaps the donation of a building or services through local cooperation.

D. Technology Increases the Need for Mediation Skills

As with all professions, librarianship must accept and apply new technologies as they become available, if these technologies meaningfully facilitate the provision of information services. Because of continuing changes and improvements in library technology, the mediation skills of librarians are especially visible. The librarian often encounters tension because of the needs to maintain the collection and to incorporate new technologies (Seiler and Surprenant, 1991). In addition, librarians must mediate not only between alternative technologies, but also between any given technology and what appears to be its best application(s) for the clientele.

It is important to remember that libraries store the information needed for the full realization of a democratic society. If this information is accessible only on or through the use of new technologies, then librarians need to adapt service provisions to continue serving their democratic mission. That is, as librarians incorporate new information technologies, their mediation skills become increasingly important in facilitating information access and making information retrieval available. This incorporation of new technologies will continue to ensure library access for all, especially for those with little means to acquire technologized information on their own.

In addition, the global network of information sources challenges the very notion of what a library is meant to be. Instead of being "where the information is," the library now is "where one *finds out* where the information is," which may be someplace other than in the library (Downes, 1990 and Weber, 1990). Society's growing reliance on online search networks and document delivery (interlibrary loan) demands that the librarian serve as an intermediary to other libraries and/or information sources. It is not reasonable to assume that library clientele will find all of the information they seek in their community library. Networks offer clients equal access to information through technology. Factors that were once considered the local public library's limitations are now rendered moot.

IV. CONCLUSIONS

This paper explores the multifaceted nature of some of the issues that engage the librarian in mediation. Mediation is described as the act and technique of objectifying issues so that attention may be focused on the facts of a dispute. It differs markedly from litigation since it involves the act of arriving at a solution rather than focusing on the decision itself. It allows for resolution without an adversarial tone, and it is a technique motivated by a desire to serve the community in seeking just solutions. Mediation also involves the recognition of tensions and limitations, as well as the desire and attempt to develop solutions.

As mediators, librarians act as information intermediaries and objectify informational issues so that attention may be focused on the facts of a dispute. Informational issues are varied and complex. The very act of imparting information to a client, for example, involves mediation between question and answer, answer and librarian, and librarian and client. Bibliographic selection and collection development also involve mediating between objectivity and the librarian's personal subjective preferences, as well as between collection needs and limited acquisition budgets.

Libraries are sites for mediation within a democratic society. They contribute self-mediation by their very existence because they provide a place where all genres, tastes, and values may be arranged, witnessed, and judged. This means that the library is an institution conducive to the art and act of self-mediation. The library is also an institution with the mission to ensure access to information for all individuals. This leads to a number of mediatable conflicts concerning intellectual freedom and censorship, multiculturalism and collection development, homelessness and the rights of clientele, and the acquisition and use of new technologies. In these and other clashes, the librarian mediates among a variety of actors including administrators, clientele, colleagues, the judiciary system, and the community in general.

There is a great need for librarians to serve as mediators. This need implies that the librarian's job may offer more tension and stress than many suspect. Some of the tensions are inherent, such as those in collection development, but they may be alleviated by leveling budget cuts and by providing real guidance when instituting such goals as multicultural sensitivity. The library's bureaucratic structure, as with most institutions, necessitates mediation between clients and the architects of the bureaucracy. The results of library administrative decisions regarding budget priorities, salary increases over acquisitions, hours of operation, and so

The Reference Librarian and Implications of Mediation

forth, are factors that affect client satisfaction. More often than not, it is the public service librarian at the reference or circulation desk who must answer the angry client. Yet, it is most often the administrator rather than the practicing librarian who often controls the very need for this type of mediation.

One solution for mitigating stress is for the library's trustees and director to include librarians in decision-making processes and policy development. Giving librarians a participatory voice in library management could alleviate the librarian's stress in carrying out service programs that may have little sensitivity to the realities of library staffing. Personnel at many libraries have turned to collective bargaining precisely so that they would have a voice in the library's operation.

Federal and state budget cuts constitute a limitation that makes the mediation skills of librarians crucial. Library administrators must mediate between budget limitations and everything needed to run a library. Librarians may be asked to forego a cost of living increase despite their already meager wages in order to free up funds for collection development to acquire a given year's best sellers. An increased recognition of libraries as necessary and important social institutions is needed to ensure not only that funding continues, but also that the librarian's role as mediator is acknowledged, valued, and supported.

REFERENCES

American Library Association. (1990). "Speakers plead the cause of multicultural education." *American Libraries. 21*(7),641-642.

Albert, M. C. (1987). "A library where the fighting stops: Can libraries serve their communities as mediation centers?" *American Libraries. 18*,822-3, 860.

Berube, M. (1991). "Public image limited: Political correctness and the media's big lie." *The Village Voice.* June 18,31-37.

Blanke, H. T. (1989). "Librarianship and political values: Neutrality or commitment?" *Library Journal. 114*(12),39-43.

Boyce, B. R. and Wallace, D. P. (1987). "In defense of 'ignorant drivel': Libraries' problems not a good reason to curtail serials publication." *American Libraries. 18*,652-660.

Des Enfants, S. (1991). "Action exchange." *American Libraries.* 22(1),44.

Downes, R. N. (1990). "Managing for innovation in the Age of Technology." In *Developing leadership skills: A source book for librarians.* Albritton and Shaughnessy, eds. Englewood, CO. Libraries Unlimited, Inc.

D'Souza, D. (1991). *Illiberal Education: The politics of race and sex on campus.* New York: The Free Press.

Dyson, A. J. (1989). "Reaching out for outreach: A university library develops a new position to serve the school's multicultural students." *American Libraries.* *20*(10),952-954.

Gaughan, T. (1991). "Mixed messages permeate the White House Conference." *American Libraries.* *22*(7),609.

Hafner, A. W. (1987). "Public libraries and society in the information age." *The Reference Librarian.* *18*(Summer),107-118. Journal issue reprinted as a monograph: *Current trends in information: Research and theory,* B. Katz and R. Kinder, eds; Binghamton, NY: The Haworth Press Inc., 1987.

Hafner, A. W. (1986). "The many facets of the public library." *Chicago Tribune.* July 24, sec. 1,18.

Healy, T. S. (1990). "Libraries in service to democracy," Keynote Address to the New York Library Association Centennial Conference. Rochester, New York, October 11.

Karim, A. and Pegnetter, R. (1983). "Mediator strategies and qualities and mediation effectiveness." *Industrial Relations.* *22*,105-113.

Kreimer v. Morristown (case no. 90-554, USDC-NJ) May 22, 1991. Opinion by H. Lee Sorokin, Judge, USDC-NJ.

Lee, R. E. (1966). *Continuing Education for Adults through the American Public Library: 1833-1964.* Chicago: American Library Association.

Molz, R. K. (1990). "Censorship: Current issues in American libraries." *Library Trends.* *39*(1 & 2),18-35.

Pearson, L. R. (1988) "Public libraries find ways to serve urban homeless." in *American Libraries.* *19*(4),250,252.

"Pittsburgh library: Mediation Center in partnership," 1989. *Library Journal.* *114* (April),24.

Pungitore, V. L. (1989). *Public Librarianship: An issues-oriented approach.* Westport, CT: Greenwood Press.

Putka, G. (1991). "Curricula of color: Course work stressing blacks' role has critics but appears effective." *The Wall Street Journal.* July 1, sec. A,1.

Rider, R. E. (1991). "Saving the records of big science: Clashes between librarians and government officials jeopardize access to research materials." *American Libraries.* *22*(2),166-168.

Schwartz, C. A. (1989). "Book selection, collection development, and bounded rationality." *College and Research Libraries.* *50*,328-343.

Seiler, L. and Surprenant, T. (1991). "When we get the libraries we want, will we want the libraries we get?" *Wilson Library Bulletin.*

Sarokin, H. L. (1991). "Letter to the editor: Vagueness, vagrants and libraries." *The Wall Street Journal.* August 6, sec. A,14.

Stevenson, G. (1977). "Popular culture and the public library." In *Advances in Librarianship.* Melvin J. Voigt and Michael Harris, eds. *7*,177-229.

Stoffle, C. J. (1990). "A new library for the new undergraduate." *Library Journal.* *115*(16):47-50.

22 *The Reference Librarian and Implications of Mediation*

Wall, J. A. Jr. and Rude, D. E. (1991). "The judge as a mediator," in *Journal of Applied Psychology.* 76(1),54-59.

Weber, R. (1990). "Libraries without walls?" *Publishers Weekly.* 237(23):S20-S23.

Weingand, D. E. (1984). *The Organic Public Library.* Littleton, CO: Libraries Unlimited.

Woodward, D. (1990). "Introduction." *Library Trends.* 39(1 and 2),3-7.

The Reference Librarian as Information Intermediary: The Correct Approach Is the One That Today's Client Needs Today

Herbert S. White

As I observe reference service taught as a required course in accredited library education programs, I see a heavy dose of exposure to a variety of reference tools and sources framed in something of a vague concept that this is what we do as service professionals. Specialized and advanced reference courses tend to concentrate on more sources of material, usually separated into subject fields such as the sciences, social sciences, and humanities, and also into types of materials containing the reference work we seek, such as government publications, prints, photographs, and microforms. There appears to be little discussion about the various kinds of reference clients we might encounter, or the suggestion that different customers might have different levels of required information interaction. Indeed, the suggestion heard increasingly that we stop teaching courses oriented to types of libraries and concentrate on a generic whole, while perhaps desirable from some standpoints, would tend to obliterate those distinctions even further and substitute some sort of generic heading called "reference in any kind of library." However, there is little discussion about what constitutes adequate levels of reference service, only about the need to answer correctly in whatever framework is provided. The issue of adequacy of services is relegated to the discussion of library budgets rather than to professional considerations, and ultimately reference service results from decisions made by nonlibrarians who control our resources, but who have no basis for making such decisions except for a preference for spending as little as possible.

Herbert S. White is affiliated with the School of Library and Information Science, Indiana University, Bloomington, IN.

© 1992 by The Haworth Press, Inc. All rights reserved.

24   The Reference Librarian and Implications of Mediation

We speak then of quality, but never within a framework of adequate resources or of approach, and rarely with a thought about determining what that should be.

It was not until my own career as a special librarian, and the opportunity for private tutorials from such intellectual giants in our profession as Mortimer Taube and Hans Peter Luhn, that I began to understand that whether we want to emphasize quality of subject analysis to make reference work simpler and largely a self-service process, or whether we prefer quick and dirty subject analysis and a concentration of sophisticated search strategies, is an option that requires serious discussion. It rarely receives consideration. Both strategies are heavily influenced by the availability of technology, although sophistication of search logic and the ability to search massive databases at a nominal cost are still more technologically sensitive than the process of subject analysis by a human being on a one-to-one basis. A case can be made for either alternative. In the first instance, we invest in an analysis process to save time at the search end where time pressures can be greater, although the existence of backlogs in subject analysis that suggest that subject headings will be perfect when and if they ever get done, also enters into the equation. An emphasis on sophisticated search strategies has the economic advantage of not "wasting" time and resources on items for which nobody will ever want to look, and there are studies that tell us that there are indeed such items.[1] Was the effort expended on subject analysis then wasted? The answer is often in the same framework as the response to a suggestion for weeding never-requested material. Somebody might want to see it tomorrow. However, the statistical probabilities from operations research are very clear, so that we do know that material not used in the first year is not likely to be used ever in the future either.[2]

The process of information intermediation, which I would argue pragmatically is the ultimate payoff in any reference interaction–did what we gave you help you?–runs into a number of barriers. Some of these originate with the patron, who brings varying levels of confidence in the ability of the reference librarian to understand let alone service the request. It has been long observed by reference librarians and teachers of reference that what we call the reference interview is necessitated by the recognition that the user frequently does not ask us what he or she wants to know. Librarians are asked what the user thinks we can understand, and usually this is at a generic level below that of the real request. They present us with simpler questions because they think we would not understand the real question. It is a phenomenon that can have formal names, but one of my students quite accurately calls it "dumbing down"

Traditional Mediation 25

the question, presumably to our assumed level of dumbness. Confidence in the reference process then obviously depends on the two individuals involved in the interaction, and that is a highly personal interaction even if the two have never met before. When librarians act as though all users are interchangeable (just ask whomever answers the phone or happens to be at the desk), we build bureaucratic barriers that may be almost impossible to overcome. In one of my consulting assignments, a corporate chemist served by a special library expressed enthusiasm about the reference abilities of his favorite librarian, whom he always consulted whenever he had a question. Puzzled, I pointed out to him that the woman was not a reference librarian, but rather a cataloger. His response, and I have since concluded the totally correct response, was "I don't care what her title is. She is my reference librarian." Edward Strable, then Head of the Information Center of the J. Walter Thompson advertising agency Chicago office, reported to my students that retired employees now living in Sun City, Arizona and Sarasota, Florida, still called their favorite reference librarian at JWT in Chicago with reference questions that could undoubtedly be handled by the public libraries in their cities. I assume that now that he is also retired, Ed Strable does the same thing.

I can certainly attest that in my own university library there are reference librarians to whom I will entrust a question and others to whom I will not. It is a combination of trust built on prior experience and of perceived attitude. Do these individuals see my question as an opportunity or as an interruption from other duties? As long as an acceptable candidate is available for me within an acceptable time frame, I have no problem. A problem only arises when there is no reference librarian available within the necessary time frame to whom I can entrust my question.

I offered a management seminar recently at a large municipal public library, where a "problem" was presented to me. Telephone reference callers, or individuals walking into the library, were sometimes reluctant to deal with the person who happened to be on duty. Instead, they asked to speak with specific reference librarians, who were not on duty at the time. I was asked how such patrons could be persuaded to conform to library schedule; I suggested instead that this was not a problem but rather a compliment. It became a problem only if there were no reference librarians to whom the client was willing to speak. I asked the group how many of them were willing to be served simply by the next available beautician or barber, and whether they ever chose a longer check-out line at the grocery because they like or trust that particular clerk. I know that I do, and that does not even involve a professional interaction of signifi-

26   *The Reference Librarian and Implications of Mediation*

cance. Managers might like to know the popular and unpopular reference librarians, and it might even suggest management actions for them, but that is another issue.

If the process of information intermediation requires the development of one-to-one trust, then why is it that only some special librarians seem to notice? Special librarians in the Indiana Chapter of the Special Libraries Association reported in an informal survey that their biggest problem concerned communication with users, and not budgets, staff, materials, or space. Communication problems, as we know, can defeat the reference process no matter how well intentioned the librarian. At least part of the reason for the problem is one I have already suggested. We subsume what is an intensely personal interaction in a maze of bureaucratic rules and procedures. It is totally absurd to set limits on how long a reference librarian may work on a question without considering the question. Some can be handled to the complete satisfaction of the need in one or two minutes, others can take two hours or two days. Is this wrong? Only if budgets drive programs rather than programs driving budgets, and that generates nonsense before we even start. The amount of "correct" reference service is a process that seeks its own level, but it should be noted in all fairness that good reference work leads to more reference work. However, can there be a better justification for budget increases? Or should we offer poor service in the certain knowledge that dissatisfied clients will not return, and therefore ease our budgetary pressures?

I would hope that no library administrator would consciously choose this strategy, although I suspect that many do indeed peg the level of service to budgets, rather than the other way around. The larger issue may concern some level of discomfort at performing reference work at all, because the premise of the library as a SERVICE institution is confused with the premise of the library as an EDUCATIONAL institution. Indeed, the two are almost directly contradictory in the strategies they suggest. Which of these models should a given library adopt? It depends on the library. School libraries may be virtually all education with very little information intermediation service. Special libraries, and particularly corporate libraries, are almost completely at the other extreme. Public libraries must do both, certainly the first as part of a transferred responsibility they accept from the school system, unfortunately rarely with either funds or credit. However, adult patrons are not in the public library to be educated, unless they tell you specifically that is why they are there. They are usually there to be served when they approach the reference desk, and pointing them in the general direction of a stack section, a card catalog, or a terminal, is not reference work. The issue can be general-

Traditional Mediation

ized. In supermarkets, when I tell a clerk that I have been unable to find a product supposedly on aisle five, I do not want to be reassured that this is where the product assuredly must be unless of course the store is out of stock. I expect the clerk to drop whatever he is doing and come look, and I will complain to management about the attitude of any clerk who offers less. Should I expect less from librarians, whose commitment to a service ethic is presumably of longer standing?

The really fascinating dichotomy is found in academic libraries. These certainly have students, and we are presumably only supposed to help them help themselves, but up to what point? Bibliographic instruction is the process designed to help eager young students to become self-sufficient for the rest of their lives, or at least until they graduate. However, I suspect that our enthusiasm for this goal may cloud any sort of realistic evaluation of how well the process works. I know that I do not care for how-to instruction in the abstract, the tactic employed in computer training. I prefer to be helped to solve specific and real problems as I encounter them, and if that instruction is useful I will be able to solve *that* problem myself the next time I encounter it. However, I will be back, because I will ask for the same kind of assistance the first time I encounter a different kind of problem or question, and I want to be helped quickly because that problem is now a roadblock for me. Are we so certain that this is not what students would prefer, and is there anything wrong with that preference? At a minimum, should bibliographic instruction not also include a component that alerts students to their rights and legitimate expectations in dealing with reference librarians, at this university and for the rest of their lives? Special librarians can attest to legions of corporate employees who expect no professional interaction because they were never offered any while they were students, and who do not even know that reference assistance is their right. They must be weaned to the reference interaction.

It is in dealing with faculty at the university level that the opportunity to provide reference service really breaks down, and it breaks down because of the assumption of three generally fallacious scenarios. The first is that all academic faculty are busily engaged in research. A number of articles by Ladd and Lipset in the *Chronicle of Higher Education* argue that only a small percentage of faculty at even major research universities are involved in original research.[3] Many others are simply milking for publication the research they undertook to obtain their doctorates. Confirmation of this judgement comes from data compiled over the years by the Institute for Scientific Information in Philadelphia for its citation indexes and the author address directory compiled from the arti-

28 *The Reference Librarian and Implications of Mediation*

cles covered in these and other publications, *Who Is Publishing in Science* (WIPIS). An astonishingly large number of individuals publish in one year but not in the next, and many of them publish once and never again.

In his own writing and research, the librarian and humanist scholar Charles Osburn dispels the myth that faculty are primarily basic researchers seeking raw material through which to sift, and that belief constitutes the second largely fallacious assumption.[4] Osburn notes that scientists long ago shifted their style of research to the patterns established by government contracts and grants. These involve not a search for knowledge but a validation of hypotheses established in obtaining the money. These are at best applied researchers, and they seek not so much raw data as proof in support of the conclusions already announced. The search for proof is a much narrower search. Osburn concludes that this pattern of information searching, always prevalent in industry, has now spilled, under the influence of similar conclusion-validating grants, from the physical sciences to the social sciences and even into the humanities. Entire disciplines of academic study have now sprung up for the simple purpose of developing proof for what the researchers stated long ago they knew. What this may suggest is that library practice in academia, which largely consists of shoveling large quantities of raw material at the faculty, may be serving a research style now increasingly rare.

The third fallacy is the assumption that faculty enjoy the process of searching through the literature for nuggets of information. Some undoubtedly do, but others abdicate and assign that process whenever they can to graduate assistants and even to others less qualified. It is this fallacy that primarily drives our insistence that end users ought to do their own database searching because deep inside they really want to, although it is of course possible that for some library administrators the argument simply serves as a convenient rationale for reducing exposed library costs by shifting them into other cost centers. Failing to consider what this does to *overall* institutional costs is irresponsible, but it is also considered financially prudent by managers who deserve little professional respect from any of us.

However, to the extent to which this is simply a case of honest self-deception we have plenty of help. Government agencies such as NASA and NTIS aim their programs at end user searching rather than at librarians, and we can understand the strategy when we realize, as government officials certainly do, that supplying information directly to engineers, scientists, economists, and business executives is more attractive to the Congress as a funding justification than a program that supplies information to librarians. The National Library of Medicine, although its name suggests a library serving other libraries, has developed an ambitious strategy aimed at freezing librarians out of the information intermediation process entirely, by gearing its program development directly to physicians through initiatives entitled "Loansome Doc" and "Grateful Med." The role that this tactic reserves for librarians is the old warehousing and supply room role, for which NLM understands clearly enough nobody gets professional credit, and that is why they would rather we do it. Never mind the overwhelming evidence that physicians do not, in general, like to undertake literature searches, and that they conduct them badly and expensively. We are not talking about quality here, we are talking about politics.

Database vendors, whose interests are quite naturally served not by fewer and better searches, but by more and sloppier ones, have even begun to amend their pricing strategies to lure end users. This is done by not charging directly for connect time (a process that rewards tightly controlled professional crafted searches), but by allowing new users to dabble at a relatively low cost.[5] Of course, once they are in the net the pricing ploys can change, as they have before.

The strategies of government agencies and commercial database vendors are reported without rancor, and even with some admiration for their understanding of both political and economic realities. Libraries are not seen either as powerful clients or as affluent ones. Better to bypass them as completely as possible as decision makers, as scholarly journal publishers have also learned to do.[6] What is less clear is why librarians would see merit for themselves in such a strategy, or for their users. As academic libraries have started training programs to teach faculty members how to do their own end user searches, they find that to a great extent faculty members do not attend the training sessions. Instead, they send their laboratory assistants, their graduate students, and sometimes even their secretaries. Corporate special librarians have known for some time that the process of information gathering and analysis is not a particularly sought-after activity, and is quickly shifted to clerks.

I have no doubt that librarians *could* play a major role in the information gathering and analysis process that shapes information intermediation. They fail to do so perhaps because the faculty, like users of the public library, do not trust them to understand the question. That lack of trust is heightened when they can not even differentiate the librarians from the student workers. However, they also sense that we are not particularly anxious to undertake reference work, in part because we claim to be understaffed and underfunded, and in part because it appears to

30 The Reference Librarian and Implications of Mediation

them that there are other things we would rather be doing. Our clients will not fight about this with us. As demonstrated long ago by Calvin Mooers, they will adapt to and rationalize an inefficient information process rather than insist that the process adapt to their preferences, because that is simply too much trouble for them.[7]

I conclude that, despite our protestations, we generally do not like to do reference work, and that may go all of the way back to the premise that the primary role of libraries is education and not information, and that we do not want to do the work of "lazy" people for them.[8] That is a serious charge to make, but I submit there is evidence. "If you can find what we have in our collection and available on the shelf, then you may have it. If the material is charged out, or at the bindery, or simply missing, then that is your bad luck, and we will certainly not seek to obtain another copy of what we already own, just because we can't supply it today. In addition, if you are so presumptuous as to ask for something we have not purchased, we will charge you for the privilege of waiting while we obtain it for you. Of course that process may take quite a bit of time." Is that our credo? There is something very backward in such a value system if we truly profess to concentrate on user information need rather than on bureaucratic convenience for ourselves. Perhaps we ought to adapt some version of the model governing Chinese medicine, under which patients pay their doctors when they are well, and stop paying them when they become ill, to give the physician an incentive for curing them. If we adopted this, there might be a fee for service but only if we provided it correctly and promptly, but there would be both a qualitative and time cross-over by which, after a while, we would have to pay the client a forfeit for our lack of performance. Some people might come to the library just to get rich.

If I suggest that our value systems do not esteem the value of reference service, it is because I see us adopting a value system that leads into almost directly contradictory directions. What we measure is not quality but quantity, as typified in academic libraries by holdings, and in public libraries by circulation. The most successful transaction is perceived to be the one that leads the user out the door with the greatest number of items; but I restate the obvious when I note that this is at best an educational and never an informational value system. Under the latter, less information, provided it is the correct information, is almost always preferred. I see this when I tell special library consultation clients that the upgraded and improved library will obtain and access more databases for their enlightenment. A look of panic comes over their faces, because they remember that they already have more materials from the library than they have hope of ever looking at, and all I seem to be promising them is more disaster. I quickly reassure them that the purpose of additional information access sources is not to provide more information but rather better information, and that it is not unlikely that the better a question is handled by the library the fewer the resources that need to be consulted by the client. Has any librarian ever attempted a management report that conveyed the *good* news that circulation had decreased, and that this clearly demonstrated that we were interacting with our users more effectively? I doubt it. The management structure, which makes circulation a part of reference, almost automatically suggests that more reference and more circulation are symbiotically related. I wrote more than a decade ago that proactive information service largely meant telling the client to stay out of the library and to concentrate on what he or she did well, while allowing us to concentrate on doing what we do well, to everybody's benefit.[9] Indeed, in an idealized information service the user does not have to ask at all, because we have anticipated the question. Selective dissemination of information services are the first cautious step in that direction.

All of the foregoing discussion still does not address the reality that there are many kinds of users, with many different information approaches, all equally valid. In a talk presented at a meeting of the International Federation for Documentation in Copenhagen, Herbert Brinberg suggested at least three kinds of users for library and information services.[10] The first group consists of traditional basic researchers, who ask for nothing more than large piles of raw materials that they will then sift, either because they enjoy the process, or because they trust nobody else to understand what they really need. In the communication shorthand of my industrial consulting, I refer to these people as classic German chemists, both because that is how these people were trained, and because every company has at least one. Brinberg's second group includes applied researchers, development people, marketing professionals, and engineers. These individuals are looking for specific answers to specific questions, and not for sources that *might* contain the answer. These people are heavily served by special librarians, and serving them correctly requires, as Grieg Aspnes has so eloquently put it, "assuming their stress and their burden onto your own shoulders.[11] For these users reference work means leaving the problem with the librarian, and either coming back for the answer, or having it sent. Academic librarians have problems with such a process, quite aside from the requirement for a large reference staff. What do these lazy people learn from such an experience? That of course is the old educational model. However, do not believe that there aren't

32 *The Reference Librarian and Implications of Mediation*

users in academia who would not welcome such an interaction. They just do not find us very hospitable.

Brinberg's third group consists of executives and managers, who are looking neither for raw data nor specific answers, but rather for options. What are the choices, and what are the pros and cons of each? Don't tell me about things I can not do anyway! That represents a process of information intermediation, and the managers and executives who require this information are potentially our most powerful clients, most particularly in academia where the number of managers has proliferated. However, these are non-clients, because we tend not to serve them at all, and they do not even have a clue that we could or would help them. Is it any wonder that the academic value system treasures collections–the *library*–but not necessarily its professional staff–the *librarian*? Have we given academic administrators any reason to feel differently?

Parts of the Brinberg hypothesis are confirmed in an excellent recent Indiana University School of Library and Information Science doctoral dissertation by Thomas Pinelli.[12] He examines the use of NASA scientific and technical reports by engineers and scientists and finds patterns quite similar to those suggested by Brinberg. My own experience at NASA as Executive Director of its Scientific and Technical Information Facility in the 1960s confirms this as well. As part of our information program we constructed more than 600 selective dissemination of information (SDI) profiles for a variety of NASA administrators, scientists, engineers, and contractors. These profiles were drawn from the terms of the NASA Thesaurus, which was used for indexing all of our documents. We originally assumed that the users themselves were best qualified to draw up their own profiles, and thereby frame their own questions. We were wrong, as those who insist on the presumed quality of end user searching have been wrong since. These users certainly believed they knew what they wanted to know, but they had no ability to phrase their request either into search terminology or into Boolean search equations. Their questions led to poor and expensive searches, and it is this expense that database vendors now seek to "forgive" to lure end users into the process. We found at NASA that it was best for the users simply to talk to us or to write us a paragraph or two describing what they needed to keep abreast about. From this we constructed the search profiles. We also found that some users had a great deal of tolerance for document announcements that did not interest them as an acceptable price for making sure that they missed nothing. These are our basic researchers, and my "German chemists." Others did not care what they might miss but became enraged about even one notice they considered irrelevant and that

Traditional Mediation 33

wasted their time. We adapted to both preferences, without judging the requestors. There was a third group that stressed convenience over information to an even greater degree. These individuals specified that they wanted to be informed only about items written in English, regardless of the subject. Their rationale was simple. First, they already had more to read than they had time to read. Second, they did not want to be made to feel guilty about material that they would not be reading in any case. These characteristics have some similarity to those of individuals who do not want to be given any facts that contradict the conclusions they have already reached, and that group may include the greatest number of our clients, even in research universities.

None of this was true information intermediation, a process in which we would tell users not only what to read, but perhaps even more importantly what not to bother to read. That last concept was proposed many years ago by Alvin Weinberg of the Atomic Energy Commission.[13] Weinberg's suggestion, echoed by Garvin,[14] was for information analysis centers staffed by fellow scientists, or perhaps fellow economists, who would decide what others needed to bother to read. Weinberg's innovative idea has never taken hold, but it is significant for us to note that he did not trust librarians with this task. He did understand, as we need to understand, that most of our users are not looking for more information. They are looking for less, but better, information. Until and unless reference librarians are able to adapt to this, and until librarians can measure something other than quantities of transactions, much education of both librarians and users remains to be done if they are to work together optimally.

Ours is a service profession, and that means that we need to bring our unique skills and preparation–both managerial and technical–to a process of user information service. What that process of interaction turns out to be is the result of negotiation, and that negotiation is ultimately based not on our preconceptions, but on what users really need in order to get on with the rest of their lives. The need will vary depending on the problem and on the user, and I have suggested in earlier writings that users are not necessarily qualified to make that judgement, certainly not all by themselves.[15] What users need is not necessarily what they say they need, and certainly not always what they say they want. We should not blame them for that inaccuracy. Users bring with them preconceptions about the library, about us, about what we are capable of doing, and about what we are willing to do. I begin my interview process for clients of a corporate library, for which I am trying to determine the appropriate level of activity, by urging these individuals not to think about the library, and not to think about what might or might not be reasonable to ask of the library.

34 The Reference Librarian and Implications of Mediation

I will tell them all that soon enough. What I want them to tell me is how, in an idealized environment of their own creation, they would like their information support services to function. It is hard to get this out of them. They feel foolish, they feel embarrassed, they feel selfish. But why? Is that not the question we should be asking them, in all information service settings? Have we beaten initiative and spunk out of them already, by our tales of overwork and the ethic of self-service, and have we subtly suggested that they are lucky to get anything at all?

One thing seems certain to me. Many of the functions now performed in all libraries, but particularly in academic libraries–functions such as document identification, document delivery, overdue notices, interlibrary loan, even cataloging–will become increasingly computerized and clerical. We have little professional future in these transactions. Our future is in the process of proactive reference work, of information intermediation, aimed not at validating a library policy but at the specific and unique needs of the person who just contacted us. And what that person needs may or may not simply be a book or even an article. However, whatever it is, that becomes our job.

NOTES

1. Kent, A. et al. *Use of Library Materials: The University of Pittsburgh Study.* (New York: M. Dekker, 1979).

2. Trueswell, R. W. "Some Behavioral Patterns of Library Users: The 80/20 Rule." *Wilson Library Bulletin* 44:458-461. (Jan. 1969).

3. Ladd, E. C. and Lipset, S. M. A series of articles written periodically for the *Chronicle of Higher Education.*

4. Osburn, C. B. *Academic Research and Library Resources: Changing Patterns in America.* (Westport, CT: Greenwood Press, 1979).

5. Spigai, F. Observations in a chapter on information pricing prepared for publication in volume 26 of the *Annual Review of Information Science and Technology* (ARIST).

6. White, H. S. "Scholarly Publishers and Libraries: A Strained Marriage." *Scholarly Publishing* 19(3): 125-129. (Apr. 1988).

7. Mooers, C. "Mooers' Law, or Why Some Retrieval Systems Are Used and Others Are Not." *American Documentation* 11(3): 204. (July 1960).

8. White, H. S. "The Role of Reference Service in the Mission of the Academic Library." In S. H. Lee. Ed. *Reference Service: A Perspective.* (Ann Arbor, MI: The Pierian Press, 1983.) pp. 17-30.

9. White, H. S. "Growing User Information Dependence and Its Impact on the Library Field." *ASLIB Proceedings* 31(2):74-87. (Feb. 1979).

10. Brinberg, H. R. "The Contribution of Information to Economic Growth

Traditional Mediation

and Development." In V. Ammundsen. Ed. *Proceedings of the 40th FID Congress, Copenhagen, 18-21 August, 1980.* (The Hague: Federation Internationale de Documentation, 1982), pp. 23-36.

11. Aspnes, G. Remarks quoted in H. S. White. *Managing the Special Library: Strategies for Success Within the Larger Organization.* (White Plains, NY: Knowledge Industry Publications, 1984), p. 8.

12. Pinelli, T. E. "The Relationship Between the Use of U.S. Government Technical Reports by U.S. Aerospace Engineers and Scientists and Selected Institutional and Sociometric Variables." Ph.D. Dissertation. Indiana University School of Library and Information Science, 1990.

13. U.S. President's Science Advisory Committee. *Science, Government, and Information.* (Washington, DC: Government Printing Office, 1963.) (The Weinberg Report).

14. Garvin, D. "The Information Analysis Center and the Library." *Special Libraries* 62:17-23. (Jan. 1971).

15. White, H. S. "The Use and Misuse of Library User Studies." *Library Journal* 110(20) 70-71. (Dec. 1985).

Back to Basics: Recommitment to Patrons' Information Needs

Claudette S. Hagle

The motto of all reference librarians probably should be the words of Samuel Johnson in Boswell's *Life of Dr. Johnson* (1949): "Knowledge is of two kinds; we know a subject ourselves or we know where we can find information upon it" (vol. 1, p. 558). Unfortunately, there appears to be a wide gap between principle and practice, and today's reference librarians are getting a very low score on their report card of correct answers to reference questions. If Dr. Johnson were alive today, he would be quite chagrined to find that those who work at reference desks in libraries seem to neither have a thorough grounding in general information sources nor can they be relied upon to give a correct answer more than 55% of the time, on average, as numerous studies have reported.

It appears that the three basic tenets of reference service frequently have been forgotten: (1) determine what the patron wants to know through the reference interview process, which includes repeating the question in the patron's own words, or rephrasing it, and obtaining patron acknowledgement that you understand the query; (2) negotiate the information location process by asking open-ended questions of the patron while mentally reviewing sources on hand or through referral; and (3) always ascertain effectiveness by asking the patron "Does this completely answer your question?" If the answer to number three is "no," the librarian should begin again with number one. This may seem an easy process, but in practice it is much more difficult, as those who work in reference services know. Meeting patrons' information needs *is* the ac-

---

Claudette S. Hagle is Director of Public Services at the University of Dallas, Irving, TX.

© 1992 by The Haworth Press, Inc. All rights reserved.　　　*37*

38   *The Reference Librarian and Implications of Mediation*

knowledged primary responsibility of reference service. This goal has not changed, though the means to attain this end have.

This article examines the severity of the problem of giving wrong, incomplete, or unacceptable answers, and suggests a return to the basics of reference work to improve accuracy by rekindling our knowledge of sources of information and by sharpening skills for conducting the reference interview. By undertaking a personal renewal program, reference librarians, as mediators between the questioning process and the answers, can more successfully bring together patrons with information needs and the sources necessary to provide that information.

SCOPE OF THE PROBLEM

Most of the literature on reference effectiveness has been highly critical of the accuracy of answers supplied to inquiries made at the reference desk, either in person or by telephone. Little has been written about methods required for making positive changes to raise the accuracy rate. Miller (1984) laments that although studies have shown that basic services are lacking, not many scholars want to discuss accuracy of reference desk service and cites as a reason that, "Few of us . . . wish to call attention to this quality-of-service dilemma, especially when dealing with our administrative superiors. We would much prefer to ignore or deny the reality, perhaps to spare ourselves embarrassment or because the dimensions of the problem are overwhelming to the point of despair" (p. 304).

Prior to the 1970's, the major way that libraries evaluated their services was through a one-page library survey sheet. This survey was generally handed out to patrons as they entered the library. Users were asked to fill out the survey form before leaving and deposit it as they exited. Those who did fill out the forms usually gave "the library" high marks. This was especially so in public libraries where a higher percentage of patrons perceived the library and those who work there in a positive and uncritical way, believing it to be a very democratic institution employing good, patient, and kind people. The questions on these forms usually did not fully or scientifically measure reference performance and effectiveness.

In order to more specifically and scientifically evaluate reference effectiveness, unobtrusive studies were developed. These studies measured the accuracy of answers to discrete questions asked by proxies (persons unknown to the reference personnel) at the reference desk. The answers

Traditional Mediation 39

to the questions were known to be available in the library under observation and they could thus be verified for accuracy.

Unobtrusive and obtrusive methodological studies have been reported in the library and information science literature for almost 25 years. These studies have continually pointed out that library personnel who work at the reference desk and answer questions in person or by telephone have failed miserably in giving correct answers to simple factual questions and providing correct bibliographic information. Burton's article in a 1990 library publication calling for client-centered service noted that unobtrusive studies have shown "reference services in academic and public libraries provide correct responses to between 50 and 60 per cent of the questions put to them by users. So frequently has this result been found that it has been enshrined in the literature as the '55 per cent rule'" (p. 203).

Crowley (1968) and Childers (1970), while pursuing their doctoral studies at Rutgers, are credited with first performing unobtrusive studies, using proxies, to measure the accuracy of answers by reference service personnel to discrete queries. Their findings, later combined in a monograph (1971) concerning the accuracy of reference service in public libraries, were confirmed by Hernon and McClure (1986), using unobtrusive methodology to examine reference accuracy in government document depositories in both public and academic libraries. Hernon and McClure came up with the same disquieting result and noted that they were most surprised that no referral was made when a librarian did not know an answer (p. 41).

Critics of these studies have mentioned that the quick factual information questions are not the sum total of reference work. Daniel (1987) notes that" . . . I like to think that library/information people are dealing with the larger problems of diagnosis, filtering, and synthesizing, in partnership with their clients, that this age demands. I like to think that the earnest minds in our profession have the opportunity to use the power of their intelligence in analyzing problems and designing systems, and that 'looking it up' is only the first step in that process and not an end in itself'' (pp. 77-78). Daniel goes further and suggests that fact provision is only an adjunct service, not the major aspect of reference, and that libraries might want to limit the number of hours this service is provided so that more time can be devoted to other services (p. 78).

Ford (1988) notes that the introduction of online database searching, most often done by appointment, has already changed the relationship of reference librarian and patron and she suggests that perhaps the best use of the reference librarian's expertise would be by appointment interviews.

40 The Reference Librarian and Implications of Mediation

This would leave the directional and ready-reference information, presumably, to trained student and library assistant staff with librarian backup. This tactic, however, has come under criticism. Hester (1988) notes that reference desk duty "can be both informative and energizing for the reference librarians . . ." (p. 584). Hester explains that time at the reference desk provides feedback from patrons that can be used for bibliographic instruction, printed handouts, needed signage, decisions on new reference titles or databases for purchase or development, and training needs for both new and experienced staff.

When the Brigham Young University Library tried just such a design as Ford suggests, Christensen, Benson, Butler, Hall and Howard (1989) report that major problems surfaced: Those working the reference desk felt isolated from the subject specialist librarians; the process of referral did not work well; training was inconsistent; and, the percent of correct answers given at the reference desk in an unobtrusive test fell to 36 percent (p. 482). In the same article the authors state that, "Providing professional-quality reference service is a complex process, requiring extensive subject expertise, knowledge of library collections and systems, and years of practical experience" (p. 468).

Durrance (1989) reports on the unobtrusive study she supervised at the University of Michigan School of Information and Library Studies. The study covers the reference environment and takes as its measure of success not only the correct answers to questions posed but also the willingness of the observers to return to the person who answered their questions. This added dimension emphasizes not only the problem of getting a correct answer but also the behavior and attitude of the personnel at the reference desk. The findings of this study suggest that reference librarians need to be identified in the environment (e.g., a sign denoting Reference Desk or Reference Librarian would help) and must sharpen their communication skills in the reference interview.

A problem-solving study conducted at Michigan State University also pinpoints the environment as a source of problems at the reference desk; the conclusion, reported in the *Journal of Academic Librarianship* by Shapiro (1987), resulted in locational changes of both the Reference and Information Desks which, in turn, provided improved service to patrons.

In an effort to improve the quality of reference service, Kleiner (1991) reports on the peer evaluation process she instituted at Louisiana State University Libraries: "Peer perceptions can be a powerful constructive influence and can motivate us to make personal as well as performance changes" (p. 358). The purpose of the formative evaluation was improvement of service, and this forced her staff to look at the social and interper-

Traditional Mediation 41

sonal skills needed to improve desk performance. Kleiner notes that the "manner and behavior exhibited while assisting patrons were perceived as equal in importance to the intellectual content of the response (p. 358).

In a much discussed article, "What's Wrong with Reference," Miller (1984) claims that the problem with reference service is staff overload and overcommitment, with constantly expanding services taking up more and more of the reference librarian's time and energy. He calls for a reordering of priorities, use of technology, alternative staffing patterns, and better training or retraining of personnel.

Reporting on an exploratory study done at five Northern California libraries, Whitlatch (1990) comments on the constraints of time in providing good reference service: "Reference librarians who were interviewed . . . observed that workload pressures often create situations in which service is not as thorough as it should be" (p. 209). She goes on to indicate that the client expects to be provided with quick, concise answers at the reference desk and that "Generally, shorter lengths of time were significantly associated with more valued service outcomes" (p. 213). Whitlatch also mentions librarian behavior and its effect on outcomes: "Librarian courtesy, interest, and helpfulness are crucial in providing successful reference service. Libraries must select and retain staff who have these service orientations toward users" (p. 213).

A TIME FOR CHANGE

Some or all of the suggestions for "fixing" what is "wrong" with reference service may help. But in the long run the "fix" has to be made by the person in the mirror. A la Pogo, "We have met the enemy, and the enemy is us." It is time to stop being embarrassed by the findings of the reference service effectiveness studies, and do something about them. A return to the basics of reference work is long overdue. A serious review of attitudes about reference desk service and the behavior exhibited while performing should be undertaken by all personnel involved, and a reordering of priorities made, if deemed necessary.

Needed is the courage to say "no" to bad attitudes and behaviors, mental laziness, and an overload of new services. And we must affirm a personal commitment to improving knowledge of (1) collections our library and other libraries hold, in paper or microform; (2) collections in electronic format and the means to access them; (3) the more elusive information sources; and (4) the network of experts and scholars who can serve as referral sources.

A significant part of the reason for giving incorrect or incomplete answers to reference queries is that we do not know information sources well enough, are not making full use of new technologies to help us, and are hesitant about referring queries to others.

SOURCES OF INFORMATION

Sources of information can be found in a wide variety of formats. These include standard print sources, electronic databases, audiovisual materials, electronic publishing, preprints, unpublished items, work in progress, networks of scholars, and experts in the local community and beyond.

To renew expertise in the standard print sources, a good starting place might be to look at Sheehey's *Guide to Reference Books* and update call numbers and other annotations in the margins. This refamiliarization with the librarian's standby can serve as a reminder of how information is organized and give some indication of weaknesses in our collections that need to be addressed. Other general reference bibliographies could be handled in the same manner to assist in the refamiliarization process. Also, reading the preface of new editions to reference continuations can alert you to changes made in coverage and organization of the work; such changes occur frequently and can provide new information. Finally, if the library owns a copy of *The New York Public Library Desk Reference*, take time to go through it, since it can provide a lot of quick information. In addition, it is quite enjoyable to browse.

It is important, however, that the search for information not be limited entirely to print sources when attempting to provide timely and accurate answers. At a panel discussion on the future of reference held at the University of Texas in Austin, Hester (1988) reminds librarians that, "While the demise of the book like that of Mark Twain has been greatly exaggerated, reference librarians would do well to remember that their destiny is tied to the book only if they are inflexible" (p. 584).

Too often in training for reference work, both in graduate library programs and on the job, the main emphasis has been focused largely on print sources of information, a core of standard reference works. During the last ten years, online catalogs and the searching of bibliographic and statistical databases, online or on compact disk, have become commonplace in reference work. This electronic information, that may in many instances substitute for print sources, has added to the supply of reference tools that librarians and patrons can use to find answers.

Overlooked sometimes is how information is organized, how databases are constructed, and the additional information that may be added by the database supplier. Alternative print and non-print sources along with the myriad of elusive, or fugitive, sources should also be in a reference librarian's "bag of tricks" and should constantly be supplemented and updated.

NEW TECHNOLOGY AS A REFERENCE TOOL

Gorman (1991) suggests that new technologies are but an adjunct to reference work: "New technologies should be seen as doing what they always do–supplementing and enhancing old technologies. It is far better to see the world of knowledge and information technology as one that grows and enriches rather than one that dominates and destroys" (p. 6). Strong words such as "dominates" and "destroys" are shared by fewer and fewer librarians today as they discover the many ways that new technologies can enhance information gathering skills, make more effective use of time, and open up new avenues of knowledge.

Hallman (1990), for one, advocates more aggressive use of technology and writes that reference librarians "have a responsibility to acquire the knowledge and skills necessary to use and teach the most efficient information techniques that current technology makes possible" (p. 204). He speculates that as a trigger for change in reference librarianship, new technology is needed for building databases to satisfy needs at the local level and also to experiment with new delivery systems. Hallman goes further and suggests that reference librarians need a wide range of skills, a good liberal education, and "a thorough knowledge of information technology and techniques is also essential" (p. 206).

PUTTING NEW TECHNOLOGY SKILLS INTO PRACTICE

Nearly every reference librarian has a list, or multiple lists, that go under various names but are generically called the Ready Reference files. They may be a neatly typed "Fifty Most-Often Asked Questions and Their Answers," a file of 3" x 5" cards with questions and referral information, a local organization list, a box of slips of paper detailing really tough questions that took a lot of digging or whatever list that appears to be an indispensable source of help at the reference desk. Update the list(s), assign subjects, and then computerize them. This is not

44 *The Reference Librarian and Implications of Mediation*

an extremely difficult task, and there are several software programs for the microcomputer to help do this.

Stover and Grassian (1989) report on a large project that they supervised that merged all of the reference information files at the several libraries on the UCLA campus and converted them into machine-readable form with the use of Inmagic, a text management software system. Future plans, depending on funding, call for sharing the UCLA files with the reference files of the Los Angeles Public Library.

Using dBase III Plus, Gallimore (1988) developed a microcomputer database for local company information at the Manchester (England) Commercial Library. This type of information on small local companies is very difficult to obtain, but through an agreement with Dun and Bradstreet they were able to secure data on floppy disks for more than 7,000 local companies. Using dBase III Plus management software for the user interface has provided flexibility, speed, simplicity, and an easily read output format, allowing lists of companies to be printed out as needed.

Librarians using the RLIN bibliographic utility have long enjoyed subject access. Now those who use the OCLC database to get correct information on titles and locations can use FirstSearch and EPIC to scan the database by subject. These additional searching techniques open up many new avenues.

One of the findings of the unobtrusive studies was that reference librarians make minimal use of online searching, and perhaps CD-ROM databases also, in order to answer questions asked at the desk. There may be many reasons for this. Cost may be an important limiting factor in online searching. There are ways to reduce these costs to a minimum, however: develop a search strategy off-line; type ahead; search later in the day for faster processing or, if using BRS, use BRS After Dark if time allows; if using Dialog, utilize DIALINDEX to narrow searches and the "SaveTemp" command to go from cheaper to more expensive databases; and download information onto disks for later printing. If there is no budget for ready reference online searching, justification to request funding can be found in the information science literature. Tenopir (1991) points out in a recent article that ". . . the most up-to-date information is only available online and database producers and online systems are rushing to enhance update schedules. Wire services are updated continuously throughout the day and night on several online systems; other databases that used to be updated monthly are now updated weekly or even daily" (p. 72).

The reluctance by reference librarians to use CD-ROM databases to answer quick questions may be related to the probability that a patron will be using the database at the time that another person asks a question that might be answered on that database. But we can establish "in-house" priorities for computer database use. For example, if the reference area does not have an OCLC terminal, we can establish the right to "bump" cataloging, interlibrary loan, or acquisitions personnel temporarily from the OCLC terminal so that we can answer a reference question for a patron at the desk. This right, however, would not be equitably applied to patrons using a database. We can limit their time spent using the database and then take our turn utilizing it, if that is the only viable option.

Telecommunications systems are becoming more important in libraries as they develop new uses and become easier to access. Through Internet and its Bitnet subsystem–an electronic mail, bulletin board, and scholar's network–it is possible to communicate with experts and build a network of sources and also request help to locate information. There are, additionally, a number of journals in electronic format that have no print equivalent. These give currency and variety to information availability and can be accessed by anyone with a microcomputer, modem, and long distance telephone line.

These, of course, are not all the new technological devices available for locating sources of information. The information field is dynamic and changing too rapidly to be described in a few paragraphs. Use of expert systems, artificial intelligence, and other means open up new ways to build databases of information. The above discussion is but a suggestion for beginning an investigation.

ELUSIVE OR HIDDEN SOURCES

Finding elusive or hidden sources, is one of the most difficult aspects of reference work. It may take a concerted effort to unearth such information as talks presented at meetings, conferences, or even at informal gatherings; technical reports; letters to the editor which may not be indexed; pamphlets, newsletters and other ephemeral materials; preprints; diaries and other personal accounts; irregularly and privately published materials; uncataloged Master's theses and senior papers; and scrapbooks and archival materials.

Very little is written in the library and information science literature about locating these sources. Reference librarians with subject specialties in the sciences probably have the most demand from their patrons for this information. An excellent article by Bates (1984) describes search techniques for locating elusive information. She suggests that it might be well to ascertain if just the information contained in an article, paper, or report is what is needed, and not the specific item. She notes, "It is in the nature of the scientific enterprise that a given set of results or ideas may be published in a number of slightly varied forms. Therefore, if the information cannot be found in one form, it may be possible to find it in another" (p. 114). Experience in online searching and working with scientific literature can help one to discover such sources.

Uncovering elusive materials requires networking with other librarians, scholars, and local experts. Asking a lot of questions is a necessity, as is good note-taking during these conversations. An excellent memory helps, too! Networking also makes referral easier, when that is what is necessary to obtain information.

THE REFERRAL PROCESS

The referral process in libraries had not received much attention in the literature until the publication of an exploratory study by Hawley (1987) which looks at the process of referral. He notes that referral may sensitize several issues such as library policy, inconvenience to the patron in being sent elsewhere, and reaction of the person or staff at the location to which a patron is referred (p. 1). Hawley discusses several factors that play a role in whether or not a librarian will refer a question: written policy statement on referral, or the absence of one which results in ambiguity; peer pressure; training; personality of the librarian; vulnerability to embarrassment and wounded pride; ethics; institutional cooperation; outside personal contacts; and costs to the patron. "Building a network of personal contacts is usually a gradual process based on the librarian's work and personal experiences in a particular geographic area" (p. 160).

A reluctance to refer a question that one cannot answer to another person or place may be viewed as an abrogation of responsibility to the patron. "No" or "I don't know" should not be acceptable *final* answers in the information gathering process. Integrity and a service orientation demand that we go farther and offer to pursue the answer by referring the question to another person at the institution or outside it. The information needed may not be available at hand, but interlibrary loan or a referral to a nearby library holding the material should always be offered.

No one person can possibly be expected to know all sources of information, and it is not unusual to have occasional memory lapses. One may want to request more time from the patron for research on the query if it appears that a number of sources will have to be consulted to arrive at the answer.

With the proliferation of microcomputers in homes and offices, and the electronic means to access information from commercial vendors as well as the ability to dial into the a library's online catalog, the ownership of materials is becoming of less importance than access to information. Therefore, referral to sources outside the library may no longer be perceived as a major obstacle to the patron.

CONCLUSION

The crisis in reference service demands action. It is now time to change attitudes and behaviors at the reference desk and return to the basics of reference service. Know yourself, your strengths and weaknesses, and know your sources. An openness to thinking about the wide variety of information sources and the many possible locations for answers may not be the entire solution to the poor showing by reference personnel for accurate information at the reference desk, but it is certainly one of the essentials.

A commitment to learn new sources that might provide answers to reference questions, new ways of finding information, new aspects of networking to help with personal sources of information, and a commitment to a personal refresher program to renew acquaintance with standard sources could bring back the excitement of the quest for information and pride in performing a valued service.

REFERENCES

Bates, M. J. (1984). Locating elusive science information: Some search techniques. *Special Libraries, 75,* 114-120.

Boswell, J. (1949). *Life of Dr. Johnson* (Vol. 1). New York: Dutton, Everyman ed. (Original work published 1791).

Burton, P. J. (1990). Accuracy of information provision: The need for client-centered service. *Journal of Academic Librarianship, 22* (4), 201-215.

Childers, T. (1970). Telephone information service in public libraries: A comparison of performance and descriptive statistics collected by the State of New Jersey (Doctoral dissertation, Rutgers University).

Christensen, J. O., Benson, L. D., Butler, H. J., Hall, B. H., & Howard, D. H. (1989). An evaluation of reference desk service. *College & Research Libraries, 50,* 468-483.

Crowley, T. (1968). The effectiveness of information service in medium size public libraries (Doctoral dissertation, Rutgers University).

Crowley, T. & Childers, T. (1971). *Information service in public libraries: Two studies*. Metuchen, NJ: Scarecrow Press.

Daniel, E. H. (1987). The effects of identity, attitude, and priority. *Journal of Academic Librarianship, 13*, 76-78.

Durrance, J. C. (1989, April 15). Reference success: Does the 55 percent rule tell the whole story? *Library Journal*, pp. 31-36.

Ford, B. J. (1988). Reference service: Past, present, and future. *College & Research Libraries News, 49*, 578-582.

Gallimore, A. (1988). Developing a microcomputer database for local company information. *Program* (Belfast), 22, 262-267.

Gorman, M. (1991). The academic library in the year 2001: Dream or nightmare or something in between? *Journal of Academic Librarianship, 17*, 4-9.

Hallman, C. N. (1990). Technology: Trigger for change in reference librarianship. *Journal of Academic Librarianship, 16*, 204-208.

Hawley, G. S. (1987). *The referral process in libraries: A characterization and an exploration of related factors*. Metuchen, NJ: Scarecrow Press.

Hernon, P. & McClure, C. R. (1986, April 15). Unobtrusive reference testing: The 55 percent rule. *Library Journal*, pp. 37-41.

Hester, G. (1988). The future of reference service: A response. *College & Research Libraries News, 49*, 584-585.

Kleiner, J. P. (1991). Ensuring quality reference desk service: The introduction of a peer process. *RQ, 30*, 349-361.

Miller, W. (1984). What's wrong with reference: Coping with success and failure at the reference desk. *American Libraries, 15*, 303-306, 321-322.

New York Public Library. (1989). *New York Public Library desk reference*. New York: Webster's New World.

Shapiro, B. J. (1987). Trying to fix "what's wrong with reference." *Journal of Academic Librarianship, 13*, 286-291.

Sheehey, E. P. (1986). *Guide to reference books* (10th ed.). Chicago: American Library Association.

Stover, M. & Grassian, E. (1989). Toward an automated reference information system: Inmagic and the UCLA ready-reference information files. *RQ, 28*, 517-527.

Tenopir, C. (1991, October 1). Predicting the future. *Library Journal*, pp. 70, 72.

Whitlatch, J. B. (1990). Reference service effectiveness. *RQ, 30*, 205-220.

Mediation in Reference Service to Extend Patron Success

Jack Alan Hicks

SUMMARY. Reference librarians have been concerned about reference performance for many years. Evaluation and study have produced statistics and guidelines but not procedures for service. Many studies dwell on failure of the librarian but offer no process for systematic remediation of reference inaccuracy. Librarians should study more closely the successful patron's approach to the reference encounter and shift the emphasis of their concern and training to perfecting the delivery of service. Service industries have long known that the skill in delivering a service is often as important as the service itself. This paper offers a beginning in the redirection of reference energies to improve upon existing performance.

MEDIATION AS A TECHNIQUE

This article is about mediation in reference service. Since librarians are either first or second parties in every transaction, and mediation implies and requires a detached third party, it is a difficult concept to define. However, it should be possible to develop a set of procedures that can be used by librarians that will allow them to mediate between a patron's expectations and the potentials of the library's resources to improve service effectiveness. A technique of mediation must be based on patron success not reference accuracy.

Librarians know that many reference transactions fail because of a flawed relationship between patron and librarian. It is productive to explore those elements of library use that separate the casual and often unsuccessful patron from the library client who generally succeeds. Those elements of success are the cornerstone of a technique of mediation that

---

Jack Alan Hicks is Director of Deerfield Public Library, 920 Waukegan Road, Deerfield, IL 60015.

©1992 by The Haworth Press, Inc. All rights reserved.   *49*

50   *The Reference Librarian and Implications of Mediation*

can extend patron success. Over the past twenty years I have observed that the relationship between patron and librarian is the crucial link in the delivery of service and the success of any transaction. Our studies should be directed not only at what patrons want when they come into our libraries but why patrons are successful.

CURRENT POTENTIALS

Just as every period probably believes it is living through a golden age, it appears that librarians are in the golden age of reference. The justification of this statement is simple. We have at our command today all of the tools and techniques that librarians have only talked about–across generations and continents. I mean that from the standpoint of both manual paper tools and all of the computer driven devices. Boolean, key-word, author-title-subject, ISBN, and adjacent searching result in bibliographic control–a tortured concept librarians have wrestled with for generations. However, the salient features of traditional reference librarianship–searching by controlled subject headings, literature searches, knowledge of tools and the collection, secondary references, intuition, and referral techniques–are still essential. Furthermore, our enthusiasm for the tools and resources now available to us should be tempered by the fact that these tools are not a guarantee of success in a patron transaction. Literature searching of any kind is still a difficult and human art. Finally, our optimism leads me to be concerned that a dark age can follow any golden period.

I am also troubled because reference librarians are delivering the same low level of service that has dominated much of our thinking and research for the past twenty years. We have the tools and techniques but we are not doing any better with them to service patrons. On the whole, reference librarians answer patron's requests correctly about 50% of the time (Douglas, 1988). Obtrusive and unobtrusive testing have shown us our faults but have not provided us with convenient forms of remediation. A survey of the literature demonstrates that reference librarians, in particular, are very concerned with measurement, testing, evaluation, and peer coaching–all with the intent of raising performance. Almost all research and articles on improving delivery of reference reach the same depressing conclusion: "We have met the enemy and he is us."

Not only is this the wrong conclusion but it also misidentifies the problem. We are not the problem, though we can improve. Attitude is a problem, but procedures, process, and motivation can go a long way to improving attitude. Stated differently, the problem of low delivery in reference performance is that the profession has not grappled with the issue and indeed does not seem to fully understand the business in which we are engaged. We are not in the accuracy business, we are not in the reference tool business, we are not in the interviewing business, and most assuredly we are not in the information science business. We are in the business of service. The form that service takes must fulfill the expectations of the patron. It is important to remember that those expectations may be unreasonable or unrealistic.

PERFORMANCE STUDIES BASED ON FAILURE

We began to set standards of performance and started measuring that performance with the issuance of Bernard Vavrek's guidelines (Vavrek, 1975) in the early 1970s and Childer's unobtrusive study done at about the same time (Childers, 1970). The results of these early tests seem to have molded the profession. We have become obsessed with inventory lists that contain every possible variable that comes to bear in a reference transaction: evaluation, standards, tests, and peer coaching. A problem with these lists–and I make them myself–is that they are useless since I can never find a librarian who embodies them, nor have I been successful in remediating staff who did not embody them in the first place. A survey of the literature will convince anyone that in reference service, failure is the coin of the realm.

One serious flaw of most of these essays–whether they are systematic or anecdotal–is the fact they dwell on failure. We always seem to focus on the shortcomings of individual librarians. But the problem is more extensive: it is in fact institutional and endemic to the profession. There is a more important flaw in almost all of these studies: the tests assume that a librarian's competence assures delivery of competent service. The profession must learn that competence and delivery of service, though intertwined, are not the same thing. Testing and measurement as used by the profession have been almost a textbook example of feeding the disease to the patient as a cure. The approach is consistent–find the button where we fail and push it harder and harder–rather than trying a different button (Isenstein, 1991). The different button should be to study the successful patrons and establish why they succeed.

Testing has been criticized by some as a faulty methodology to gauge reference performance (Von Seggern, 1989). Cold questions posed in a vacuum represent to a high degree the expectations of many clients, but

52 *The Reference Librarian and Implications of Mediation*

also point clearly to where the deficiencies arise: failure of the librarian to engage the patron, lack of knowledge of the tools, inability to understand the question, routinized lack of interest on the part of the librarian, lack of specific knowledge of the internal details of the tools, and finally the foolish belief that the librarian can interpret answers that the patrons cannot interpret themselves. Much of this reverses the concepts that drive the Deming quality process–that institutionally we have looked only at shortcomings and failures of deficient libraries and librarians. Deming would say that these failures lie with management, which did not ensure quality control (Walton, 1986).

Quality control in most library transactions is assumed by the client and not the librarian. Deming insists that quality control comes out of the board room, not off the shop floor. We have always practiced do-it-yourself librarianship because most patrons let us get away with it–and there generally are not enough librarians to go around during peak hours. Seen from the perspective of retail trade we never have adequate staff on hand to meet service challenges.This is a failure of management to lead and not worker failure. How many supervisors does one observe at a reference desk overseeing quality? How many directors initiate policy, training, and supervision plans geared solely to control quality? The profession talks about service, but it is just a sacred cow and false piety with very little emphasis in actual practice. Instead of being obsessed with reference accuracy, I am much more concerned that many librarians have no idea what the goal and mission of their library actually is. Accuracy is as much a product of motivation as it is of skill (Alvarez, 1987).

Another common complaint about the measurement and testing of reference service is that somehow reference librarians "do more than just answer questions." To an extent that is true. There are collection development, filing, weeding, phone calls, and all the other housekeeping tasks and accoutrements associated with the reference desk, but answering questions is the reason that we have that desk in the first place. All standards and measurements must and should come from analyzing the effectiveness of the work done there. A collection without successful patrons is a useless collection. What good does it do if the reference staff is proficient at the reference process, and knows the resources, tools, and techniques, if this knowledge is not applied to answering questions that patrons pose? We may as well not have the materials, processes, and staff, if the patron does not benefit from them. Rashid's (1990) study of book availability demonstrates that collection measurement is a valid use analysis of a library's resources to fulfill patron expectations.

This does not mean I am satisfied with the state of research in librarianship. Too much of what passes for research has been done by librarians who have never faced a patron or delivered the services on which they pontificate. Right now, we need more performance evaluations, tests, and measurement to insure a higher quality of service delivery. But guidelines and statistics have not been standardized into the procedures the profession needs to approach basic problems. We must also avoid the gestalt argument that some people get their questions answered incorrectly and, therefore, what the librarian did was incorrect. In practice the librarian can do everything right and still be wrong.

ROLE OF THE LIBRARIAN AS MEDIATOR

Librarians are at a serious disadvantage in the patron/librarian transaction. We are neither data producers nor data users, nor can we vouch for the accuracy of any of the answers we deliver. We have tried for years to play all roles: producer, interpreter, user, apologist. Our task is to mediate between willing and unwilling patrons and a complex set of tools, resources and techniques. Many librarians fail in this role. The talents needed to be a functional reference librarian should be well known, but often they are not. Successful reference librarians must have wide-ranging knowledge and authentic intellectual curiosity, and intimate and specific knowledge of the tools and resources available. Most important, they must possess the human relation resources to deal closely with patrons. They must avoid the prescriptive and pejorative. They also must have the ability to be guided by the patron. I have not found these qualities in all reference librarians I have worked with or trained. Additionally, I have known librarians in the past few years who were essentially nonliterate which does not make this task easier: I would judge this a failure of standards, not of supervision nor evaluation. Some staff members should not have gotten through library school.

We have tried to define ourselves as information providers, thriving in an information age, yet we bewail the information explosion. We also tend to ignore the realities of our professional life: we are not data providers, we are data facilitators. There will always be a profound difference between data users and data facilitators. Librarians do not create data and cannot qualify as data providers. Furthermore, we are not information specialists since we seldom, if ever, understand or can interpret the data ourselves. Instead of complaining about the information explosion, we should embrace the fact that we need more, not less information.

54 *The Reference Librarian and Implications of Mediation*

THE SERVICE ENCOUNTER BUSINESS

We should address the reality that we are working in a service industry that demands that we become more goal directed instead of task directed. We must develop standardized procedures and techniques that mediate between client expectation and the potentials of our collections, mechanical resources, and mediums of resource sharing. The number one goal of our business is patron success in their service encounter. As I will repeat, service is the fulfilling of the patron's expectations. Also, as far as the patron is concerned, perception is reality (Albrecht & Zemke, 1985).

Librarians reject or ignore the idea that we are in the service encounter business. Search the literature for research or anecdotal articles on the service encounter principle and one will discover that they do not exist. Yet the service encounter concept dominates the thinking in all service professions except librarianship. Hotels, banks, sales organizations, and retail stores have long since identified the key element of success in their various professions as success in the service encounter, i.e., not the product but the encounter. The concerns of business articles are reminiscent of those in *Library Literature* but they acknowledge and deal head-on with solving the problems. They diagnose favorable and unfavorable service encounters, quality of service, service improvement, and service to the customer as the keys to survival. These business articles define what customers really want–service, beyond products–service-based strategy (Sellers, 1990). Performance evaluation, monitoring service delivery, imperatives for improving service quality, and delineating mistakes that service companies make are seen in the light not only of improving customer service, but also altering the customer's perceptions of service quality. These articles are designed to give a company a competitive edge, break the cycle of failure in service, and declare war on mediocre service (Schlesinger & Heskett, 1991).

Unlike library articles, business articles usually identify the problem and assign specific responsibility for remediation and the need for service excellence in order to remain competitive in the marketplace. The literature assumes that quality and control will come from top management. The library literature dwells on our failures as individuals. This is a disservice to our profession. Many librarians I work with are talented, hard working, and bring great insight to every transaction. We should never underestimate the value of what we do.

There is a common thread to the business articles–responsibility for output and training (Hensel, 1990). Blame is assessed for failure but the thrust of most articles is how to increase service effectiveness. This ap-

Traditional Mediation 55

proach usually avoids guidelines and standards and suggests positive steps to take in order to gain an edge over the competition in quality of service. Prescriptions are made for daily, weekly, and monthly training programs to reinforce the corporate goals. All marketing and service professions are customer driven: find out what the customer wants and get it for him (Whiteley, 1991). These articles do not precisely translate into the library environment in each instance, but they do illustrate the principle of quality control over service delivery.

The library profession has used the phrase "marketing" for the past 15 years in a dangerous context–not really understanding the basic idea. We have confused publicity with public relations, marketing with advertising, all the while failing to perceive that we should be customer driven. Libraries and librarians have had many successes–but a signal failure of the profession has been public relations. Our status and image suffer if the public is not familiar with our services, what we can or can not do, but it is even worse when our facilities do not fulfill their role if the public does not use them–and to a large measure they do not. If we do not make ourselves indispensable to our constituencies and stop posing as something we are not, we will be eliminated.

How did I reach these conclusions? My library has been concerned with reference accuracy, and performance, and delivery of effective service for many years. Our surveys demonstrate that our service levels coincide with the 50% averages that other libraries experience (University of Illinois Graduate School of Library Science, 1988; Stephen Edwards Associates, 1991).Exceptions are made for service delivered by exceptionally skilled and clever practioners, i.e., not all librarians are equal nor can all librarians be trained to deliver effective reference service.

MEDIATION BASED ON SUCCESS

A survey of the patrons who use our library with regularity revealed that although the general patron probably receives the same mid-range level of service, there is also a special class of user who is always successful. This led me to surmise that I should not study remediation based on failure, but rather should study the techniques used by successful patrons and then apply those techniques to mediate service to the user–even if he or she only has a one-time transaction.

Our internal surveys have also shown that very few patrons actually know or understand the resources and services offered. For instance, casual users of the Business Reference collection often criticize it and

56   *The Reference Librarian and Implications of Mediation*

complain about its limitations. Scholl Communications, a Deerfield Library patron and a premier business reference publisher, thinks we have a fine collection (Stephen Edwards Associates, 1991). Who is right? Both the critical patron and Scholl Communications are correct–the patron has no idea what we hold or how to use it and Scholl does. Staff expertise, bibliographies, brochures, and displays have not educated patrons so that they can succeed, thus, we fail in their assessments. Yet bibliographic instruction, signage, and enduser training dominate our activities. Patrons do not absorb information we present to them unless they have a specific need to know that information, and they do not retain the information any longer than they have to. This phenomenon does not deter the successful patron.

After an analysis of the successful patrons I decided that they really belong to a classification all their own–so I term them clients. Now client is a term that has been used loosely by many librarians to somehow inflate the status of the profession. I believe there are two classes of reference users–the larger group of patrons, who are general library users, and clients.

The general characteristics of patrons are that they often know little about what the library can or cannot provide, what a librarian can or cannot do for them, or what can be expected from a reference department. They often ask what I term the "non-question," which in fact has no answer, and the librarian and patron alike do not recognize this. Publilius Syrus noted that "It is not every question that deserves an answer." It is equally true that not every question has an answer. The unraveling of the non-question seems to be beyond many patrons and librarians–"I want a copy of the de facto law, a copy of the Green River Ordinance, a picture of an egg of the ninja turtle"–and takes up much of what passes for reference transactions.

Clients are easy to define: they are always successful in their reference encounter. Like ordinary patrons they generally know absolutely nothing about how a library works and are not to be considered endusers. I was tempted to define the client as an enduser, but I have rejected that notion. In fact, it should be rejected by the profession as quickly as possible. It is a clever ploy though, to define the patron as the problem and make him or her and not us, responsible for the encounter by turning the user into a surrogate librarian. I reject the enduser concept completely for a simple reason: I have only been partially successful at making full-fledged librarians into endusers and have failed miserably with others. We do a lot of training for "situational users." Since they immediately forget everything we have taught, I hesitate to term them endusers.

Traditional Mediation 57

ENDUSER: A FLAWED CONCEPT IN A PUBLIC SETTING

Experience has taught that I can never turn a patron into a database searcher, surrogate librarian, or even a very good searcher on an online public access terminal. Patrons can search author/title catalogs with a degree of facility but that is only about ten percent of what a good reference librarian can bring to a transaction. Of course, there are true end-users–those who access their own material from their computers and subscribe to the various databases and information vendors–but they bear little weight in our environment. Their needs are hybrid and specialized and fulfilled through access to a small number of sources. When they come into the library for other reasons they are fish out of water just like any other patron. I have a large number of patrons who fit this category and their limitations are typical of the general population. Yet I have heard library pundits predict that this user is, or shortly will be, the general patron. I think not.

This is as it should be. Information is hard to locate and interpret, and it is difficult to classify and control. We should not apologize for the fact that any discipline or body of knowledge is not mastered instantly. Yet a common expectation and response from patron to librarian is, "I didn't think it would be this hard." Libraries are not easy to use and OPAC catalogs are difficult to teach; additionally, around this difficulty of organizing and making information systematic, librarians have erected an enormous–obtuse and obdurant–seignorial apparatus to control and systematize library mechanisms. There is no escaping the fact–libraries are hard to use successfully. Once a library builds a tradition of poor reference service, it will outlive any individual staff member and be spread by word of mouth to every patron. Conversely, a library that takes the time to build a positive reputation for excellence in service will reap benefits beyond the tenure of any single staff member.

Phrases like "libraries without librarians, libraries without walls" are meaningless phrases created by nonpractitioners. We should stop being apologists or depicting ourselves as something we are not. Librarians are needed now more than ever to facilitate the use of the materials. Most patrons do not possess the skills or the inclinations or can not or will not use those skills. It is up to the librarian to mediate between the unwilling or unknowing patron, their expectations, and the resources at hand.

ANALYZING THE SUCCESSFUL CLIENT

Once I fully understood that there really is a category of client who is always successful in library service encounters, I set out to compile a list of individuals, their range of needs and questions over the time I have known them, and to see if I could identify any common techniques that would help me to understand why they are consistently successful. The list of patrons I classified as clients grew to include about fifteen people. These clients use the library with regularity, yet it was clear to me they are not endusers. They actually know little about libraries but they have established a direct relationship with the reference staff through their own mediation skills.

They embody a list of similarities, but the most striking thing is that their transactions are always conducted through a procedure of mediation in which they lead the librarian, yet rely completely on the skills and resources of the librarian. The key seems to be their approach to the interview–they clearly know what they need and expect from the service encounter, but they do not know how to get it except through a mediation technique that unwittingly forces the librarian into the role of service provider–not information scientist, not cultural maven, and certainly not enduser instructor. Analyzing these clients also led to the conclusion that success in the reference transaction has almost nothing to do with accuracy, tools, currency, or the reference interview. Reference success is attitudinal, and what counts is not the attitude of the librarian alone but rather more importantly that of the client. Clients insist on, and get, the proper data to fulfill their needs and they accept nothing less. Over time they have taught me a lot about reference service.

The librarian is at a disadvantage in the encounter. Librarians must ask themselves at least eight fundamental questions with each reference transaction–Did the patron ask a non-question? Did the patron ask the question correctly? Did the patron understand the question and the range of answers sufficiently to pose the question? Did I hear the question correctly? Do I have the tools to answer this query? Did I understand the question? Did I read the tool correctly? And is the tool accurate? The issues must be faced with each question and there is nothing we can do about that except to remember that it is up to the librarian to ask or answer these questions, and there is nothing we can do to eliminate them.

How does one judge if the patrons obtained the information they needed? And how does one judge success, especially if one is not in a position to know if one was successful? My experience is that the patron often does not know, but the client always does. Yet unsuccessful patrons often do not complain, come back, or try again. The reference process has not bewildered, confused, or angered them. It simply failed to enter their range of experience and patrons will never be library users if they just walk away. Surveys done in Maryland show that reference success

Traditional Mediation 59

rises substantially if the librarian simply asks the patrons if they got what they wanted–which is a pathetic comment on the engagement given by too many librarians (Stephan, Gers, Seward, Bolin & Patridge, 1988). Do librarians lack the human resource skills needed to engage patrons? I fear that the answer is yes, but these skills can be taught and learned.

All successful clients approach their transaction with the same attitude: as if they are entering a dark room, they assume there is a switch that will turn on the lights, and it is up to them to find a way to locate it. These clients are neither thrusting nor aggressive personalities, persistent and professional yes–aggressive, no. I have yet to see an adversarial relationship develop between a client and librarian although this is not uncommon between patron and librarian.

ELEMENTS OF SUCCESS

Although this approach varies from client to client, I feel certain that I have identified the key elements that clients employ in their search for information, data, and materials. I call these the ''elements of success'' and they are not complicated. They are as important to reference work as the tools consulted or the skills of the librarian.

We can use the elements to format a style of mediation to be used by all desk staff, whether circulation or reference, to ensure success not only by fulfilling patron expectations–unrealistic or not–but also by matching needs with the reality of the collection and backup resources. None of the elements involve any library skill at all. The successful client,

1. Assumes a personal relationship with the librarian.
2. Assumes ownership for the transaction.
3. Is always prepared to accept the information provided and then evaluate the data.
4. Comes as prepared as possible–tries never to pose a question in a vacuum.
5. Is persistent, stopping the query only when he or she has all the information needed.

How does one use these ''elements'' to deliver reference success? I wish I had easy and facile answers. What has worked for me has not worked for all of the librarians I supervise. Another question I cannot answer is what makes a person off the street, one who has never been in a library in his or her life, behave as a perfect client? I do not even know why a client behaves like a client. I have always advised my staff to "slip-stream" a patron–follow closely and look over his or her shoulder, so to speak, to find out what he or she really seeks. How can we replicate client behavior in every transaction? I do not have the answer. I guess the most frustrating part for me is that I have dealt with so many patrons for so many years, and so few of them have become clients. I know that it means that librarians must work in closer proximity and contact than is comfortable for some of them. This is an area that needs systematic study: Why do clients behave the way they do and how can we replicate that behavior? I assume it is because they are people who have developed abilities to help them actualize their own self interests. If there is one element that seems to be most important, it is the willingness to take the data away with them for off-site evaluation and an equal willingness to return for more or corrected data when necessary.

All of this–working closely with the patron, engaging the patron at a personal level, and disclosing our lack of knowledge–exposes us and makes us vulnerable. The classic reference transaction is a one-to-one relationship in which the librarian is in command. Slipstreaming a patron requires close contact, revealing shortcomings, asking all eight questions about the transaction, plus bringing energy and enthusiasm to each transaction. As individuals we realize that time constraints, personality traits, world experience, and collection knowledge limit the degree to which we may engage a patron or mediate the transaction.

All too often we think that the patron/librarian relationship is one of the blind leading the blind. Then into our department come assertive patrons who call us by name, know what they want, and force us to deliver the service they require. And we come out from behind the desk and deliver the service we have been trained to give. As a profession, we do not have to worry about clients–they will get the service they desire–we have to direct our energies to patrons.

This is where the concept of a mediation technique can enter the transaction. When patrons come to the desk, they usually assume that the librarian will take over and deliver what they need. As I have detailed, this does not happen. What occurs is a bi-polar relationship–both the patron and the librarian want the other to take responsibility and complete the transaction successfully or at least quickly. What should happen in the mediation process is not the "perfect" interview but the question should be stated, restated and rephrased–fine-tuned–as the librarian learns from the patron and the patron learns from the librarian. All the while, the job of the librarian is how to get the patron to take on three or four of the characteristics of the successful client. The point is to mediate

Traditional Mediation

61

between the potentials of the collection and service resources and the patron's needs.This can consist of a restating of the elements of success to the patron, using one or two of them, or doing the whole transaction alone. The goal of each interaction should be to provide service to the level of the patron's expectation.

LIBRARIAN AVOIDANCE TACTICS

Looking at the "elements of success" will make many librarians uneasy. The first point deals with human relations. Librarians must make personal contact with the client and they must encourage interaction by the patron. The second point, ownership, must be stressed from the outset. It is the needs of the patron that are being serviced–not the librarian's. The patron "transfers" ownership of the transaction to the librarian–"it's your problem"–and all too often the librarian accepts this transference. The third point–accepting the data and evaluating it off-site–is difficult. Patrons want the whole transaction wrapped up in a neat package–but how can this be realistically accomplished if no one knows whether the data is right, wrong, or appropriate? As long as the librarian accepts ownership of the transaction it will remain unsuccessful. The patron must be encouraged to take the data home and evaluate it and then come back, if he or she needs additional information.

Many patrons will have totally unrealistic expectations when they come into the library–often embarrassing low or impossibly high–about what the librarian can hand them across the desk. In this area librarians must stand their ground and put these expectations into a reasonable perspective. Librarians and patrons alike have always hated the "smiling no" that is given in lieu of service at many desks. More subtle and more insidious is the "impossible dream" scenario, a common and far more undesirable response to a patron query. Generally this technique is used to terminate the encounter–promise the moon, if the patron will leave. Dealing with realistic expectations is really the first order of business. Serious disservice is done by librarians when they deal fraudulently with patrons. Too many librarians do not understand the basic truth that often the most professional thing they can do for a patron is to say no.

I have observed that librarians use what I call "escape and evasion" techniques that are subtly employed to disengage from a patron; for example, answers like "If we only had the tool I had at the University of Michigan," or "We used to own that book but we don't anymore," or "We don't have access to that computer." Tools, equipment, and reference skills are important, but we have put too much stress on them. Service is more important and the trick is not to fail because we do not have the tool of choice at hand. The librarian's training and experience allows him or her to succeed by using other tools that the library does own. Knowledge of the tools and listening skills are important but when the transaction is finally evaluated, only the data users can measure the success or failure rate. If they do not receive the service they feel they deserve, the process is unsuccessful. Failure of the librarian or failure of the collection does not have anything to do with the success of the patron. Success implies the pursuit of service excellence.

CONCLUSION

The process and the problem that librarians face when they try to begin mediating with the patron is four fold: attitudinal, procedural, intellectual, and interpersonal. This is where failure begins–the librarian fails to develop or even desire a client relationship. Librarians not only fail to listen to the patron, they fail to learn. Librarians fail to develop the skills needed to get the patron to disclose his or her needs. And, finally, they accept transference of ownership from the patron. Again, these things have nothing to do with library skills. They have to do with mediation skills; they have to do with service skills, and they have to do with people skills. What good does it do if the librarian knows technique, process, tools, and resources, if patrons do not get what they want? We can coach skills, but we can never coach attitude. Supervisors must act to control quality of service (Butterfield, 1991). Their goal must be to evaluate, test, and review the service of their staff to ensure that the patron's expectations for service are being met.

Success means commitment to the service encounter, and this means dealing with the mysteries of the human psyche. We make a very human process difficult because of the way we have institutionalized our service. We have insisted on technology as salvation for far too long. A patron's enthusiasm and willingness to stare blankly at a computer screen and excitedly accept a meaningless free-text search does not validate the existence of these machines or this service approach. We must now make service excellence the primary factor in our organizations, and we must project an image of the profession's commitment to excellence. Every reference transaction has a life of its own–a short lived phenomenon–that requires energy and enthusiasm. The energy and enthusiasm to deliver technical expertise is our main professional responsibility. We often pay lip service to the idea of public service–it is the profession's piety–but too often there is no real commitment.

We need more research. There exists a vast body of knowledge concerning retail trade, staffing, sales technique, motivation, telephone use, stock, and prices, but I do not see the same level of operational knowledge in library publications. Descriptive statistics and measurement yes, but not the same kind of synthesis of data into workable techniques and procedures. At the same time, we need more theory and library philosophy, if we are to be sustained as a profession–Library Theology–if technology in its most banal forms is not to become our master. We face the future with a prevailing sense of uncertainty. If we are to thrive, it will be through a technique of mediation between client expectations and resources that guarantees success in the delivery of service.

Where this theology will come from I cannot say. There is no dominant writer or editor in our field, who is currently shaping the direction of our thinking and guiding our research. We are a profession of wise and wonderful voices who have left the writing to non-practitioners. We are not a profession of information scientists. I see a direct link between the decline and closing of library schools and the use of titles like that to define or enhance our profession. If we are to be judged by any of the criteria used to judge a scientific discipline, we would fail. Yet that is how our constituencies judge us when we apply inappropriate descriptions to what we do as librarians. We have yet to confront the implications that library school closings will have on the ultimate fate of our profession. We will need a sustaining paradigm of library philosophy if librarians are to carry on and thrive in the post-computer era.

REFERENCES

Albrecht, K. & Zemke, R. (1985). *Service America: Doing business in the new economy.* Homewood, IL: Dow Jones-Irwin.

Alvarez, R. S. (1987). *Library boss: Thoughts on library personnel.* San Francisco: Administrator's Digest Press.

Butterfield, R. W. (1991, March). Deming's 14 points applied to service. *Training: The Magazine of Human Resources, 28,* 50-59.

Childers, T.A. (1970). *Telephone information service in public libraries: A comparison of performance and the descriptive statistics collected by the State of New Jersey.* Doctoral dissertation, Rutgers University.

Douglas, I. (1988, Fall). Reducing failures in reference service. *RQ, 28*(1), 94-101.

Hensel, J.S. (1990, January). Service quality improvement and control: A customer-based approach. *Journal of Business Research, 20,* 43-53.

Isenstein, L.J. (1991, February). On the road to STARdom: Improving reference accuracy. *Illinois Libraries, 73* (2), 146-151.

Rashid, H. F. (1990, October). Book availability as a performance measure of a library. *Journal of the American Society for Information Science, 41,* 501-508.

Schlesinger, L. A., & Heskett, J. L. (1991, Spring). Breaking the cycle of failure in services. *Sloan Management Review, 32,* 17-28.

Sellers, P. (1990, June 4). What customers really want. *Fortune, 12,* (13), 58-68.

Stephan, S., Gers, R., Seward, L., Bolin, N. & Partridge, J. (1988, Winter). Reference Breakthrough in Maryland. *Public Libraries, 27,* 202-203.

Stephen Edwards Associates. (1991). *Survey of Deerfield Public Library use.* Deerfield, IL: Stephen Edwards Associates.

University of Illinois. Graduate School of Library Science. (1988). *Deerfield citizen survey.* Urbana, IL: University of Illinois.

Vavrek, B.F. (1975, May). Sacred cow no. 4: Implications of the new information services guidelines. *American Libraries, 6,* 294-295.

Von Seggern, M. (1989, Winter). Evaluating the interview. *RQ, 29* (2), 260-265.

Walton, M. (1986). *The Deming management method.* New York: Dodd, Mead & Company.

Whiteley, R. C. (1991). *The Customer-driven company: Moving from talk to action.* Reading, MA: Addison Wesley Publishing Company.

II. MEDIATION
AND THE ELECTRONIC WORLD

Books and Screens,
Readers and Reference:
Bridging the Video Gap

John Swan

The issue of the mediator's role in the library of the electronic age takes on peculiar forms in that part of the library that has felt the impact of the new technology most heavily. It is true that some types of libraries and some fields of inquiry are being overtaken in their entirety by full-text computerization and other forms of total paperlessness, but in general there is a balance, albeit an uneasy one, between the computer and the materials that the computer is there to access. The patron typically uses a computerized catalogue or index or online search in order to get at something that is itself not on a computer. In the reference area, however, the primary paper tools, certainly their most recent, most frequented portions, are themselves being displaced. This is most obvious among the indexes, but it is increasingly the case among dictionaries, encyclopedias, and a host of other sources as well, as the power of the CD manifests itself to both publishers and their customers.

This is not in itself a bad thing, indeed, is often a very good thing. The new machines are getting better and better at allowing patrons to

---

John Swan is Head Librarian, Bennington College, Bennington, VT 05201.

© 1992 by The Haworth Press, Inc. All rights reserved.

66   *The Reference Librarian and Implications of Mediation*

find a great deal more a great deal faster, and their user-friendliness–and the sensation of enhanced well-being that goes with it–entice more people into using them. It is doubtful that even the most hardened Luddite in the reference business would claim that any paper index, however approachable, enjoys the powers of seduction inherent in a video screen.

There are problems, however, that stem in part from that very seductiveness. They are familiar to anyone who has experience in a significantly computerized reference area, but they also immediately confront those who have only taken the first modest steps toward that electronic access utopia. An informal survey of some academic libraries, my own included, recently yielded a number of common examples of misuse of electronic reference, all of them unintentional and certainly unmalicious. At a workstation providing selective or full-text coverage of company profiles, wastebaskets are filled daily with ten- to forty-page full-text printouts from which nothing but the name and address of the company has been torn off and taken away. At many computerized journal indexes, patrons, apparently hypnotized by the power of the hundreds of citations without any preliminary screening, often with the intention of using but a handful thereof. In one case, at a station without a limit on its "multi-print" feature, a young man pushed that button, then went off to get himself a cup of coffee outside the library. One sign of the success of such computer indexes is the lines that form in front of them–often populated with people waiting for that particular machine not because it will provide them with the best or most relevant information, but because it is quick and easy to use.

Over and over again, the universe of information is reduced to the half decade or so of a select half thousand or so journals, accessible via index terms which may or may not suit the conceptual needs of either the patron or the articles subjected to such inevitably simplifying manipulation. Online catalogues commonly provide better subject access to a larger percentage of the portion of that universe that happens to reside in a given library or network of libraries. However, there are many similar misunderstandings about just what can and what cannot be summoned up with a keyboard, and certainly a parallel lack of comprehension about the relationship between the machine-readable and non-machine-readable worlds. In a library (such as the small one I work in, but also in some very large establishments) that still has significant collections accessible only via the paper catalogue, "frozen" or otherwise, the process of luring people back to fingering cards as well as keys is as difficult as convincing them that there are still many more journals in many more years to be found in paper indexes than on compact disks.

In the library world, or at least on all its leading edges, these problems

Mediation and the Electronic World 67

are usually seen as the natural cost of transition. All the promise and all the solutions are electronic, in this view. The challenge of educating the public in the effective manipulation of the electronic library takes precedence over paper instruction for the very good reason that the future of the library, certainly of reference, is electronic. Paper, even paper reference, will continue to be useful, no doubt, but for an even smaller and more specialized population. Scholars who need paper sources will have, or know how to get, the training to use them. The most familiar paper sources, such as the Wilson indexes, will serve more and more in a back-up role and, unless they all undergo complete retrospective electronic conversion, in the capacity of historical reference. For the general public, the most urgent demand for service, and need for instruction, will naturally require the ever more focused energies of the librarians involved.

Just as inevitable is the advance of computer-assisted instruction into the fray. "Using technology to teach technology," the thesis of one effective new anthology on the subject,[1] is a phrase that sums up many different activities in this area. They all rely on the basic assumption that the properly employed workstation is itself the most efficient and attractive method of drawing patrons to other workstations, particularly for a public more and more attuned to them as the first line of reference. I have sat through several demonstrations of HyperCard applications in this area, in which it has been proven conclusively that a mere three hundred hours of professional time will yield up, via menu-driven magic, a set of instructional screens, replete with illuminating and witty graphics, that unlock the secrets of a given library with such dogged, mind-numbing and tedious simplicity that I personally would prefer to wander lost through the stacks, throwing myself to the gods of serendipity. I know this puts me among the problem patrons, and certainly among the backward in reference thinking. It is true, however, that CAI of this type has had its successes (some of them breathlessly reported in these same demonstrations as the conversion of dozens of students to the joys of "self-paced" instruction–dozens, I note, in five-figure student bodies), and that more success is on its way.

Indeed, according to Virginia Tiefel, an extremely reliable source, success is already here, as Ohio State's Gateway project has earned widespread praise as a truly friendly integrated workstation system that links the online catalogue and a multitude of journal index, encyclopedia, and biographical databases on one plain-English-driven screen:

> It strives to lead users to the best information for their needs regardless of the materials' format. As the "front end" to the online catalog, the Gateway takes users far beyond the catalog, providing

68   The Reference Librarian and Implications of Mediation

instruction and guidance in identifying which materials likely will best meet their information needs, where the materials are, and how to evaluate and use them.[2]

Beyond the integrated institutional system lie the network systems forging national and international connections from reference department to reference department–or more accurately, from workstation to workstation, without any such spatial limitation, within or beyond the library building. The advent of OCLC's enhanced systems, including the First-Search online reference service, means that patrons now will be able to perform their own subject (and author and title) searches of the vast OCLC bibliographic database, tap into multiple subject databases, and do their own interlibrary loan ordering. According to OCLC's CEO, K. Wayne Smith, another very credible source, "In five years, you will look up a journal through OCLC data bases, punch a button on the computer, and get the document in your hand."[3] Adaptations, improvements, and linkages are inevitable, and it is very likely that within a similarly short period, OCLC's patron-oriented workstations will have all the features of friendly, integrated instruction described so well by Gateway's Tiefel.

It may well be true, then, that within a few years all of the high-priority tools of the reference section, as well as of orientation and most of the other "front-end" public service activities of the library, will be electronic. This does not make the gulf between the screen and the printed page disappear. There will still be a problematic distance between information codified for access via computer and the reason for that manipulation of data, the packages of information and knowledge, a great portion of which is and will continue to consist of words on paper. The electronic triumph also will not mean that the larger issues of information access and comprehension, and their impact upon the role of the librarian, will go away either.

A decade ago, in an influential and prescient article on the changes likely to be wrought in reference and bibliographic instruction by the "Online Age," Brian Nielsen wrote that the traditional intermediary role will become less and less necessary with the advent of machines that invite end-user access:

In academic libraries, the development of online catalogs may . . . . lead to the intermediary role becoming an anachronism. Catalogs *must* be user friendly, or at least have the appearance of friendliness; if they were not, the amount of time required for staff assistance would be staggering. . . . Those who favor exclusive practice of an intermediary role lock themselves into the practice of a specialty that is rapidly approaching obsolescence due to continuing economic and technological change.[4]

As Nielsen and many others foresaw, the information industry has a powerful motivation to make their electronic access machines useful and attractive to the user. This contact occurs by way of friendly library computers, but also, increasingly, via cable, modem, or whatever emerges in the rapidly evolving world of transmission, in offices, homes, cars, hotel rooms, wherever the ever-more-transportable tools of electronic connection will go. Smart librarians have long since begun to adapt to this by working toward the goal of making their institutions as multiply connective to their individual communities as their budgets and staffs could afford. They have also largely yielded to the necessity of change in both their intermediary and instructional roles. It does no good to interpose one's highly professional body between a patron and a computerized index if the patron already expects to be able to use it without help. Herb White summed up our situation in the world of multiple information paths succinctly:

> Information service is not a morality play. It is a strategic decision, and some clients will want to do all of it, some a part of it some of the time, and some none at all. If we refuse to interact on that basis they will find others who will, because while we have expertise we don't have exclusivity.[5]

There are many threatening issues of professional identity lurking in all this, to be sure: the reference librarian becoming an anachronism or a seldom-needed specialist, or the process of library instruction dwindling to the role of holding the hands and soothing the anxieties of those who turn phobic or slow-witted in front of video display terminals. Many librarians already find themselves monitoring lines of users, preventing obvious abuse of machines or performing emergency surgery upon them, clarifying instructions, and generally attending to the management, often crisis management, of machines. It may be a form of bringing together people and the information they need, but in many such situations, being an information manager feels, and looks, more like being an information janitor.

But the issue is larger than that of professional identity, or even survival. Someone will always be needed to process materials, whatever their form, wherever they are physically or electronically stored; someone will always be needed to tend to the machines and the people, even if it is as information janitors. The real problem is much larger than our pro-

70 *The Reference Librarian and Implications of Mediation*

fession; it goes to the core of our collective experience as a culture undergoing a revolution in the way we absorb information. Barbara Ford is among a number of leaders who have cast this problem in terms of information literacy:

> Today, most of us have too much information; this overload is one of the challenges we should address. In an information-rich environment, consumers must learn to overcome information anxiety and to digest and utilize information in decision making. New computer tools help us manage information, but also bring us more of it. The changes in formats and organization of information mean that users need guidance and may have unrealistic expectations because computers can create the mistaken impression that library research can now be accomplished quickly and effectively.[6]

Every librarian will recognize this as an accurate summary of some large, if familiar, challenges. A good deal of the motivation behind the creation of versatile, friendly, and more powerful and inclusive computer gateway and reference systems is the desire to make those patron expectations less and less unrealistic. In fact, however, the "mistaken impression" that library research can be done quickly and effectively is–from the point of view of many, maybe most of the library computer patrons–not mistaken at all. Even if they run off a half dozen company profiles in order to tear off a few lines of printout; even if the confine their bibliographies to the most recent dozen journal citations that can be found in the library, they know they can do an effective enough job more quickly than in the days before these tools existed.

Most people who think about it at all know that they have too much information flowing into and around them, but they deal with this burden by shedding or ignoring as much of it as is necessary to keep the burden manageable–and the decisions as to what stays and what goes have little to do with the intrinsic quality of the information, at least for most of us. This phenomenon is hardly an artifact of the electronic age, but it is important to understand that our new machines do not make it a thing of the past. They certainly provide the opportunity for the retrieval of more good information more quickly than ever before, a potential that is surely the major impetus behind driving most of the reference books to the back of the reference area, behind the machines. But let us recall that the central icon of all of this video, the television itself, is a tool of mass information of unparalleled power. It is, however, at the very least an open question whether this tool is principally in the service of enlightenment through its informing powers. A recent critical analysis of the hypnotic television coverage of the Gulf pointed to a familiar, but always uncomfortable question:

> The numbing effect of hours of television-watching is obviously inimical to ordinary rationality. Isn't it possible that for many in the television audience, it is more desirable to be numb than to be informed? . . . Surely, the fulfillment of the common desire to be anesthetized is one of the primary functions of television. In this sense, one tunes in in order to tune out.[7]

It may seem unfair to heap upon the brave new world of online reference the sins of the Vast Wasteland. After all, people who do spend longer time in front of the screens of the library actually learn more, not less; they are often enough the same serious types who got a great deal out of paper reference, and it is extremely doubtful that comfortable numbness is their goal. Fair enough, but our machines do exert their own mild form of anesthetic effect—we have all seen that stare—and more seriously, they do often create the illusion that with a few keystrokes the patron has access to a customized universe of all the relevant information. A well-designed menu-driven system such as that described by Virginia Tiefel can only do so much to disabuse those for whom quick efficiency has a higher priority than through inquiry—and in the pressures of modern life that is hardly confined to the population of lazy students out for a shortcut.

Many libraries engaged in orientation and instruction as well as in the improvement of reference service have confronted these problems of misuse, abuse, or underuse of the new machines. Many of their solutions involve not only the new design of hardware and software, but evolution of both their teaching and mediation roles, the necessity of which was so clearly foreseen by Brian Nielsen. However, the overwhelming thrust of that evolution has been in the same direction as the development of librarianship itself, that is, electronic.

The electronic direction has meant either "using technology to teach technology," or increasing the user-enticing qualities of that technology itself. This is understandable, and entirely appropriate, but it is also seriously incomplete. The balance between paper and machine may be uneasy, as indicated above, and it may tilt inevitably toward the machine. However, it is not mere Ludditism to believe that if the balance disappears entirely, even in the reference section, our individual and collective understanding will suffer massively.

72 *The Reference Librarian and Implications of Mediation*

The simple truth is that the world of paper knowledge and information is and always will be a major and necessary portion of the human record. Except for some special libraries with a specific focus on current data and analyses, books and other paper documents will therefore be forever a vital part of library usage. This is so obvious–except, perhaps, among those who believe that Plato and Tolstoy, as well as every map, picture, score, diagram, and problem looks better on a screen–that it hardly needs saying. The thrust of all our cutting-edge management in reference and elsewhere is, however, toward that on-screen future. There are many good reasons for this, but the accompanying rhetoric as well as the intense focus upon planning and implementation all this requires often obscure the fact that librarianship must now and forever be a holistic enterprise.

A few years ago, David Isaacson wrote a ruefully amusing parable about an ace paper-based reference librarian, Argos Fervor, who is pitted in an epic battle for citations with a computer and its online searcher. Argos wins, coming up with a few more relevant citations than the computer, but like John Henry the steel-driving man, he is killed by his exertions in competition with the machine.[8] Argos dies with generous praise for his opponent on his lips, but part of the point, surely, is that we do tend to treat reference books, despite the unabated activity in producing them, in a somewhat patronizing, if not exactly elegiac, manner, at least on the level of our fast-track leadership.

Most of us, dealing with the realities of money and staff as well as the real daily needs of library users do offer service that combines paper and computers, still often with a heavy tilt toward the former. We usually find that the problems associated with getting people to make the best, or at least decent, use of the machines are not unlike the old problems of getting them to use the paper indexes and other tools with something close to their real potential. The optimism (and success) of a few bibliographic instruction mavens excepted, most of us recognize the cruel fact that the majority of our patrons ignore or make too little use of the majority of our reference sections, even in paper, and it has ever been thus.

There are no simple solutions to the multiple conceptual and educational challenges inherent in bringing people together with either books or machines. It will always require the tenacity and ingenuity and devotion that ever characterize successful reference and BI. It will also require that librarians bring a fuller understanding of the whole, connected nature of their domain to the task of helping other people in this ever-evolving process of learning how to learn. Philosophers and pundits of the video age are forever reminding us that a general shift from verbal to visual

Mediation and the Electronic World

consciousness may be well underway in our culture. We certainly see the signs of it in the library, and not only in the prevailing drift to the machines (yes, there are words on those screens, but in that context their significance is generally much more functional, and one-dimensional, than on the page). We have not yet come to terms with this shift, however, except in ways that emphasize, even celebrate, the video side of the video gap. We are eager to go with the flow.

This is not the place to sing the praises of the library as one of the last refuges of individualized, self-directed exploration, or as natural repository of the book, the tool most eminently suited for that precious relationship between the self and our collective verbal culture. This sort of language only confirms everyone's suspicions about terminal (no, not as in computer, but as in dead end) nostalgia. This is especially so in a time when more and more public libraries proudly announce that their videotapes circulate more vigorously than their books, and more and more academic libraries insist that they are not mere libraries but nodes on an electronic network. But the critic Sven Birkerts recently reminded us that there are indeed major values at stake as we enter the ''Electronic Millennium'':

> One day soon we will conduct our public and private lives within networks so dense, among so many channels of instantaneous information, that it will make almost no sense to speak of the differentiated self.

He does leave room for a qualified optimism:

> It may turn out that language is a hardier thing than I have allowed, that it will flourish among the bleep and the click and the monitor as readily as it ever did on the printed page. I hope so, for language is the soul's ozone layer, and we thin it at our peril.[9]

Birkert's guarded hope is our professional responsibility or at least a vital facet thereof. If we cannot preserve the library, of all institutions, as a place for the whole panoply of human tools for learning and research, there is little reason to believe that anyone else will nourish our relationship to language. Preservation in this sense is not a rear-guard action; it will require full, intelligent engagement with ''the bleep and the click and the monitor.'' It will also require that a good many librarians retain an allegiance to the printed word–or more to the point, a commitment and knowledge deep enough to embrace both the book and the screen.

NOTES

1. Linda Brew MacDonald et al., eds. *Teaching Technologies in Libraries: A Practical Guide.* (Boston: G.K. Hall, 1990).

2. Virginia Tiefel, "The Gateway to Information: A System Redefines How Libraries Are Used," *American Libraries* 22 (9) (October 1991), 859.

3. David L. Wilson, "Researchers Get Direct Access to Huge Data Base," *The Chronicle of Higher Education*, October 9, 1991, p. A24.

4. Brian Nielsen, "Teacher or Intermediary: Alternative Professional Models in the Information Age," *College and Research Libraries*, 43 (3),(May 1982), 188.

5. Herbert S. White, "Libraries and Librarians in the Next Millennium." ("White Papers") *Library Journal*, 115 (9, (May 15, 1990), 55.

6. Barbara Ford, "Information Literacy" (Guest Editorial), *College and Research Libraries*, 52 (4) (July 1991), 313.

7. Ernest Larsen, "Gulf War TV," *Jump Cut* No. 36 (May 1991), p. 8.

8. David Issacson, "A Martyred Manual Searcher: A Remembrance of Argos Fervor," *National Librarian*, November 1986, pp. 4-7.

9. Sven Birkerts, "Terminal Reading: Into the Electronic Millennium," *Boston Review*, XVI (5) (October 1991), 20.

Electronic Reference Services: Mediation for the 1990s

Anita K. Evans

Fifteen years ago, the choices for mediated electronic reference services were few, and the hardware requirements straightforward. Libraries that provided any online service usually subscribed to one or two online vendors, such as DIALOG and BRS, and accessed these using a dumb terminal at 300-baud. Issues of service at that time revolved around free vs. fee arguments and whether or not any reference librarian had the innate skills to become a good searcher. With the advent of ready reference searching at the desk, public terminals for OCLC and other utilities, end-user products like Knowledge Index, videodiscs, CD-ROMs, electronic full-text, OPACs, regional and national networks, and hypermedia, the electronic world has become an intricately complex array of service possibilities.

Just as the rapidly expanding bibliographic instruction programs of the late 1970s forced a recognition that a well-defined philosophy of service and established limits were needed to forestall staff burnout (Miller, 1984), so too will libraries today need to make hard choices about what level of support to offer patrons accessing electronic information as these technological products come of age. At the same time, however, worrisome trends are evident. The library's role in the electronic information loop often is not recognized by the popular press or is sometimes neglected in disciplines outside of our own. Commercial enterprises are marketing electronic information sources for the home that have been traditionally viewed as ''reference'' or library materials. Campus computer centers for a number of years have been redefining their roles as information providers.

What services libraries will select to mediate, and at what level, and those which they choose not to offer must be based upon a careful reading of the value added by that mediation within the context of the mis-

---

Anita K. Evans is affiliated with the University of Wisconsin, LaCrosse, WI.

© 1992 by The Haworth Press, Inc. All rights reserved.

76   *The Reference Librarian and Implications of Mediation*

sion of the library and staffing and budget limitations. In planning for the future of mediated electronic services, libraries will need to be decisive in carving out their niche, but be willing to define areas where direct patron access to the information source without any library involvement or mediation is preferred. At the same time, the role of the reference librarian is evolving, shifting from one where online service mediation is required in the form of one-on-one tutorials or search sessions, to that of program manager, consultant, advocate. Developing even more close-working alliances with the technical services and automation staff and the academic computing personnel, reference librarians will take a more active part in advocating command standards and user-friendly interfaces and general product quality.

To talk about the changing nature of online mediation, one must look at the near future for most libraries by reviewing some of the recent developments in electronic services within libraries and in the commercial markets.

CD-ROMs

Most of us have a high comfort level now with at least a few CD-ROM titles. The bugs that plagued some of the software of the mid-1980s largely have been eradicated from mainline products. In many cases, we have moved beyond the stand-alone one product stations to daisy-chained drives and LAN configurations. Instruction in CD-ROMs has been integrated into BI programs, and many libraries have staffed CD-ROM clusters with paraprofessional or student employees, thereby reducing the one-on-one mediation of librarians.

More CD-ROM products are being linked up with software programs that transpose the disc data into another form. Pro-Cite and Biblio-Link, which have been serving the traditional online community for many years, are now available for CD-ROM stations so that disc citations can be translated into bibliographic formats. An increasing number of Government Documents depository items are being offered as CD-ROMs, and many products can be used in tandem with a database program to manipulate the raw data. If these products are to be used at library stations, we are assuming another layer of instruction and the familiarity of librarians or paraprofessional staff with software programs such as dBase.

With all CD-ROM vendors we need to press for products with adequate screen prompts, clear tutorials, templates, and documentation. Particular vigilance may be needed with the federal depository discs whose designs are subcontracted with various firms. The experimental *Congressional Record* on CD-ROM reviewed by depository libraries in the Spring of 1991 exhibited major shortcomings. We cannot allow bad designs to take time away from significant mediation encounters. As voice, pictures and hypertext movement are added to CD-ROM products, other issues may arise. Will a grade school child be confused that President Kennedy is heard on an encyclopedia CD-ROM reading his own words, but an actor is reading the "Gettysburg Address?" As we evaluate newer multimedia products, we will need to be aware that, indeed, the "medium is the message," and some misleading cues may be built into the audio or pictorial design components.

ELECTRONIC INFORMATION SERVICES AND THE PRIVATE CONSUMER

By 1988, there were more than 22 million microcomputers in homes, up from less than one million seven years earlier (U.S. Bureau of the Census, 1990, p. 759). It is not surprising that a number of commercial operations are seeing a rich market for online services and CD-ROM products. For a monthly fee of $12.95, Prodigy offers dial-up access to travel services, financial services, a handful of periodicals including *Consumer Reports* and *Sports Illustrated*, and the *Academic American Encyclopedia*. GEnie advertises travel services, headline news, again the *Academic American Encyclopedia*, a number of bulletin boards, and, with expanded service, the *Wall Street Journal* and a number of investment services. Compuserve, Bix, and American People/Link (see Walsh, 1990) offer home online service and the Baby Bells are entering into the Information Industry as well. David Coursey (1991) in *InfoWorld* declares that "online services are becoming the public libraries of the 1990s" (p. 40) and proceeds to compare the relative costs of using Dow Jones News/Retrieval, Dialog, NEXIS or IQuest (Compuserve) with a trip to the public library to obtain a copy of a *Business Week* article. Factoring in mileage, copying and labor, the article shows the library as the most expensive option.

This thinking is also reflected in an article in *The Futurist* (Cetron & Davies, 1991) which in summarizing from *Crystal Globe: The Haves and Have-nots of the New World Order* states that "More private companies will market large electronic databases, eventually replacing university libraries" (p. 18). The ideas expressed here are not entirely new, though now home access to electronic services is more technically feasible. In

78   *The Reference Librarian and Implications of Mediation*

The Age of Discontinuity, Peter Drucker (1969) more than 20 years ago stated that "there is no technical reason why someone like Sears Roebuck should not come out tomorrow with an appliance selling for less than a TV set, capable of being plugged in wherever there is electricity, and giving immediate access to all the information needed for school work from first grade through college" (p. 25).

The number of home use CD-ROM products also is growing. Barbara Quint (1991) in an RASD-MARS sponsored program at the ALA Annual Conference mentioned a new Information Access Company product called *Magazine Rack*. This CD-ROM exclusively marketed to home users offers the full-text of some 300 journals for one year. The CD-ROM format is also being advertised to a scholarly audience. The "Optical Disks" section of the *Chronicle of Higher Education* has listed products like "GeoRef" and "PAIS International." As more microcomputers with CD-ROM drives are marketed, and a large consumer base for CD-ROM products is created, this trend will gain momentum.

The onslaught of the cheap paperback did not put public libraries out of business, and the advent of home online services and CD-ROM products will not bring about their demise either. Individual access to online services, either popular or scholarly, however, may force a modification in what online services and other resources are offered by libraries. Naisbitt and Aburdene (1990) state in *Megatrends 2000* that "without a structure, a frame of reference, the vast amount of data that comes your way each day will probably whiz right by you" (p. xix). Reference librarians will need to monitor the developing market of consumer products. They then can better assess what electronic services libraries need to offer or not and will be in a good position to provide an essential service in directing users to appropriate commercial or library products, thus "structuring" information for patrons.

At some point, a critical number of people in a library's user group may have direct access to a service, obviating the need to offer the product at the library. However, libraries will need to be cognizant of whether or not dropping a service is creating a class of information poor in the potential user community. If the library does offer a mediated service for a product, is the library providing information retrieval significantly beyond what the patron can provide for him or herself? As users begin to subscribe to services in their homes, there may be some manifestation of what might be called the InfoTrak Syndrome. Some users will assume that they can access "everything" they need by dialing into several services; libraries through public relations efforts will need to get the message across that there is a diversity of information sources available.

Successful mediation of online services entails not only explaining the use of a service or conducting the search, but also indicating the limits of an electronic source while referring the user to other relevant materials.

THE ENHANCED SUPER CATALOG

The library catalog, at one time the primary domain of catalogers and technical services staff, now is a tool reflecting the applications and intentions of numerous library units. Integrated systems means just that–the distinctions among the function responsibilities of units are no longer clearly delineated. Circulation and acquisitions information, for example, is displayed in the online catalog. Since the flexibility of a number of online catalog systems allows for the modification of screen prompts and help screens, reference librarians can make a major contribution in determining those user interfaces. Reference librarians are in the best position to observe typical patron behaviors and difficulties (beyond statistical data garnered by the system) as well as any changes in the level of sophistication of user groups. Are we as involved as we need to be in actively pursuing improvements with automation and technical services staff? Creating clear screen directions, search examples, and help screens not only reduces user frustration, but also has the effect of limiting the number of questions asked at the reference or catalog help desk. This secondary, indirect mediation is supplanting direct mediation and is becoming increasingly important as more databases and other choices are added to the menu offerings.

Our successes with designing various interfaces could be shared more broadly. Bob Walton, President of CLSI, Inc. remarked in an interview that he had "to go to the electrical engineering literature" for information on how to "design a screen on a terminal to make it really effective," and added that reference librarians who would be the ones best able to, do not write up their experiences (Gaughan, 1991). A number of recent articles do address local development of front-ends that standardize or simplify the use of the online catalog. Notably, Virginia Tiefel (1991) reviews the Gateway Apple-based front-end designed at Ohio State University. In Indiana, the IBM hypermedia software, LINKWAY, provides an easy interface for school, public, and special library users accessing SULAN (State University Library Automation Network) libraries that use NOTIS (Bobay, Stockey & Popp, 1990). The LINKWAY product was designed with idea in mind that "the traditional role of reference librarian as an 'intermediary,' answering questions of those users who ask,

80 *The Reference Librarian and Implications of Mediation*

cannot meet the needs of remote users'' (p. 55). Simple, graphic interfaces alleviate the make-work business at the reference desk and solve, in part, the difficult mediation issues connected with remote users who have great variations in skill levels. However, the design of some graphic interfaces or library expert systems from the ground up is probably a venture that should be entertained by some of the larger institutions that have the staff, expertise and funding for the project. Some of these campus-based experiments will be packaged commercially and then can be adapted for use at other libraries (see Fadell & Myers, 1989).

Beyond the screen displays of front-ends, the even more daunting question around the corner for many libraries will be what commercial or local databases or access points will be added to the basic online catalog to comprise a local or consortium ''super catalog.'' Again, reference librarians are in the best position to advocate certain choices on behalf of users and should participate in any planning process as equal players with automation and technical services staff. Numerous vendors of integrated systems currently are offering the same search protocols for tape-loaded indexes and abstracts or full-text databases that are used for the online catalog. The search software chosen will be critical, impacting significantly on the level of needed mediation. Georgia Institute of Technology has been using BRS search software for a number of years for the online catalog and a handful of index sources. Search languages employing commands like those used by BRS, which requires two periods preceding a command, are not intuitive for users negotiating the system for the first time. If command-driven systems are chosen over menu-driven systems, the search language should be quickly understood by the average user with the aid of screen prompts and examples.

If the task is not too difficult now in deciding to add to the OPAC a number of Wilson Indexes, ERIC, PSYC, PAIS, and a few basic reference sources, how far can we go before users respond to the menu of choices with bewilderment? Even in 1987, Hildreth spoke of ''navigational confusion and frustration'' (p. 652) as being one of the common problems experienced by users of second-generation OPACs. What databases or access choices will we want to reserve for staff-use-only terminals requiring full mediation?

Another layer of complexity is the idea of ''content-enriched access'' (see Van Orden, 1990 and Michalak, 1990). In addition to the basic MARC catalog record, book analytics, table of contents, indexes, or reviews of that book, and even reader comments or other ''online marginalia'' such as circulation statistics and related citations could be loaded (Koenig, 1990). How will adding a significant number of access points, i.e., moving away from controlled vocabulary, affect the precision of unmediated patron searches–will significantly more personal assistance be required or can screen prompts and displays adequately lead patrons through a more convoluted online environment?

Since many libraries will be selecting the new generation of integrated system in the next few years, it is also incumbent upon reference librarians to see that they are well represented in the system selection process. Advocacy for the user at this point is critical as a preventive measure: as OPACs become more complex, mediation necessarily will be required and the interface design should be as intuitive and self-explanatory as possible as well as easily modifiable to meet institution needs or to respond in the future to observed changes in patron use patterns.

THE INTERNET AND LIST SERVERS

The web of networks crisscrossing the country now raises even more questions. Internet, a super network composed of local, regional, and national networks, allows entry into a large host of databases including more than 100 online catalogs. Information about Internet is wide-spread beyond the scholarly community. *Boardwatch Magazine* which bills itself as the "leading monthly publication covering electronic bulletin boards and online services" discusses Internet in its July 1991 "telebits" column and mentions the availability of PACS-L (Public Access Computer Systems Forum, the University of Houston based list server on online library catalogs). In the directory of bulletin boards and online information services listed in this issue, CARL (Colorado Alliance of Research Libraries), The University of Texas-Austin, and University of Minnesota online catalogs appear along with bulletin boards such as "Herpnet/ Satronics" and "Dave-Barry." As catalog access extends across the nation, and even internationally, the potential remote user base becomes increasingly more culturally diverse. Depending upon the level of service defined in each library for non-primary clientele, these differences may have to be considered as interfaces and help screens are designed. Telephone mediation offered to remote users may have to be curtailed if the volume of usage significantly increases.

For our local users of Internet, there are other considerations. On some campuses with academic computing centers, there may be a trend for the staff to give seminars on accessing the Internet. Certainly, academic computing personnel are in a position to explain network protocols, but once the link with an information database is established, a librarian is

82   The Reference Librarian and Implications of Mediation

uniquely qualified to explain the efficient navigation and search strategy formulation of another catalog. And access to remote catalogs naturally ties in with other library related functions, e.g., interlibrary loan. As yet, the Internet is not formally indexed, and it is not easy to get a handle on all that it provides. Kalin and Tennant (1991) in a good overview of the Internet mention a number of lists and guides including the NSF produced *Internet Resource Guide*. The Internet represents a vast unexplored sea, and may in due time exhibit certain service undertows as well. Again, we may be able to provide needed directory information, basic access procedures, and information on searching online catalogs, but how far we will be able to go with mediating specific files that may not be designed with any standard search protocols in mind remains to be seen. Being careful not to promise too high a level of unrestricted service, however, seems wise.

A LOOK AT STANDARDS

As terminals or microcomputers have been added to Reference areas, some libraries have resorted to signs advising users: "This is not an online catalog terminal." This problem of multiple electronic stations hosting different products is resolved in part by integrated online systems that offer the same search interface for mounted databases and for the online catalog. The user is still handicapped when accessing online catalogs at other institutions where a different interface is in place. The work on a Common Command Language by a committee of the National Information Standards Organization (NISO) is a critical step in providing users (and librarians) with command protocols that can be recognized across systems (Klemperer, 1990).

Setting standards for clear, intuitive search language (terms like "find" and "display") addresses the verbal aspect of the command-driven interfaces, but as more graphic front-ends come into use, easily recognizable pictorial cues will be equally important. These screen "road signs" need to be universal icons that have the same semiotic significance from one user to the next.

INFORMATION LITERACY EDUCATION

User group instruction will continue to be a significant measure to reduce the one-on-one mediation at the Reference Desk related to the use of online systems. In class instruction, it is possible to explain online sources within the context of an integrated research strategy that recognizes a use for all media and access vehicles. This instruction, however, should be "unlike tool and format-specific instruction," instead "provid [ing] generic information for finding, evaluating and using information, regardless of storage and retrieval media" (Baker, Huston, & Pastine, 1991, p. 220). The traditional limits of one to two hours for instruction sessions cannot be taken up with the mechanics of various search interfaces; selecting thesaurus-based search terminology, boolean operations, and other philosophical considerations need to take precedence.

BACK TO SQUARE ONE: ONLINE VENDORS

Coming back full circle and looking at our roots, we may ask whether or not we can afford the time to keep abreast of all the traditional services and databases added over the years. The number of available databases has grown from some 300 in 1975 to 5,600 in 1990 (Tenopir, 1991, p. 96). Many libraries have passwords for Dialog, BRS, Orbit, Wilsonline, and more recently EPIC. Some have NEXIS, VU-TEXT, and STN among others. A few services such as Wilsonline may have been dropped already by some libraries acquiring CD-ROM products. The level of activity in some of the services may raise the question of cancelling any service that is accessed only a dozen or fewer times during the course of a year. There are real costs in the time required to keep up with any changes in the service and monitor separate billing.

Traditional mediation requires an hour or two to complete the search and process the paperwork; can we really afford this generous ratio of one client to one librarian for an hour or two? Also, if only a select few faculty are searching the databases, it may be more practical to train them to search an online file such as *Chemical Abstracts* where the user in most cases has a far greater knowledge of the field. Costs can be assumed more readily by the library if the paper copy of the index is cancelled. Undoubtedly, the "scholar workstation" will have as a chief component access to the principle bibliographic, data, or full text files of that scholar. Many scholars will applaud not only the convenience of accessing information from their offices, but also avoiding the "intrusion" of the librarian into the process. Marilyn Schmitt (1990) in the *Chronicle of Higher Education* describes a library search procedure: "A reference librarian interviews you to find out what information you want and then conducts the search. You are grateful to receive some 30 "hits"

84   The Reference Librarian and Implications of Mediation

(references), but leave with the nagging worry that you might have found more information if you had been able to browse through the material yourself'' (p. A44).

IN CONCLUSION

Certainly there are looming complications that can be added to the picture already presented: computer files (machine readable datafiles) often requiring statistical packages to manipulate the data, electronic journals, and advocacy for handicapped users of electronic sources (particularly in light of the 1990 Americans with Disabilities Act). New technologies will continue to appear on the scene. Reference librarians are facing a double-edged sword: with the burgeoning number of electronic services and the definite movement away from ownership to access, we must carefully choose the services we mediate–and the level of mediation–and at the same time not abdicate interpretive responsibility for online services that reasonably should be offered by a particular library. A gap in providing the online information service and mediation users need will result in patrons relying on themselves or computing center personnel or, perhaps, information brokers. Library Reference Departments do not have the resources not to allocate some of the business to these others, but this allocation should be conscious and strategic.

As we look ahead, a number of statements can be made about the near future:

1. More users will acquire CD-ROM products and online services for home and office, possibly viewing commercial sources as the ''primary information provider,'' rather than the library. Librarians will need to monitor the popular press as well as sample the literature in other scholarly disciplines to realistically appraise and plan for the library's position in this new order. Where can users be self-sufficient and in what contexts is mediation, at any level, advised?

2. Ubiquitous end-user searching will result in the virtual end of the long professional debate about the necessity of a trained intermediary to insure the quality of search results. There are few professional drivers on the road, but most people are able to negotiate the highways well enough to get to their desired destination.

3. Reference librarians will need to even more rigorously serve as advocates for users with vendors, promoting standards for search protocols, icons, and system interfaces that can be easily navigated by users.

Reference librarians will need to work closely with the technical services and automation staff on these issues.

4. Reference librarians will continue in a strong role as "reader services librarians," in this case with emphasis on electronic mediums, advising users of strategies to identify relevant electronic sources.

5. One-on-one mediation will significantly diminish. Reference librarians will be more active in long-range planning for electronic services, including next generation integrated systems, designing or adapting online aids that obviate the need for significant, direct mediation. However, a critical point in the design of these system interfaces is the inclusion of messages at key locations indicating that a librarian can provide further direction or additional sources, thus referring the user back to a human interface and, subsequently, needed paper technologies.

REFERENCES

Baker, B., Houston, M. M., & Pastine, M. (1991). Making connections: Teaching information retrieval. *Library Trends, 39*(3), 210-222.

Bobay, J., Stockey, E., & Popp, M. P. (1990, Fall). Library services for remote users with LINKWAY. *Reference Services Review,* 53- 57.

Cetron, M. & Davies, O. (1991, September-October). Trends shaping the world. *The Futurist,* pp. 11-21.

Coursey, D. (1991, August 5). The cost of information. *InfoWorld,* pp. 40-41.

Drucker, P. F. (1969). *The age of discontinuity: Guidelines to our changing society.* New York: Harper & Row.

Fadell, J. & Myers, J.E. (1989). The information machine: A microcomputer-based reference service. *Reference Librarian,* 75-112.

Gaughan, T. (1991, May). Who is Bob Walton and why is he saying these outrageous things? *American Libraries,* pp. 406-407.

Hildreth, C.R. (1987). Beyond Boolean: Designing the next generation of online catalogs. *Library Trends, 35*(4), 647- 667.

Kalin, S. W., & Tennant, R. (1991, August). Beyond OPACS . . . The wealth of information resources on the Internet. *Database,* 28-33.

Klemperer, K. (1990). The common command language. In M. Gorman (Ed.), *Library and Information Technology Standards: Papers Presented at the Second National Conference of the Library and Information Technology Association, October 2-6, 1988; Boston Massachusetts* (pp. 12-19). Chicago: American Library Association.

Koenig, M. (1990, October). Linking library users: A culture change in librarianship. *American Libraries,* pp. 844-849.

Lyman, P. (1991, January/February). The Library of the (not-so-distant) future. *Change,* pp. 34, 36-41.

Michalak, T. J. (1990). An experiment in enhancing catalog records at Carnegie Mellon University. *Library Hi Tech*, 31, 33-41.

Miller, W. (1984, May). What's wrong with reference: Coping with success and failure at the reference desk. *American Libraries*, pp. 303-306, 321-322.

Naisbitt, J. & Aburdene, P. (1990). *Megatrends 2000*. New York: Avon Books.

Quint, Barbara. (1991, June). *New lamps for old: substituting online for traditional*. Paper presented at the American Library Association RASD MARS Preconference, "The electronic library: linking people, information and technology," Atlanta, GA.

Schmitt, Marilyn. (1990, November 11) Scholars must take the lead on computerization in the humanities. *Chronicle of Higher Education*, p. A44.

Tenopir, Carol. (1991, April 1). The most popular databases. *Library Journal*, pp. 96,98.

Tiefel, V. (1991, October). The gateway to information: A system redefines how libraries are used. *American Libraries*, pp. 858-860.

U.S. Bureau of the Census. (1990). *Statistical Abstract of the United States: 1990*. (110th ed.). Washington, DC: Author.

Van Orden, R. (1990). Content-enriched access to electronic information: Summaries of selected research. *Library Hi Tech*, 31, 27-32.

Walsh, T. (1991, August). On-line bonanza . . .via offbeat trails. *AmigaWorld*, pp. 29-32.

Response to Swan and Evans: "Problems and Opportunities"

Michael D. Kathman

John Swan and Anita Evans present a summary of the issues that face librarians, at a time when all libraries are incorporating electronic information sources into the range of materials available. The issue each addresses is how reference librarians can mediate these electronic sources along with the paper resources, not converted, in order to meet the users' needs. This problem is compounded by the availability of electronic services from outside vendors similar to those offered by libraries. Computing centers, not-for-profit, and for-profit vendors offer services that can be made available anywhere that a patron can plug a computer into a phone line. The forms of electronic information will change over the next five years as will the players. Rather than focusing on specific technologies and players as Swan and Evans have, I would like to look at what can be generalized from their observations. These generalizations might best be expressed in a series of questions.

What value can or should librarians add to the various forms of electronic information available? If we do not add value then why are we involved? Will the definition of "mediation" in reference change during the next five years? What will the role of the "professional" librarian be in the next decade? What work should be done at the local level and what should be done at the regional or national level? What should bibliographic instruction encompass during the next five to ten years? Should it be significantly different from what it has been in the past? Will the issue of "fee" vs. "free" or the "information rich" and the "information poor" be any different in the next five years than in the past? As we answer these questions in our individual libraries and as a profession we will be better able to cope with the ever-changing technol-

---

Michael D. Kathman is Director of Libraries and Media and Academic Computing at The College of St. Benedict and St. John's University, Collegeville, MN 56321.

© 1992 by The Haworth Press, Inc. All rights reserved.

ogies that are and will remain a part of our professional lives. We need to look further than the individual technologies and the problems they bring to find the answers.

In general, the other players in the information market are of little concern. If they can provide service better and more efficiently than libraries, we should applaud their efforts. So much needs to be done and therefore there will always be enough work for libraries and librarians. Our "competitors," in reality, take on the "easy" tasks or those where economies of scale give them an advantage: Librarians, as Evans says, "need to monitor the popular press . . . to realistically appraise and plan for the library's position in this new order."

This "monitoring" could take far too much of our time unless we figure out how to do it as a profession rather than as individual librarians. The same is true with many of the experiments being done locally. We must be careful not to "re-invent the wheel" with costs we can ill-afford (interfaces, computer assisted instruction, HyperCard applications, etc.). How many of us can afford, as Swan suggests, the three hundred hours of professional time to create a HyperCard application with "a set of instructional screens, replete with illuminating and witty graphics, that unlock the secrets of a given library with such dogged, mind-numbing and tedious simplicity that I [Swan] personally would prefer to wander lost through the stacks . . ."?

The technologies that are and will be available, along with the many non-library information providers, offer an unparalleled opportunity for the profession. We have complained for decades about the amount of clerical work we have to do, the number of "dumb" questions we have to answer, and the lack of user sophistication. Now, the technology and our outside competitors will force us to move away from simply providing answers and require us to work on what has been called the "front" and "back end" of the reference process. We will need to spend more time helping users decide which of the many sources available should be queried and then how to evaluate the results.

These two articles bring up to date some of the issues that have been facing the profession, but I wonder if the basic issues are any different than they have been for the past century. There may be more players in the game, but as Evans points out, "The onslaught of the cheap paperback did not put public libraries out of business, and the advent of home online services and CD-ROM products will not bring about their demise either." I do not believe technology is the issue. The real issue is defining our role as professional librarians. This debate has been going on for a long time, but these articles show clearly why it is time to bring it to closure. If we cannot, we just might become a vestigial organ of the information system. The threat suggested by Swan of "the reference librarian becoming an anachronism or a seldom-needed specialist, or the process of library instruction dwindling to the role of holding the hands and soothing the anxieties of those who turn phobic or slow-witted in front of video display terminals" is real if we do not choose to act now.

The problems of mediation have been around for a long time. Very big libraries before the age of electronic information had a large number of paper indexes and other reference tools available for users and reference librarians. The electronic age has simply moved a larger number of resources to smaller libraries and even into users' homes and offices. All libraries as Evans suggests, will now have to "make hard choices about what level of support to offer patrons accessing electronic information as these technological products come of age." She gives clear direction on how libraries should make the "front end" decisions I suggested earlier. She thinks that selection criteria for what libraries should mediate ought to "be based upon a careful reading of the value added by that mediation within the context of the mission of the library. . . . " The problem with this, as she points out, is that "libraries will need to be cognizant of whether or not dropping a service is creating a class of information poor. . . . "

She goes on to suggest that "libraries will need to be decisive in carving out their niche, but be willing to define areas where direct patron access to the information source without any library involvement or mediation is preferred." Her solution, and I think one that is on target, is to be selective about what we support and to train users to do as much as possible on their own. This training, as she notes, cannot be format specific; it should be generic in terms of finding information and, perhaps even more important, in evaluating the large quantities of information found.

Finally, Evans' suggests that librarians will need to take an active role in designing user interfaces both in our own libraries and in consultation with electronic vendors. We need to move away from the hundreds of proprietary interfaces to ones that are intuitive and common if information seekers are to be able to search many different databases without assistance.

Swan looks at the "back end" of the reference process. He watches patrons "print out hundreds of citations without any preliminary screening" and realizes that they are not necessarily getting the best or most relevant information. He is concerned with the patrons' ability to comprehend these hundreds of citations. We have all experienced the same prob-

90 *The Reference Librarian and Implications of Mediation*

lem in trying to assist users at CD-ROM workstations. "It does no good to interpose one's highly professional body between a patron and a computerized index if the patron already expects to be able to use it without help." How do we assist users to evaluate the results of their searches if they do not see the need? Our patrons know they have too much information but, as Swan suggests, "they deal with this burden by shedding or ignoring as much of it as is necessary to keep the burden manageable."

Although there is no simple solution to this problem, Swan looks to bibiligraphic instruction as at least a beginning. The problem will "require that librarians bring a fuller understanding of the whole, connected nature of their domain to the task of helping other people in this ever-evolving process of learning how to learn." Both Swan and Evans suggest the solution for both the "front" and "back end" questions is that librarians will have to spend more time both in-house and with vendors on the design of interfaces; that librarians will have to make hard decisions regarding information sources they will and will not support; and finally, that they will need to be more involved in teaching than in answering questions.

The two articles make it clear that these issues can no longer be addressed solely at the local level. Experimentation must be done there, but as a profession we will have to publicize our mistakes as well as our successes faster and to a broad audience. List servers like PACA-L are a way to use the current technology to our advantage, but I believe there is a very important role here for professional associations. For every problem there is an opportunity. These two articles point out many problems, but at the same time they show that as a profession we are in a time of great opportunity. We can look at strategic alliances with other information providers, whether they be giant corporations or our local computing centers. We have a unique opportunity to become true information professionals. We can use the background and knowledge we have to train patrons to use appropriate resources and to better evaluate the results they obtain. Professional associations could move out of bureaucracy and navel gazing into what they should really be doing–helping librarians add significant value to the information delivery process.

III. SPECIALIZED MEDIATION

Information and Research
Support Services:
The Reference Librarian
and the Information Paraprofessional

Carol Hammond

SUMMARY. Organizing reference services to use paraprofessionals as information providers can help academic libraries adapt to new technology, provide staff support for resource sharing, and assist reference librarians in developing new and enhanced roles on campus. It is a staffing alternative that can facilitate the integration and use of electronic reference resources, such as Online Catalogs, CD-ROM databases and end user searching by providing more assistance to users. Placing responsibility for teaching library clients how to use document delivery with the same staff who help users identify needed materials makes access easier for requestors, and resource sharing more readily accepted by students and faculty. And by separating Information and Research Support activities and sharing the workload between staff at different levels, reference librarians can provide an advanced level of research assistance, spend more time on support for faculty research collection development, classroom instruction, and the development and improvement of programs. Training of the paraprofessional staff and practice of the referral process are essential to the librarian-paraprofessional

---

Carol Hammond is Head, Research and Information Access Services, Arizona State University West, Phoenix, AZ.

© 1992 by The Haworth Press, Inc. All rights reserved.   *91*

92 The Reference Librarian and Implications of Mediation

partnership this model requires. This article describes how parapro-fessionals have been used in reference at a new academic library, and how the role of the reference librarian has been redefined as a result.

The future of reference. Balancing the demands of collection development and reference. Library instruction methods for the electronic library. The teaching role of librarians. Coping with multiple priorities. Adapting to automation. Doing more with less.

These are some of the current issues being discussed at conferences and workshops, articles, reference offices and reference department meetings. They reflect the rapid change that the profession of librarianship has experienced, and especially show how those changes have affected reference librarians. There is no doubt about it; there are now new roles for reference librarians to play, additional obligations to meet, new skills to demonstrate, and revised expectations to meet. The question is, what can be changed to handle the new workloads, to manage the additional priorities, and to structure the jobs of reference librarians so that they can all be done and done well? To begin this process, a re-examination of traditional job descriptions may be in order. If the ground rules have changed, other changes must occur as well.

The unusual event of the birth of a new university campus and a new academic library at Arizona State University West has provided an ideal opportunity to restructure the role and responsibilities of reference librarians. Could librarians more fully demonstrate their unique professional expertise, develop a model partnership with the teaching faculty, utilize and promote the capabilities of all the new technology, and at the same time build library programs and collections from the ground up? The answer to this challenge was yes. But it was unlikely that all this could be accomplished by doing things the way they had always been done. It was an opportunity to change traditional responsibilities and provide the instruction and assistance that patrons would require to use the different kind of library envisioned, and the support which librarians would need to meet the challenges that lay ahead.

LIBRARY PROGRAMS FOR A NEW INSTITUTION

Some of the parameters for library programs were established by the institution's definition of itself and the proposed curriculum. Others that were identified early in the planning process were the definition of the kind of collection the library would have, the concept of using resource sharing on a large scale to meet student and faculty research needs, and the integration and use of technology in library services. The development of the library's own vision along with these parameters were responsible for how staffing and services were developed.

Arizona State University West. Established as an upper-level institution in 1984, ASU West offers courses at the junior, senior, and graduate levels only. Academic programs are offered in Business, Education, Human Services, Arts and Sciences, and Engineering. Many of these programs are designed to reflect the increasingly interdisciplinary approach to knowledge and problem solving. An urban university which is part of a multi-campus system, ASU West serves the higher education needs of students who may transfer from the many local community colleges, or who are returning to school for various reasons. Many are non-traditional students. These include a large number of working adults attending classes on a part-time basis; 67% of the students are over 25 years of age, 74% are enrolled part-time, more than 50% are married, and 63% are women. Enrollment at the campus is projected to reach 20,000.

Library Collections. As a new branch campus, reliance on the much larger and stronger collections of the main campus in Tempe, 35 miles away, is not only essential but a great benefit to a developing library. An on-site collection of both current and retrospective publications and media is being built to support the ASU West curriculum. A strong reference collection is considered a basic need. Periodicals and journals are provided primarily in microform; very specialized titles and extensive backfiles, available on the main campus, are not generally duplicated. Rare and non-curricular research materials are not collected.

Resource Sharing. The West campus library does not attempt to duplicate the research level collections available in Tempe, but does provide convenient access to them. Using a shared Online Catalog for identifying materials and a strong document delivery program, some 15,000 items a year are provided to ASU West library users primarily from the Tempe campus collections. The delivery of those materials, and helping users work with a delivery system to supplement the more traditional help-yourself-from-the-shelves system, are major parts of the service program.

Electronic Technology. The arrival of CD-ROM technology coincided with the initial planning of the library. Many sources, such as *ERIC* and *Psychological Abstracts*, have never been available in the library except in electronic format. Additionally, a deliberate decision was made to provide access to certain indexes through online searching as needed, and

94 *The Reference Librarian and Implications of Mediation*

not to purchase them in any other format. The ASU Online Catalog has been in place since the ASU West library opened; it provides access to all the books in all the ASU libraries, as well as seven different periodical indexes, a full-text encyclopedia, gateways to numerous other online catalogs at other institutions, and a selection of in-house indexes and guides to special collections. Just as the document delivery program allows for access to a much greater wealth of material, the use of electronic tools in reference also improves access for users. At the same time both of these systems create the need for new approaches and techniques in reference, bibliographic instruction and circulation.

The Vision. In addition to the above, the development of library programs has been guided by some basic principles and organizational values. These elements are part of the library's mission and vision. By identifying them first and building consensus about the vision, programs were able to develop with these goals in mind. To begin with, it was recognized that no organization trying to meet many needs can do all things to perfection, and that the library needed to select what it could do well. The ASU West Library selected three areas: providing a high quality, targeted collection, excellent information services, and convenient access. Services should be client-centered, service-oriented and user-friendly. One result of this goal is that staff in all units operate with a caring attitude for patrons and their needs. Programs would strive to enhance both the role of the librarian, and the role of the library within the university. Staff should select the best from tradition but constantly seek better solutions. Qualities that are valued in the organization in addition to a strong service orientation are openness to change and the ability to be excited by challenge (Gater, 1989 and 1990).

A NEW PLAN FOR REFERENCE: INFORMATION AND RESEARCH SUPPORT

The staffing plan that has been developed reflects the library's vision, the "differentness" of the programs–the reliance on the electronic tools and the need to use document delivery from another collection to obtain materials–and the information finding and gathering behaviors of students. It is designed to meet these needs and at the same time provide the support that makes possible a different role for the reference librarians. To provide the appropriate individualized and personal service for each user, a partnership between librarians and paraprofessionals for the delivery of information has been established.

Establishing a two-level service is not a new idea; information desks, to filter out and answer directional questions and provide some basic assistance in using catalogs or serials lists have been around for quite some time. These rely on the existence of a reference desk or desks somewhere else in the building, staffed by librarians with reference expertise, to whom other kinds of questions can be referred. Having a reference desk staffed by a combination of librarians and paraprofessionals, where an effort is also made to sort out questions and utilize referral, is also not uncommon. Some institutions have used student help rather than regular library staff to provide information services. Trying to sort out user needs and questions that truly require professional expertise, and directing those to the level of staff where they are best answered, has been one objective of these efforts. Trying to use skill and the time of those reference experts to the best advantage is another. Estimates of the number of questions asked at reference desks that can be handled without professional expertise usually are in the 80-85% range; although this may vary by type of library, studies done at the University of Illinois, the University of Nebraska, and other places have provided some basis for this estimate (Boyer and Theimer, 1975; Aluri and St. Clair, 1978; Woodard, 1989; Deeney, 1990). Another study suggests that only six minutes out of an hour at the reference desk are spent providing professional reference service (Jestes, 1974).

What is different about the model at ASU West is the use of paraprofessionals as a key element in managing the integration of electronic tools into the information process for users, including both the "finding" and "delivery" aspects, and the use of that staff to change and enhance the role of the librarian. Paraprofessionals serve a role similar to that of the laboratory assistant, with the library as the laboratory. The librarians' reference training and expertise is used for teaching, consultation and referral, and more of their time is allocated to other priorities in the library program.

Paraprofessional Information Providers. The Information Desk, which is the first service point users come to in the building and the only desk in the reference area, is staffed by paraprofessionals. They answer directional and information questions, and when it is appropriate they conduct a reference interview with users and determine which source or sources to use. They meet the initial reference needs of users, and play a strong role in library instruction. This is particularly so in providing assistance with electronic resources, and implementing the document delivery system for access to materials that are on the Tempe campus or elsewhere.

Assistance with Electronic Resources. The need for individual instruction at the point at which the user arrives to find information is particularly necessary, we have found, when using electronic tools. Nothing has been as effective, or able to replace, the one-on-one assistance by a trained staff member when students are ready to search an online or CD-ROM database, even when a classroom lesson has been provided. This same conclusion was reached at Texas A&M, another library that relies heavily on CD-ROM technology (Anders, 1990). Non-traditional students have been less willing to commit their limited time to instruction in using electronic tools except at the time of need. Attempts to provide this instruction in a variety of out-of-the-classroom situations were widely promoted but poorly attended. Instead, providing support on a demand basis has been a more effective way of accommodating the information seeking behaviors of this group of students.

In fact, assisting students and faculty with a lack of exposure to any of the electronic library tools, especially those who may suffer from varying degrees of technophobia, is a major activity at the Information Desk and one that is handled effectively by paraprofessionals. The variety of databases available on the Online Catalog, and the reliance at ASUW on the remote collections it lists, make it the most frequently used tool in the reference collection. Instruction and assistance in using the catalog have replaced instructions on how to use the *Reader's Guide* as the most repetitive task in reference, besides directing people to pay phones, restrooms and copy machines. In addition to the Online Catalog, the reference collection includes nine different CD-ROM databases, and on an average, first-time CD-ROM users may need as much as 30 minutes of individual assistance, no matter what classroom instruction they have had. Using paraprofessionals has allowed for the level of staffing this instructional support requires. Because of the intensive demand for this assistance, staff experience and expertise with the systems has become very strong. Periodic tests given to the staff by the librarians on CD-ROM search strategy and use of system commands have produced highly positive results, and serve as evidence that confidence in the ability of paraprofessionals to assist in the library-laboratory has not been misplaced. Providing personal assistance to users to complement or replace some other instructional methods has also given the library a reputation for user-friendliness and helpfulness. Student input from our ''How are We Doing?'' Comments and Suggestions forum provide many thanks and testimonials in support of the personal service received in the library.

Because of the success the paraprofessionals showed in providing instruction to CD-ROM users, their role was expanded to be the front line coaches for students taking advantage of the end-user search service,

Specialized Mediation 97

which is treated as just another tool that may be used in the information gathering process. With already strong skills in using electronic databases, the training needed to go online with simplified search strategies available through *BRS After Dark* or Dialog's *Knowledge Index* did not require a great leap in expertise. With specialized classroom instruction and worksheets for planning search strategies provided by the librarians to selected classes, students with some assistance from paraprofessionals were able to execute their own online searches. It was another way the library was able to provide individual assistance with electronic resources.

Telephone Reference. One of the serious distractions at almost any reference desk, and one which can be most annoying to users who are standing and waiting for assistance, is the interruption of the ringing phone. In an environment where staff are frequently occupied in one-on-one instruction, answering the telephone is almost impossible. Two different month long samples of telephone calls showed that about 85% of the calls were for information about the campus and questions that could be answered through the Online Catalog. A re-evaluation of telephone reference services was made, and a station for providing this service was established in the office area away from the desk. An Online Catalog terminal, a shelf of reference books, phone books and other campus information is available to the telephone reference staff. Forms are available for recording questions which cannot be answered from the station, and those calls are returned after the reference collection is consulted and the answer found. The Information desk paraprofessionals are scheduled in telephone reference as part of their daily routine.

Document Delivery. The Information Desk staff are also responsible for implementing the first step of the document delivery process, which provides convenient access to materials that are elsewhere. They not only help users identify what they need but explain and start the process of delivering the items. This is also an instructional process, and a repetitive one, as procedures are explained to each user. Once again, providing the personal assistance of staff in working with users to facilitate an unusual concept in library use has made a difference. It is more hassle-free for users because they need not go to another desk, and repeat part of the transaction. The library has been able to avoid establishing an additional service point, or duplicate a great deal of staff training, by simply extending the role of the information provider to include initiating document delivery for users who have identified needed materials. Printouts are used from the electronic resources whenever possible and citations, locations and call numbers verified by the same paraprofessionals who assisted in the search process and who are already familiar with the tools.

Most requested materials are available for pick-up at ASU West within 48 hours. Paraprofessionals have met this important, and time-consuming, user need effectively.

Referral. Questions that are very specialized in nature, requiring more subject expertise or knowledge of reference sources than the paraprofessional may have, are referred to a librarian. Office hours are maintained to ensure that a librarian is always on hand, even though he or she may not be physically at the desk. Users who may need a consultation, for lengthy assistance in how to use the library or how to approach a research assignment, or who may need an online search, are also referred to the librarians.

This model removes one of the most time-consuming, and for some the most cherished, aspects of reference librarianship and entrusts it to paraprofessionals. The librarians train library assistants in interviewing, information gathering, verification, and referral skills; this is another aspect of their teaching and instruction role. It is an ongoing and continual effort that includes formal classroom instruction for staff as well as informal and individual mentoring. Research support, including the answering of complex, difficult, and in-depth questions requiring subject expertise, knowledge of specialized databases and resources is reserved for them. Paraprofessionals serve as mediators in the person-to-person part of information delivery and often suggest that users make an appointment to meet with a librarian. Mary Biggs describes this as "Gourmet Reference Service" (Biggs, 1985); similar and variations have been suggested by others as well (Ford, 1989; Miller, 1985; Freides, 1983).

Research Support Services Librarians. The different job titles given to the librarians better describe the new role of the reference librarian, and more accurately reflect the responsibilities as they are now defined. There is a greater emphasis on teaching, marketing, staff training, and liaison activities. With a reliance on electronic databases as an alternative to the purchase of sources, knowledge of available databases and expertise in accessing electronic tools is of greater importance. Because of the demands of creating an entirely new library, collection development is given a high priority, as is program development.

Research Support for Students. Research Support Services Librarians interact with students and faculty in the classroom and during office hours, when online searching and individual consultation and assistance with library research projects are provided rather than at the reference desk. Library instruction often takes place in the campus computer lab or in the classroom building where students usually meet for classes. The use of appointments for consultation is heavily promoted; librarians distribute their personal business cards to students during all of the classes they teach to encourage students who feel the need for the librarian's expertise to use them as they would another professional service provider: by appointment. Meeting office hours to work with students who need advanced research assistance and being available for the referrals is another responsibility, as is encouraging and promoting a referral process that provides the right level of assistance and expertise for each user.

Instruction and Staff Training. Developing a staff of skilled paraprofessional information providers, who are capable of handling the basic reference and instructional responsibilities at the desk is an extension of the librarian's instruction responsibilities. The instruction is on-going, with intensive training in reference sources provided for the paraprofessionals at the time they are hired. The training is coordinated by the Information Delivery Specialist, who supervises the staff, with instruction and follow-up exercises provided by all of the research support services librarians. Interviewing techniques are also covered. Training in subject areas and reference tools is considered to be an ever present need, and classes are given for the paraprofessionals on a regular basis. Contribution on a regular basis to the staff training program is, in fact, an expectation of all of the research support services librarians. Often, it is offered as the result of a particular session prepared for a course, providing the staff with expertise to work with the students when they come to the library after classroom instruction. Others are inspired by questions at the desk, or requested by the paraprofessional themselves.

Research Support for Faculty. The liaison role of librarians has been expanded to include a strong element of marketing and an unusually high level of library support for faculty research. Adjusting to more extensive use of indexes that are available only in electronic form, and resources that are only available through document delivery is a new kind of library concept for faculty as well as students. Library support for research is a strong personal and professional need for faculty, and a factor that has great impact on their careers and success. Changing the model that is familiar to them creates uneasiness among the faculty, because of the high cost to them if it does not adequately meet their needs.

As part of the responsibility to market the new library, librarians have become part of the recruitment process for faculty, and meet with all candidates for faculty positions who visit the campus. This time is used to explain how access to research level collections is conveniently provided through document delivery, and to illustrate the ways in which individual librarians and the organization are prepared to assist in the research and teaching goals of the faculty. Very often the librarians suc-

100   *The Reference Librarian and Implications of Mediation*

cessfully alleviate the candidate's fear that the ASU West library is too small to accommodate his or her research agenda. When new faculty are selected, librarians have already had an opportunity to find out about their needs and be prepared to address them, as well as establish an image of the librarian as a partner in the academic enterprise.

Librarians have been able to assist in the transition to a different kind of library by spending more time with faculty and by having the support to provide personal service to them as well. Online searching is supported through the materials budget, as just another form in which information is provided. Being aware of faculty research interests and responding to requests from them for support are given high priority. The librarians also coordinate document delivery requests from faculty. Faculty members provide anything from a stack of notecards to a printed bibliography, and the paraprofessional staff verify citations, gather and if necessary copy the materials from our collections or place requests for document delivery. It is not at all unusual for a faculty member to drop off a list of 30 citations, all of which are collected, copied, and delivered to his or her office two days later. Faculty recognition of the expertise of the librarians as online searchers, as experts who can teach the use of traditional and electronic sources to students in their classes, and as facilitators of reference queries and document delivery is expressed in several ways. In the annual survey of the faculty, in which all programs and services are rated, the library is viewed as an institutional strength by 80% of the faculty (ASU West, Office of Institutional Planning and Research, 1991). The faculty scholarship committee, in a recent progress report to the provost, identifies library support, and specifically the individual liaison librarians, as a strength for the institution in the area of support for faculty research. Librarians are members of the Faculty Senate, with many of them holding key elected positions and committee appointments. Librarians are appointed to search committees for faculty and administrators. They have successfully competed for campus research grants. The library budget requests receive administrative support. Our model has contributed to the enhanced position of librarians on campus, by allowing librarians to demonstrate the expertise they have, and the contributions they can make.

Collection Development. Building library collections including books, journals, and media from the ground up has been an important responsibility of the research support services librarians, and another aspect of the liaison role. Time for collection development activities is more available because less time is demanded for covering the desk. Paraprofessional staff at the Information Desk also provide support for collection develop-

Specialized Mediation 101

ment activities, such as checking bibliographies, which are assigned to them by the librarians.

THE EXPERIMENT AND THE PRACTICE

What have been the problems with this model? The lack of a good career ladder and good salaries for paraprofessionals has resulted in high turnover; well-trained staff are lost, and time is invested anew in training and developing new staff. This takes a good deal of mentoring at the desk and on-the-job teaching. The referral process is difficult to perfect. Studies done at Brigham Young University (Christensen et al., 1989), by Egill Halldorsson and Majorie Murfin (1977) and by Marjorie Murfin and Charles Bunge (1988) identify some of the problems, and these are genuine. It works best when it is easy to do; calling someone who is in an office is not the easiest thing to do when the desk is busy. Librarians feel that spending less time at the desk and using various tools has resulted in their reference skills becoming less sharp. To address all of these concerns, the librarians have opted to spend some hours working on the desk along with the paraprofessionals. A different mix of reference librarian and information paraprofessional staffing may evolve, an alternative suggested by others (Courtois and Goetsch, 1984; Christensen, 1989).

The model has been in place for four years, providing time for development, practice, experimentation, and modification. Use of the library has increased by more than 100% in almost all areas and the staff size has tripled during that time. What is the success rate of paraprofessionals in conducting an effective interview and answering questions? Beth Woodard (1977) puts it at 70%. Halldorson and Murfin (1977), who studied problems with paraprofessionals conducting the reference interview, suggest they do less well with this aspect of the process than professionals for a variety of reasons. Murfin and Bunge (1988), in studying paraprofessionals and reference service, find librarians score significantly higher by comparison in tests of user success and satisfaction. Although informal feedback has been encouraging and user response to our service model has been positive from the evidence we have, a more accurate evaluation of the quality of information services has not been, but should be, conducted. The costs of such a service also need analysis. While salary dollars may be saved, does this truly offset the costs of training and providing referral?

ASU West might be the ideal test site for evaluating the effectiveness of paraprofessionals as information providers. Some of the elements that

102   *The Reference Librarian and Implications of Mediation*

have been identified by others as contributing to the success of paraprofessionals in reference are in place at ASU West (Christansen et al., 1989; Halldorson and Murfin, 1977; Mufin and Bunge, 1988). The library has made a strong commitment to the idea, which has been in place since the library was established and which has wide acceptance. The paraprofessionals are all full-time staff who are scheduled to provide information services at least 75% of their time, and often more. The library and the librarians have invested a good deal of time and effort in developing and delivering a strong, on-going training program. Staff have been selected with academic background, familiarity with computers, service orientation, and interpersonal skills as prerequisites. Annual evaluations include input from the librarians on the appropriate use of referral, ability to handle the reference interview, knowledge of reference sources, and expertise with electronic resources. The activity of partnership is emphasized, and the whole department, librarians and paraprofessionals, meet regularly to discuss policies, issues, and questions.

What has been most successful? One great success of this model is the credit and acknowledgement of the faculty, who have benefited from the expertise and extended services they have received from the librarians to support teaching, research and recruitment of new faculty. Much of this evidence has been noted earlier. The librarians have had time, and faculty support, in developing a strong, course integrated instruction program. Collection development has been tremendous, as the book collection at ASU West has grown from 40,000 volumes in 1989 to 167, 000 today. Library instruction services that give individual users personal assistance have helped students adapt to using electronic sources. Many non-traditional students have become fearless searchers of various databases. In a recent survey, 96% of the students queried rate the library as a service as "Important to very important." The library was higher on the list of important services than any other item, including free parking and food! The same survey shows 45% of the students are extremely satisfied with the library, and 83% indicated they were satisfied to extremely satisfied (Firat and Behaegel, 1991). Library users, including the most prolific faculty scholar on campus who alone requests hundreds of items every year through document delivery, has developed an attitude of acceptance for the system as a viable alternative to ownership of materials (Pyne, 1988). New programs have been developed and librarians have to their credit some very notable and outstanding individual achievements, including publications, research projects, and elected offices.

How much would have been possible without the support of the paraprofessionals? The time they have provided for the librarians to carry out

Specialized Mediation

other responsibilities has been very substantial. Until more expert systems and gateways are developed, the demand for the assistance with electronic tools will most likely continue. The need to develop ways to share resources between libraries will escalate, as it has already. The demands on reference librarians to meet changing roles and additional demands will probably not diminish. A model that uses paraprofessionals as information providers, mediators, and instructional assistants has been a large part of the solution to these circumstances at Arizona State University West.

REFERENCES

Aluri, R. & St. Clair, J. W. (1978). Academic reference librarians: An endangered species? *The Journal of Academic Librarianship. 4*, 82-84.

Anders, V. (1990). The Wiley laser disc service at Evans library, Texas A & M University. In Stewart, K., Chiang, B., Coons, B. (Eds). *Public Access CD ROMs in Libraries: Case Studies.* (pp.179-191).Westport, CT: Meckler Publishing Company.

Arizona State University West. Office of Institutional Planning and Research. (1991, Spring). *Faculty and Professional Staff Annual Survey.*

Boyer, L. M. & Theimer, W. C., Jr. (1975). The use and training of nonprofessional personnel at reference desks in selected college and university libraries. *College and Research Libraries. 36*, 193-200.

Biggs, M. (1985). Replacing the fast fact drop-in with gourmet information service: A symposium. *The Journal of Academic Librarianship. 11*, 68-74.

Christensen, J. O., Benson, L. D., Butler, H. J., Hall, B. H., Howards, D. H. (1989). An evaluation of reference desk service. *College and Research Libraries. 50*, 468-483.

Courtois, M. P. & Goetsch, L. A. (1984). Use of nonprofessionals at reference desks. *College and Research Libraries. 45*, 385-91.

Deeney, K. (1990). The role of paraprofessionals at the reference desk. *Bulletin of the Medical Library Association. 78*(2), 191-193.

Firat, A. F. & Behaegel, E. (1991, September). ASU West Student Survey.

Ford, B. (1986). Reference beyond (and without) the reference desk. *College and Research Libraries. 47*, 491-4.

Friedes, T. (1983). Current trends in academic libraries. *Library Trends. 31*, 457-74.

Gater, H. L. (1989, April). Arizona State University's westward expansion: Mapping the route. In panel presentation *The road less traveled: Two libraries find new ways to meet traditional needs.* ACRL 5th National Conference, Cincinnati, OH.

Gater, H. L. (1990, August). State of the library address. Arizona State University West Library Staff Association Meeting, Phoenix, AZ.

104   The Reference Librarian and Implications of Mediation

Halldorsson, E. & Murfin, M. (1977). Performance of professionals and nonprofessionals in the reference interview. *College and Research Libraries. 38*, 385-95.

Jestes, E. (1974). Why waste valuable professional time on directional questions? *RQ/Reference Quarterly. 14*, 13-16.

Miller, W. (1985). Logic and reason at the reference desk. *Journal of Academic Librarianship. 11*, 551-554.

Murfin, M. E. & Bunge, C. (1988). Paraprofessionals at the reference desk. *The Journal of Academic Librarianship. 14*, 10-14.

Pyne, S. (1988, Special Edition). A faculty perspective. *ASU Libraries.* p. 6.

Woodard, B. S. (1989). The effectiveness of a reference desk staffed by graduate students and nonprofessionals. *College and Research Libraries. 50*, 455-483.

ADDITIONAL SOURCES

Emmick, N. (1985). Nonprofessionals on Reference Desks in Academic Libraries. *Reference Librarian. 12*, 149-160.

Hawley, G. S. (1987). *The referral process in libraries.* Metuchen, NJ: The Scarecrow Press.

Jahoda, G. & Bonney, F. (1990) The use of paraprofessionals in public libraries for answering reference queries. *RQ/Reference Quarterly. 29*, 328-31.

Miller, R. (1975). The paraprofessional. *Library Journal. 100*, 551-554.

Oberg, L. (1991). Paraprofessionals: Shaping the new reality. [Guest editorial]. *College and Research Libraries. 52*, 3-4.

Parmer, C. (1988). Paraprofessionals in the literature: A selective bibliography. *The Journal of Education for Library and Information Science. 28*, 249-51.

Riechel, R. (1989). *Personnel needs and changing reference service.* Hamden, CT. Library Professional Publications.

St. Clair, J. W & Aluri, R. (1977). Staffing the reference desk: Professionals or non-professionals? *Journal of Academic Librarianship. 3*, 149-153.

Woodard, B. S. & Van Der Laan, S. (1986/87). Training professionals for reference service. *Reference Librarian. 16*, 233-54.

Response to Hammond: "Paraprofessionals at the Reference Desk: The End of the Debate"

Larry R. Oberg

The emergence of paraprofessionals as a distinct class of employee within librarianship is a phenomenon whose impact upon the profession may yet equal that of automation. As a topic in the literature, the deployment and utilization of paraprofessionals remains to be fully analyzed, yet another casualty to our unerring ability to avoid or deny many of the most pressing problems.

Over the past quarter of a century, vast numbers of support staff have been pressed into service not only at reference desks across the country, but in technical services and most other areas of libraries as well. Today, they perform tasks newly created or reordered in the status hierarchy of library work by the rapid change that automation, networking, and other forces have created. Paraprofessionals also perform tasks shed by librarians increasingly preoccupied with fulfilling their faculty status obligations of research, teaching, and governance. This massive transformation of the library workplace has occurred at the grass roots level, independent of any decision-making counsels and unfettered by national standards or policy guidelines.

The shift to paraprofessionals of tasks traditionally performed by librarians has blurred the roles of both groups and confused patrons. Many librarians contribute to this role blurring by persisting in the performance of work that no longer qualifies as professional despite the availability of talented and competent paraprofessionals. It comes as no surprise, therefore, that clients and the administrators to whom we report often fail to distinguish between librarians and support staff, fail

---

Larry R. Oberg, is Director of Libraries, Stockwell-Mudd Libraries, Albion College, Albion, MI 49224.

© 1992 by The Haworth Press, Inc. All rights reserved. *105*

106 *The Reference Librarian and Implications of Mediation*

to acknowledge librarians as colleagues or experts, and deny them full professional status.

The use of paraprofessionals at reference desks has been a subject of intense debate for many years. My 1990 national survey of the role, status, and working conditions of paraprofessionals, however, indicates that the matter has been laid to rest, in practice, if not in the literature.[1] I found that 88 percent of the Association of Research Libraries (ARL) and 66 percent of the smaller college and universities libraries nationally regularly assign paraprofessionals to work at their reference desks.

The data also indicate that few restrictions are placed upon their performance. It seems to me that we are doomed to disappointment if we expect a return to the halcyon days of the reference desk as the last refuge of the true professional. What remains to be debated and resolved, in my opinion, is not whether paraprofessionals should or should not be used at the reference desk–the troops have voted with their feet on that one–but rather how they may best be utilized and what can be done to assure the conditions necessary for their success.

The separation of information and research support services at Arizona State University West offers a welcome model of how the judicious use of paraprofessionals to perform tasks appropriate to their education, competencies, and classification can improve services and free librarians to concentrate on their higher-level work. It also focuses attention upon the long ignored but important distinction between basic information provision and research support and, most importantly, the implications of this distinction for staff deployment.

The Arizona State model promises to improve services and free librarians for their highest level work, but it should not be accepted uncritically. For one thing, it places primary responsibility for triage and referral in the hands of those least qualified to make these decisions. Of course, were librarians to expand significantly their liaison activities and bond with their primary clientele, they might succeed in getting students and faculty to comprehend, accept, and respect this new order of things. Nonetheless, changing the stereotypes, habits, and expectations of researchers may be more easily accomplished on a new campus with a non-traditional student body than in an established school where perceptions and expectations have been ingrained over generations. It may also be easier to implement in a school populated exclusively by upper-division and graduate students than in an undergraduate college.

Hammond's description does not reassure one that a clean separation has been achieved between information provision and research support. Where is the line drawn between the inquiries handled by paraprofessionals and those handled by librarians? When and how are referrals made?

If significant task overlap exists, the distinction between the two classes of employees will remain clouded and intensify the role-blurring that already plagues the profession.

It is also likely that this new model will require a new method of evaluation, if it is not to become self-referential. Traditional instruments may prove inadequate. One is also left to wonder whether librarians are filling their additional time with appropriate research-related work and even if they become rusty when they are no longer required to use standard reference tools and techniques on a regular basis. Finally, the changes in reference that will inevitably be brought about by the creation of new automated services should be, but are not, discussed.

Hammond also indicates that adequate staffing structures and a level of compensation that ensures staff stability have yet to be achieved at ASU West. Clearly, if we ask paraprofessionals to do what they have watched us doing for years without offering them appropriate compensation, training, incentives, and status, we will ensure dissatisfaction, resentment, and even failure. Job satisfaction studies already indicate that support staff are less satisfied with their lot than are librarians.[2] Anecdotal evidence and my own research make it abundantly clear why this should be the case: Their pay and status are not commensurate with the responsibilities we ask them to assume.

It seems to me that the profession has focused quite enough attention upon whether we feel comfortable permitting non-MLS staff to work at the reference desk and whether we believe they can do a good job. The vote is in and it is time to move on. We should now work to become active agents in the change process that will ensure adequate and appropriate training, compensation, and status for the paraprofessionals to whom we increasingly entrust many of the most complex tasks.

Not all of us have the opportunity to create our own library from scratch. As a new school, ASU West is well suited to serve as an incubator of a new model of reference services, one that will be welcome indeed, if it contributes to resolving role confusion, rationalizing staff deployment, and upgrading services and the profession.

NOTES

1. Larry R. Oberg et al. "The Role, Status, and Working Conditions of Paraprofessionals: A National Survey of Academic Libraries." *College & Research Libraries*, in press.

2. See, for example, Patricia A. Kreitz and Annegret Ogden. "Job Responsibilities and Job Satisfaction at the University of California Libraries." *College & Research Libraries* 51 (July 1990):297-312.

Breaking Through:
Effective Reference Mediation
for Nontraditional Public Library Users

Sally G. Reed

Public libraries are committed to providing equal access to information for a widely diverse clientele. Getting beyond the rhetoric to make libraries and the information they provide truly accessible to all is the real challenge and arguably one which we have not always met with great success. It seems safe to say that in the view of many, the public library is an elitist organization primarily serving a white, well-educated, middle class clientele. Historically, patterns of use have borne this out.[1] This stereotype is further narrowed when such articles as "Click! The Feminization of the Public Library"[2] are taken into account. If the perception exists that we offer a service of limited value because it is designed for and delivered by a limited segment of our population (i.e., white, middle class, female) and if we are indeed committed to providing equal access to a diverse clientele, then we must make greater efforts to provide service that is flexible enough to aid an infinite variety of patrons.

The information services that public libraries provide their patrons demand such flexibility. Here a paradox exists, namely, that equality of access necessarily means aggressive and unequal service. Patrons who do not fit into the traditional mold are unlikely to receive equal service unless we, as librarians, are committed to serving them in a special way. We must not only remove barriers to access (these typically being physical, such as providing handicapped accessibility, and financial such as removing fees), we must also provide and promote service that takes into account patrons' needs as well as their abilities to assess and use the information we provide. For patrons with mental impairments and educational handicaps, information retrieval is only half the picture–the very

---

Sally G. Reed, is affiliated with the Ilsley Public Library, Middlebury, VT 05753.

© 1992 by The Haworth Press, Inc. All rights reserved.

110 *The Reference Librarian and Implications of Mediation*

information itself might well be unintelligible, unmanageable and therefore, inaccessible.

Reference and public services librarians who are committed to delivering not only information, but information that is meaningful must identify patrons with special learning or understanding difficulties and work closely with them to mediate their information quests. Although there are many "nontraditional" groups that are likely to be underserved by traditional library reference services (e.g., foreign speaking, dyslexic, physically handicapped), this paper will address the special needs of two groups that are increasingly seeking reference services in public libraries, namely, those with mental impairments and illiterate or newly literate adults.

FACTORS AFFECTING SUCCESSFUL REFERENCE TRANSACTIONS WITH MENTALLY IMPAIRED PATRONS

Over the past decade, the trend to mainstream certain mentally impaired citizens into the community has meant an increase in the use of the public library by them. Typically comfortable with institutionalized settings, people with mental impairments naturally enough have found their way into the library seeking refuge, socialization, and traditional library services. Unfortunately, it is often the case that due to the special needs and behaviors of the mentally impaired, barriers are erected by the institution itself in its traditional design for service.

The first barrier a patron with a mental impairment is likely to face is a negative or at least suspicious attitude on the part of library staff and reference personnel. This might be most readily exhibited as a lack of respect for the question itself or a failure to take the request as seriously as we do those of other patrons. Although recognizing that the request for librarian assistance may stem from a desire simply to socialize, to assume that this is the case is a form of discrimination because we do not typically make such judgements of all requests before discussing them.

A negative attitude toward the patron acts as a barrier if the librarian feels or shows discomfort with what may be deviant behavior on the part of this patron. Chief among these behaviors are communication skills that often translate into overly loud talking and an inability to define the question (which is experienced to a greater or lesser degree with all patrons). It is also possible that mentally impaired patrons will find it difficult to make the information provided fit into their own framework of knowledge and therefore will be unable to determine for themselves if they have received satisfactory answers to their questions.

Accepting different behavior, not being embarrassed by it, and having patience with the patron are key factors in mediating a request successfully.

Specialized Mediation

It is likely that without patience, frustration on both the part of the patron and the librarian will detrimentally affect the outcome of the transaction.

Once a comfortable rapport has been established, it is important for the librarian to determine the comprehension level of the patron. This is a tricky business because it involves labeling (that nemesis of equality), at least to the degree that the patron is identified as having "special" needs, and it requires an avoidance of the inflexibility in attitude that labeling so often produces. In *Mainstreaming: Library Service for Disabled People*, Emmett and Catherine Davis point out that, "Though diagnosis is necessary, its shadow–diagnostic categorization–is dehumanizing, unless classification is precise. . . . "[3]

Another barrier to a successful reference transaction with a patron who is mentally impaired is the limitation of time. However pressing demand is at the reference desk, it remains clear that to deliver "equal" service to this patron will almost certainly mean that extra time must spent with him or her. Time must be taken not only to understand the reference query, but to understand what limitations this patron will have in understanding and using the "traditional" sources in the library because both content and format themselves can significantly restrict access.

The Davises encourage librarians to ask themselves, "Are the modes of learning to be auditory, visual, tactile, kinesthetic, or multisensory? What are the potential user's interest level, interest area, reading level, visual and auditory decoding level, and general developmental level?"[4] It is necessary that the librarian be even more flexible in using a wide variety of formats to assist the patron than is normally considered. It may well be that the librarian will depend almost exclusively on audio/visual materials such as videos or audiocassettes to provide information.

If there is some degree of reading ability, the children's collection might prove helpful. Books that have been published for children can provide a wealth of information that is often enhanced by clear illustrations, simple charts and maps, and more careful and deliberate explanations. The limitations of our collections will become clear when regular materials (designed for the "traditional" reader) are found to be virtually useless to those with unique learning disabilities.

Because our collections may well be of limited use to the patron directly, it is incumbent upon the librarian to work with the patron to help him or her understand and make use of what is available including, if necessary, actually reading aloud to the patron–again a time consuming, yet necessary component to delivering useful information. It is this particular need of librarian intervention that is likely to make esoteric strategies such as on-line searching of limited value. Although full-text searching could be used, the degree of difficulty in interpreting the information

112 *The Reference Librarian and Implications of Mediation*

retrieved even with the librarian's help will make this a less than satisfactory choice in most cases. Bibliographic databases that will only send the patron on a more complicated search will bring about frustration but probably not positive results.

If database searching only complicates the reference transaction, so too will any secondary searching. Because of significant learning and memory handicaps, a mentally impaired patron is not likely (or is less likely) to benefit from interlibrary loan or referral. A delay in providing requested information may cause a loss of continuity for the patron, and this makes immediate, in-house completion of the transaction even more important.

Once information is delivered in a manner that works for this special client, it is reasonable to assume that the librarian will also have to interpret the material. It is possible that a mentally impaired patron will be unable to incorporate the information into his or her body of knowledge in a meaningful way without assistance. It may be that the patron is unable to differentiate fact from fiction, conjecture from report. In order to make the material specifically meaningful, the librarian will have to understand how the information is to be used and, perhaps, why the information is needed (knowledge which should, of course, be garnered at the onset of the reference interview).

If it seems obvious that extra time and mediation will be needed to help a person with limited learning ability, it is also true that the librarian will at some point have to decide just when to disengage from the interview. It is not always easy to find a way to sensitively pull out from this interaction because it is likely that the patron will want to continue with the dialogue and/or search long past the time the librarian is truly able to render assistance. As important as it is for the librarian to interpret materials retrieved, it is also necessary to show the patron where materials that he or she can use are housed, how to find what might be of interest, and even how to participate in such general library procedures as obtaining a card, checking materials out, and what the procedures for returning materials are.

FACTORS AFFECTING A SUCCESSFUL REFERENCE TRANSACTION WITH NEWLY LITERATE OR ILLITERATE ADULTS

Tackling the problem of illiteracy in this country has provided a strong mandate for public library service to illiterate or newly literate people.

Specialized Mediation 113

American Library Association Past-President Richard Dougherty found literacy to be so fundamental to library service that he dedicated his term of office to raising the consciousness of both the country at large and those in the library profession to the need to eradicate what has been termed our "national embarrassment." The Bell Atlantic Charitable Foundation has awarded substantial sums of money to the ALA for community-centered family literacy projects.[5] Barbara Bush has lent the prestige of her name and position to volunteer literacy projects and the one portion of Library Services and Construction Act funds that gets support from President Bush is that which provides funding for literacy projects in libraries.[6]

The important strides taken by the library community and others will have the added effect of encouraging a more positive and flexible approach by librarians in providing services to illiterate or newly literate adults than might be the case with mentally impaired library users. It is an interesting contrast that although illiterate or newly literate adults can also be considered "nontraditional" users, the problems they encounter in using the public library are likely to be dramatically different than those found by mentally impaired users.

Our self-imposed mandate to work toward elimination of illiteracy has imbued adult new learners with new respect and, on the whole, our efforts to serve them probably reflects this. Although mentally impaired patrons and their requests for information may not be accorded the respect typically given to more traditional patrons, it is likely that during this decade of literacy awareness, adult new readers will find that their needs will be met.

The problem in delivering information services to this particular group, then, may lie more in their own assumptions and fears about the library than in actual practice by public service librarians. The library as an institutional setting existing to house the very nemesis they are now trying to overcome–the written word–can be an extremely awesome and even terrifying place. In *Read With Me*, Walter Anderson relates the following story by an illiterate woman coming into the library to meet her literacy volunteer for the first time: "I opened the car door and walked into the library. But when I saw the books, I couldn't breathe. I couldn't breathe! It was as if a hand were squeezing my heart. It hurt. It was terrible."[7]

Ensuring a meaningful reference transaction with people who are unfamiliar and uncomfortable with the surroundings necessarily means that the librarian must first work to establish a feeling of comfort and trust. Although it is often the case that mentally impaired patrons feel comfortable both in the library setting and in asking questions, the oppo-

114   *The Reference Librarian and Implications of Mediation*

site will likely be true for the adult new reader. A feeling of fear of both the institution and the librarian who represents authority, makes a more aggressive yet thoughtful approach necessary.

Additionally, patrons with mental handicaps might be readily identifiable, but illiterate or newly literate adults are not. In order to identify and to increase the comfort of new readers, many librarians have established connections with tutors and administrators of adult basic education programs and have worked with these educators in bringing adult new readers into the library. The security of coming into such an intimidating place as a library with support is invaluable. When these opportunities do arise, whether created by the librarian or by chance, meeting new readers on a one to one basis, describing the types of services available to them, and how to use the library's resources will personalize the experience, and it will increase the chance that in the future when these patrons need assistance they will be less reluctant to ask because they have someone to ask for by name.

If the statistics on illiteracy are at all believable (Anderson says the estimates range from 67 million Americans to a low of 3 to 4 million; his own estimate is closer to 27 million,[8] then it is probably safe to assume that public services librarians will be called on to serve illiterate adults unaware of their disability. So how are we to help mediate searches for those who cannot read the materials we provide if they do not identify their problem (and of course, often they will not)? Standard reference interview techniques are crucial here, probably the most important technique of which is following up each search with, ''Does this answer your question?'' Librarians should always be alert to responses that might indicate an inability to read. Many illiterate adults have developed coping techniques which, of course, they have practiced all their lives. Such patron responses as, ''I forgot to bring my glasses, could you read this for me,'' or ''I'm afraid I really don't understand this, what do you think this means?'' are pretty good clues.

If there is a certainty or even suspicion that the person receiving information services will have difficulty making sense of the material provided, the librarian must work with the patron so that the material can be understood. Unlike mentally impaired patrons, however, there is no reason at all to believe illiterate adults will have trouble understanding the information on an intellectual level.

In addition to reading to the patron (and offering supplementary materials in audio and/or video format, if available), mediation will also include establishing the patron's reading level if he or she is a new reader, explaining how charts and graphs work as well as interpreting their

Specialized Mediation 115

meaning if it seems necessary, translating jargon, and introducing the patron to available materials that will be of interest and useable so that this patron will feel more comfortable with some degree of self-directed use of the library in the future.

Like the frustration a librarian might experience with a lack of useful materials for mentally impaired adults, frustration may surface with the library's minimal collection of a wide variety of high interest, low reading level materials. This affords a chance, of course, to analyze the collection and its relevancy to a wide array of community members. In addition to the "high-low" materials one can provide, the children's collection should not be overlooked for its ability to provide clear, concise, well explained and illustrated information. If this collection is used, it makes sense that the librarian avoid possible embarrassment on the part of the patron by either sending for relevant materials to be delivered from the Children's Room or by explaining tactfully to the patron that the library is at fault in not having the appropriate materials available in the adult collection but that often the reference sources in the Children's Room prove helpful.

Serving the illiterate or newly literate patron requires the same degree of patience, tact, time, mediation and commitment to service that most nontraditional patrons require. It seems to be true that the typical public library is geared to handling reference queries in a traditional manner. When patrons do not fit this mold, librarians must be ready to work more closely with both the patrons and materiel to ensure that access is being provided in its fullest sense.

CONCLUSION

Until illiteracy is eradicated, libraries must continue along this new and hopeful path of ensuring that the public is aware that libraries are working to support literacy campaigns and that libraries can not only serve but have much to offer illiterate and newly literate adults. Likewise, librarians must not only welcome patrons with mental impairments, but invite them in and be responsive to their unique needs. To do this, of course takes commitment of the kind difficult to come by in these times of financial hardship. In *Public Libraries and Nontraditional Clientele*, Marcia J. Nauratil says that, "We are paralyzed by our own divided loyalties. Even while we recognize the existence of special needs and the universal right to public library service, we are reluctant to formalize that recognition in our annual budgets."[9]

116   *The Reference Librarian and Implications of Mediation*

As important as financial resources are, meeting the information needs of nontraditional library users will take more than money. It will take the recognition of and commitment to the belief that if we intend for all our patrons to have equal access to information, they must be provided with reference services that are delivered with sensitivity to different behaviors and skills and that recognize differing abilities to use the materials we provide. It will require librarians to work with patrons to interpret, understand and make some sense of the overwhelming world of information.

NOTES

1. Marcia J. Nauratil. *Public Libraries and Nontraditional Clientele: the Politics of Special Services.* (Westport, CT: Greenwood Press, 1985), pp. 9-10.
2. Carol Hole. "Click! The Feminization of the Public Library," *American Libraries* (December 1990): 1076-1079.
3. Emmett and Catherine Davis. *Mainstreaming: Library Service for Disabled People.* (Metuchen, NJ: The Scarecrow Press, Inc., 1980), p. 24.
4. Ibid., p. 57.
5. Christina Carr Young. "Libraries and Literacy." In *The ALA Yearbook of Library and Information Services*, 1990 ed.
6. Ibid.
7. Anderson, Walter. *Read With Me.* (Boston: Houghton Mifflin Company, 1990), pp. 88-89.
8. Ibid., p. 6.
9. Nauratil, p. 162.

ADDITIONAL REFERENCES

Hodges, Laura J. *Library Services for Persons Who are Mentally Retarded: Guidelines.* Tallahassee, FL: Florida State Department, Division of Library and Information Services, 1987.

MacCann, Donnarae, ed. *Social Responsibility in Librarianship: Essays on Equality.* Jefferson, NC: McFarland & Company, Inc., 1989.

Response to Reed:
"Unequal but Appropriate Service"

Emmett Davis

Sally Reed is correct: "Equality of access necessarily means aggressive and unequal service." Unequal service, however, means not "special" service, but rather appropriate service. If two patients arrive at a hospital, one requiring surgery and the other aspirin, I hope that they receive unequal service. There is no doubt that, except in rare cases, libraries are failing to provide equal access to many portions of their service community, including the two populations Sally Reed focuses on: people with mental impairments and those who are illiterate or newly literate. We must continue to improve access.

We ourselves, our institutions, and our profession need to decide on what we are about. If our objective is to have a positive impact on people's information needs, then we must be clear about this. Sally Reed's discussion of how X number of persons will need a nontraditional portion of time reflects our profession's awareness of standards for delivery systems and our insensitivity to standards concerning their impact.

Not wanting to settle the primordial question concerning purpose as a byproduct of a response, let us assume that our goal is to positively mediate between people who need information and the information sources themselves. That is, people who once did not have the information they needed now have the information and if possible can now acquire that information themselves. Given that, we must improve our mediation skills and knowledge, as well as our other resources.

Emmett Davis is Librarian at More Information, St. Paul, MN 55105. (More Information provides knowledge and information support service to businesses and nonprofits.)

© 1992 by The Haworth Press, Inc. All rights reserved.

118   *The Reference Librarian and Implications of Mediation*

Consider the situations set before us by Sally Reed, including coming to grips and overcoming

- negative staff attitude toward mentally impaired patrons;
- mentally impaired clients' poor communication skills and restricted capacity to absorb new information;
- the fearsome awe some illiterate and newly literate peoples have toward libraries.

For the problems of both of these groups and others, our profession needs a better model or framework of what is happening and what can be done, and more knowledge and facts to flesh out that framework.

Consider illiteracy: If the obstruction to literacy is a mental impairment (short term memory or mixed dominance of the hemispheres of the brain, for instance), then no number of easy to read books will do nor will heroic tutorial efforts. If I need glasses in order to read, then I *NEED GLASSES*. This is a very important idea. It is the blindspot of our information profession. If I cannot read because I cannot see, then what good will tutoring do? Get me glasses, then tutor me, and then stand out of my way.

Go where the problem is. Have a model of the community that allows for discovering problems and resources outside the boundaries of a two minute reference interview and the walls of a library. Have a model of service that will allow for solving problems with lateral thinking, innovation, and teamwork with other professionals and community members.

Here are two examples: A Chance To Grow is a regional nonprofit organization that works with brain injured children and adults. Two years ago they applied their skills to nonreaders in the early grades of the Minneapolis Public Schools. In a pilot project using a control group, they diagnosed and worked on the mental impairments that kept most of these children from reading. Crawling, coordination games, eye patches and exercises, and other exercises supplemented traditional reading drills. In six months, these children often exceeded not only the control group, but the remainder of the cohort that had no reading problems. Secondly, consider that the distribution of the meaning of knowledge has a social component. When mentally impaired persons have a restricted capacity to absorb meaning from information, consider transmitting that information both in library and nonlibrary settings. Provide the information to both the individual and to persons who normally supply information and meaning to the individual. Calvin Klein does not communicate by phone to just you about his jeans. He communicates to your peers, who in turn

Specialized Mediation 119

indicate to you your dullness for not wearing his jeans as they do. Look for specific capacities to access information in individuals and then tap those capacities. This we should do everyday for everyone.

Traditional library practices and resources work for ''ordinary'' library users because the practices suit some portion of how they learn. If potential users cannot learn within the parameters of these practices and resources, then implement new medalities. If you do not get the impact you want, then change your behavior.

Mediation and Schemata Theory in Meaningful Learning: The Academic Librarian's Role in the Educational Process

Barbara Doyle-Wilch
Marian I. Miller

A young woman walked reluctantly up to the reference desk. Her face was sullen, and she responded to the question "May I help you?" with a hesitant, downward glance. "I need a book with statistics. I think my professor said something about *Statistical Abstract*. I gotta stick some numbers into my paper for EN 101." The student clearly did not want to be in the library and even more clearly was only interested in doing with minimal effort what her professor asked. As the reference interview began with the standard questions such as "What is your topic? What statistics are you trying to find?", the student's lackluster answers suggested to the librarian that the information seeker had little ownership in the quest.

This assessment of the student's apathy led to a tactical change in questioning. The librarian began to ask questions to determine the student's experience with her topic of effectiveness of motorcycle helmets in reducing injuries. The student disclosed the assignment was to write an argumentative paper and she had chosen to argue for a helmet law because a friend who had not worn a helmet had recently died in a motorcycle accident. Her reference to the friend's death led to a sharing of the librarian's experience in witnessing a similar tragedy. This self-disclosure was a catalyst for changing the student's demeanor. At the point where the interview became more of a conversation in which two people were sharing concerns, the investigation of the resources moved from the

---

Barbara Doyle-Wilch is Director and Marian I. Miller is Bibliographic Instruction Coordinator at Augustana College Library, Rock Island, IL 61201.

© 1992 by The Haworth Press, Inc. All rights reserved.

121

122 *The Reference Librarian and Implications of Mediation*

need for a quick fix for a paper due the next day to a personal experience. Through the reference interview, the librarian determined the student's understanding of her subject and helped her use that knowledge with statistical resources. Information on motorcycle helmets was no longer "stuff to add to the paper" but had increased in value to the student because it had personal significance for her; it was a part of her schemata.

The notion of schemata and the process of comprehension based on attachment to the personal knowledge base of the individual has been discussed by psychologists since 1920 (Head, 1920 in Brewer & Nakamura, 1984). However, a review of the library literature suggests that librarians have not recognized their roles as mediators in this cognitive process. Traditionally the reference interview has been viewed as a method for determining the library user's information needs. The reference interview can also serve as a vehicle that enhances learning by helping the student attach his schemata to the classroom information. This theory of learning and comprehension can strongly influence the role of the librarian.

As humans move from experience to experience, they organize what they have learned from these situations and build upon this personal knowledge. "Schemata are data structures for representing the generic concepts stored in memory" (Rumelhart & Ortony, 1977, p.101). Information becomes knowledge when it is attached to an individual's schemata or personal knowledge base.

According to Gage and Berliner (1984),

> Some theorists hold that the schemata brought to an instructional situation are as important as the actual oral or prose message that makes up instruction. . . . If the relevant schemata do not exist, then a teacher needs to provide a context . . . for what is to be learned. . . . Unless the teacher provides these contexts, the students will provide their own, which may be inappropriate. (p. 317)

Bjorklund and Green (in press) describe the memory research based on schemata:

> In memory research with both children and adults, higher levels of recall are achieved when subjects relate the target information to themselves, during either encoding or retrieval. For example, in research by Lord, adult subjects were asked to determine whether each adjective on a list was like them, their fathers, or Walter

Cronkite. He reported that items identified as being related to them were remembered significantly more often relative to the other words.

Such meaningfulness is based on familiarity or logical organization. Hence, if a learner finds a task to be meaningful, the experience can be more easily encoded and, therefore, retrieved (Gage & Berliner, 1984, p. 313).

In the case of the hurried student seeking statistics on motorcycle accidents, once she became engaged with the subject, she stayed for hours. Research presented (Gage & Berliner, 1984, and Bjorklund & Green, in press) suggests that because her information need had become more meaningful, her ability to remember this experience and to use it in other situations was enhanced. Specifically, the location and use of statistical evidence had become part of her schemata.

The following is a simple example of a librarian facilitating the classroom learning process. At the end of a public speaking class session, the professor asked the students to do some research on euthanasia and come prepared to debate the issue. A student, having no experience or schemata with the term, went to the library to look up "youth in Asia" planning to talk about his own siblings, adopted from Korea. When the student sought help from a librarian, the librarian's familiarity with the professor's assignment helped raise a mental red flag in the course of the interview. This prompted questions probing the student's understanding of mercy killing. The librarian's intervention saved the student wasted effort and potential embarrassment.

The college library has the potential to be more of a center of learning than it is purported to be. Librarians, however, have concentrated their attention on determining information needs and providing that desired information, rather than on the cognitive processes of learning. Joan Bechtel (1986) suggests that librarians move away from the "information business" and "begin to think of libraries as centers for conversation and of [librarians] as mediators of and participants in the conversations of the world" (p. 219). By viewing libraries as a setting in which today's scholars hold conversations with other scholars, past and present, librarians have opportunities to participate in and mediate these exchanges.

Fister (1990) views students as participants in these conversations as well, if these students are taught to approach research "as a constructing process rather than a gathering process" (p. 506). When librarians help students attach their schemata to these conversations, the students have a foundation on which to participate in such conversations. Such participation in turn reinforces knowledge.

124 The Reference Librarian and Implications of Mediation

As librarians move away from the paradigm of information brokers to mediators of the learning process, the reference interview becomes a vehicle for applying schemata theory. The interview process helps the student attach his schemata to the classroom instructor's information or to the vast "conversations" of the literature of mankind; this is information literacy. To mediate this attachment, the librarian must extend the interview to investigate the personal knowledge base of the student in the area of inquiry.

Often librarians are in a better position to clarify or reinforce classroom objectives. Students unable to discuss an assignment with the instructor for fear of negative assessment will talk with the neutral librarian. Nigel Ford (1986) writes of this important role of the librarian in the learning process.

> The vicious conflict between assessment and learning, between judging students and helping them to learn, can render teachers even more impotent than librarians in facilitating and encouraging deep, meaningful and valued learning. Librarians to a large extent stand outside the arena of formal assessment. Consequently, their perceived role may be more akin to that of priest than boss. Priests and librarians can reach the parts of students that others cannot reach. They must capitalize on this quality. (p. 59)

If librarians see themselves as facilitators in the learning process, they must have knowledge of the curriculum and the educational process. Familiarity with curriculum includes developing and maintaining working relationships with individual faculty members. There have been many "teachable moments" lost in libraries because the librarians do not have the information from the faculty to clarify or reinforce the classroom instruction.

In order to apply schemata theory to the reference interview, librarians need to have a broad base of knowledge from which to generalize. They need to be able to make relationships between contemporary issues (be it politics, rock music, geography) which may be a part of the students' schemata and historical or foreign issues, which are probably not. Librarians with multifaceted schemata can more easily have a dialogue with students and faculty and draw into the conversation relationships and experiences.

Conversations, lectures, and papers on reference interview technique frequently include discussion of active listening. (Smith & Fitt, 1982 and Aron, 1988 are two examples.) This act of focusing verbal and nonverbal attention on the student seeking assistance is extremely important in establishing rapport with the user in order to investigate the schemata of that person tactfully and skillfully. Such interviewing takes time: time to listen and time to converse. This is often a luxury not available at a busy reference desk. Such opportunities more easily avail themselves in small colleges, rather then large university settings. However, librarians in larger academic settings might consider practical ways to mediate these conversations in order to facilitate learning in their respective communities.

Application of schemata theory is not appropriate, not to mention practical, in all reference transactions. Many students have enough understanding of their topics and/or information sources that a little guidance is all that is needed. However, when a student gives verbal and/or non-verbal messages that suggest frustration, anger, or other negative emotions, the librarian might take that as a signal to probe further into the student's knowledge of the subject matter and library materials. If understanding is lacking to the point of impeding progress on the project, questioning could focus on a schematic point for attachment.

A student seeking information on Latvia for a short speech seemed confused when the librarian suggested using subject headings such as "Union of Soviet Socialist Republics" and "Baltic States." This confusion led the librarian to the conclusion that the topic had little significance to the student because he had no personal knowledge of the region. When the librarian compared Latvia to states in the United States and asked the student to imagine that Illinois had been forced to become a part of the United States against its citizens' will, the young man's interest increased. Through this comparison with something in his schemata, the student was better prepared to find additional information on Latvia as well as comprehend what he found. Without the interaction with the librarian, the student's situation was not hopeless. Because of this intervention the student was in a better position than he would have been if he were simply directed to possible sources on his topic. This information helped the student not only in a cognitive way but also in an affective manner. He seemed to relax and to be more comfortable with the task at hand. "Providing schemata or helping the learner bring his or her own appropriate schema [schemata] to an instructional situation is how one insures meaningful learning" (Gage & Berliner, 1984, p. 319).

There are students who understand their subject matter but who do not have strong library backgrounds. Actions to attach to their information literacy schemata are in order. For example, when introducing a student to a specialized periodical index, a simple query such as "Are you familiar with *Readers' Guide?''* could serve as transfer point for schemata attachment.

Although there will always be many students who benefit from the vast resources of the library without mediation or guidance from anyone and students who will get the necessary guidance from their instructors, there will still be those students who could enhance their learning, comprehension and retention with that conversation (reference interview) that would connect with their schemata. The assignments of a paper arguing motorcycle helmet laws or the speech on Latvia would have been executed within the parameters of the assignments; however, the mediation of the librarian enabled more effective, intrinsic learning.

In his discussion of librarianship education, Ford (1986) suggests librarians must get away from research "into the processes whereby students access and use information . . . and increase emphasis on understanding the psychological and social aspects of the processes of information accessing and use in relation to their effects" (p. 59). As librarians enhance the learning experience by applying schemata theory, greater potential for the use of this vital learning process will become evident.

Understanding this very powerful cognitive process alters the librarians' relationships with students and faculty. Applying schemata theory results in many changes: adjustments in reference interview techniques, shifts in the staffing of the reference desk to allow release time for librarians to consult with faculty and students away from the desk, and certainly a reevaluation of the communication skills and educational backgrounds needed by librarians. Librarians can and should play an important role in the education of students beyond information accessing and servicing. As academic librarians recognize and explore their roles as educators and colleagues with their classroom teaching faculty, the effectiveness of learning will be greatly enhanced.

REFERENCES

Aron, G. (1988). Active listening in the reference interview: a Tafe perspective. *Australasian College Libraries, 6(1)*, 29-31.

Bechtel, J. M. (1986). Conversation, a new paradigm for librarianship? *College & Research Libraries, 47(3)*, 219-224.

Bjorklund, D. F. & Green, B. L. (in press). The adaptive nature of cognitive immaturity. *American Psychologist.*

Brewer, W. F. & Nakamura, G. V. (1984). The nature and functions of schemas. In R. S. Wyer & T. K. Srull (Eds.), *Handbook of social cognition.* Hillsdale, N.J.: Erlbaum.

Fister, B. (1990). Teaching research as a social act: collaborative learning and the library. *RQ, 29(4)*, 505-509.

Ford, N. (1986). Psychological determinants of information needs: a small-scale study of higher education students. *Journal of Librarianship, 18(1)*, 47-61.

Gage, N. L. & Berliner, D. C. (1984). *Educational psychology* (3rd ed.). Boston: Houghton Mifflin.

Rumelhart, D. E. & Ortony, A. (1977). The representation of knowledge in memory. In R. C. Anderson, R. J. Spiro, W. E. Montague (Eds.), *Schooling and the acquisition of knowledge*. Hillsdale, N. J.: Erlbaum.

Smith, N. & Fitt, S. (1982) Active listening at the reference desk. *RQ, 21(3)*, 247-249.

Questions and Answers:
The Dialogue
Between Composition Teachers
and Reference Librarians

Sarah R. Marino
Elin K. Jacob

SUMMARY. In the composition classroom, writing teachers regularly communicate different ideas about library research–a necessary component of the research paper–than reference librarians do. The contradictions confuse the student. And a lack of mutual understanding limits the dialogue between composition teachers and reference librarians. A survey of pedagogical theories about the research process in the composition classroom and the reference library illustrates the discrepancies. Although no one solution for this rift in communication is possible, understanding the different approaches is necessary to restore the dialogue between the two fields.

For composition students embroiled in the frightening task of writing a research paper, the movement from the composition classroom to the library often involves more than a leisurely stroll across campus. Although their fear of and distaste for the research assignment contributes to their hesitancy, the composition students are also aware that writing teachers communicate different concepts about the research process than reference librarians do, which impedes them from casually entering the library and requesting information. Various developments in the pedagogy of research assignments imbricate the composition teacher, the refer-

---

Sarah R. Marino is affiliated with the Department of English, University of North Carolina at Chapel Hill. Elin K. Jacob is affiliated with the School of Information and Library Science, University of North Carolina at Chapel Hill.

© 1992 by The Haworth Press, Inc. All rights reserved.   *129*

130   The Reference Librarian and Implications of Mediation

ence librarian, and the students in a triangular relationship—a singularly misshapen triangle flawed by a lack of communication. The earnestness of all three participants adds a tragic element to the twisted design.

A review of the different philosophies of teaching the research assignment in the composition classroom and of the different methodologies in teaching bibliographic skills allows for specificity in locating a break in communication between the composition teacher and the reference librarian. Unfortunately, the students remain silent subalterns caught in the vicissitudes of professional debate. While locating the problem can not immediately restore the lines of communication anymore than it can relieve student anxiety, it will allow the reference librarian and the composition teacher to achieve a clearer understanding of the conflicting philosophies that inform their respective practices.

Although the lack of communication among the three participants varies according to the specific community, it is not an isolated problem for only one campus. The latest survey on the status of the research paper estimates that 84% of composition programs offer research paper instruction (Ford & Perry, 1982). In teaching any assignment requiring research, the composition teacher relies considerably on the friendliness and good will of reference librarians to help those students who do not know the mechanisms—differing in complexity according to the size of the school—of the university library system. The reference librarian looms as a demi-god of information enabling students to meet the challenge of the research assignment. Yet, despite the indication that 76% of composition programs require either a library tour or a presentation to prepare the students (Ford & Perry, 1982), in pursuing the assignment, students encounter the library on their own.[1] Many libraries rely upon informal, individualized instruction to introduce students to basic research skills, either through the auspices of scheduled appointments for term paper counseling or in response to queries at the reference desk (Mensching, 1989). The solitary positions of students in completing the research assignment, along with the potentially differing views held by the composition teacher and the reference librarian about the research assignment and the role of the library, create a variety of communicative gaps that subvert the dialogue between the three participants.

Those empty spaces that interrupt the geometric wholeness of triangular communication are not always in the foreground, even though they are incipient in certain tensions. It may seem pedagogically unproblematic for the composition teacher to supply the assignment sheet to the students—who then ask the reference librarian for aid in finding the sources, but the reconceptualization of both the process and goals of research

Specialized Mediation 131

complicates this simple relaying of information. Summarizing changes and developments in any field automatically effaces the diversity and differing practices of intellectual movements. But the transition from a product-oriented approach in teaching writing to a process-oriented approach has dramatically affected the pedagogy of the research paper from that of the traditional research assignment that relies upon a linear, goal-oriented approach to an exploratory, recursive method of gathering information.

Yet a residual emphasis on writing as a product lingers in requiring research for a piece of writing. The traditional research paper is frequently still taught as a formalized, end-of-the semester project that terrifies students, overwhelms teachers, and flurries reference librarians. In a traditional research assignment, students choose or are assigned a topic: they walk into the library with a predetermined subject and do their research, asking questions of the librarian. The next step involves writing the papers. The final, and most traumatic stage, is handing them in for evaluation. Composition teachers evaluate these products on several levels: how they have developed their research skills, incorporated their resources, and written the paper. Although writing is always a multi-leveled activity, the research paper embodies the many different levels in a material form; yet an artificial linearity erases the necessary synthesis between the research process and the writing process.

Besides misleading students about the interaction between research and writing, the traditional research assignment in the composition program suffers from the same contradictions that overburden other assignments in the composition classroom. These courses–intent upon providing a service to the academic community–focus on preparing students for the various "writing situations" typical of other classes. The widespread introduction of "Writing Across the Curriculum" programs directly confronts or responds to this phenomenon, yet the research assignment in the traditional composition classroom covertly institutes the course as a supplement to the rest of the academic university community. But the improvement of student writing–detached from any disciplinary allegiance–also factors into the composition classroom. The research paper replicates the dual nature of the composition classroom, challenging the students to master a topic and then write a cogent essay about it. The myriad hopes and goals that circulate around the research paper in the composition program can only hint at the number of teachers and students who wilt under the pressure.

But the reference librarians keep them company. With the prevailing philosophy of introduction in mind, many composition programs incorpo-

132 *The Reference Librarian and Implications of Mediation*

rate a library tour, either formally sanctioned by the university or informally arranged by the individual teacher, to help the students become acquainted with the library instead of simply assuming that students can negotiate this unfamiliar and intimidating situation on their own. These tours or presentations struggle under the same dual responsibilities enacted in the composition classroom. The librarian recognizes that the freshman research paper may be the primary–if not the only–opportunity to provide students with those bibliographical skills deemed important for a successful university experience. As well as addressing the students' future needs, the librarian must struggle to suit the presentation to the immediate task: the research paper. This imperative to disseminate not only the techniques of the research process particular to one assignment but to a whole range of potential needs creates the same schizophrenia endemic in the research assignment: when dealing with a specific question, the librarian frequently feels compelled to formulate a response that addresses both at once.

Despite the double burden, the librarian and the composition teacher work together effectively in implementing the traditional research paper and in attempting to aspire to the various goals and values that inhere in it. But the concept of the research paper has changed considerably in the composition program, causing a considerable decline in its status. Although the larger institutional conflict–between the composition classroom as a service or as a separate discipline–frames a great many of these developments, the pedagogical problems of the research paper are central. First, the common description of the methodology informing the teaching of writing focuses on the key word: "process." Composition teachers are emphasizing the steps involved in writing an effective paper rather than concentrating on the product. The traditional research paper naturally assumes a product status because the initial steps involve a focus on research, not writing. Furthermore, the pairing of the words "research" and "paper" institutes them as separate entities and confuses the students about the purpose of the research paper. In the students' eyes, the "research" of the topic dominates the actual writing of the "paper" –a problematic situation in any writing class (Schwegler and Shamoon, 1982). And, in a study surveying students' logs of a research process (Quantic, 1985), it seems that when students do recognize the interaction between these two activities, they become paralyzed at the immensity of the task. They find that "the neat linear model outlined in so many research manuals and composition texts" does not adequately encompass the variety of organizing, synthesizing, and writing tasks involved (Quantic, p. 225).

With all of these problems, many composition teachers conclude that the traditional research paper does not accomplish its goals; it functions, instead, as an empty exercise that haunts both the composition teacher and the students. Larson (1982) argues that the traditional research paper is "a concept without an identity, and that to teach it is not only to misrepresent research but also quite often to pander to the wishes of faculty in other disciplines that we spare them a responsibility that they must accept" (816). In addressing the institutional rationale that dictates the form of the research paper and places it in the composition classroom, Larson does not devalue research; instead, he considers a variety of options to make the research a meaningful part of the writing process. Furthermore, Larson's stance typifies the attitude of many teachers who translate the research assignment into the classroom. Rather than forcing individual interests into a linear, goal-oriented research model, teachers are urging students to consider the research process as a means of development, a cornucopia of discovery, a medley of questions, and, ultimately, a symphony of serendipity.

In attempting to institute a new philosophy of research assignments, teachers consider a variety of different approaches, many of which either subvert or respond to the institutional framework that identifies the composition classroom simultaneously as a site of good writing and as a service to the academic community. In addressing the first concern, one approach—the I-search—centers around using the students' interests, rather than the library, as the initial informative resource so that students learn their own critical thinking processes before they become overwhelmed by a variety of textual material (Macrorie, 1984, 1988). Connected with Macrorie's emphasis on finding information from within is finding information from around—in other words, asking the students to use a variety of sources that do not originate in the library (Tyryzna, 1986). Another development requires students to write as they are doing their research (Strickland, 1986; Schmersahl, 1987; Kleine, 1987; Williams, 1988). In responding to the problematic of adequately preparing students for other courses, an alternative perspective uses the research assignment to introduce students to another discipline, be it science (Jeske, 1987), philosophy (Coon, 1989), or a general interdisciplinary approach (Lutzker, 1988). These approaches have affected composition classrooms considerably, changing not only the nature of the research assignment but the students' demands upon the library's resource.

Summarizing these different approaches minimizes the variety of pedagogical theories that inform the different permutations within one perspective, as well as negating the many different implementations that can occur within the classroom. But such a summary illustrates the ways in which composition teachers have revised the linear model of the research paper. With the notion that students should first study their own resources, composition teachers demarcate the library as the last step in the discovery process of research. If the students do use the library, the specificity of their questions predicates a predetermined and often inflexible thesis. In moving the research outside the library, the responsibility of reference librarians for directing student research disappears, even though students who believe that the library is the only place to do research may appear at the reference desk occasionally. The third variation, which asks the students to work recursively on research and writing causes more problems for the reference librarian, precisely because this approach, focusing as it does on the research process as development, subverts the linear strategy encouraged for most beginning students. In this variation, teachers often ask students to do research without having any definite goal in subject matter; instead the writing process surrounding the research task is more important.

And another method of teaching the research assignment–or, to be more explicit, of teaching writing–further complicates the relationship between the composition teacher and the reference librarian. The influential social constructionist view of language has significantly altered the course of composition theory, particularly in its insights into collaborative learning and language as a social construct that defines the communities that use it. This theory asks students to contextualize their writing within a certain community; at the same time, they must learn the written conventions that govern that community–a far different prospect than simply learning about the community. According to Bruffee (1986), rather than displacing research, this approach "places reading and writing unequivocally, where (in my professionally self-interested opinion) it belongs, at the center of the liberal arts curriculum and the whole educational process" (778). Teachers who ask their students to discover the writing conventions of a community require an entirely different approach to library research. To ensure that this process is not reduced to an empty exercise in analysis, students need to discover the context–defined in this instance as the practice of the profession that enables the production of these written conventions–that surrounds the texts defining a certain community (Blalock 1991).

This approach often asks students to walk into the library without either a specific goal or a definite subject. In fact, students have only negligible boundaries: a community. To abbreviate a lengthy assignment cycle, a series of assignments generated from the idea of exploring differ-

Specialized Mediation

ent professional communities follows a generalized pattern: students work on brief exercises that combine writing and research to discover the context and the written conventions of a specific community; then the students must choose a particular problem in their field–for example, the cost of malpractice insurance for doctors–define the problem, review a variety of solutions, and argue that one particular solution is better than the others (*Freshman Committee*, 1991). The second step in this process requires a significant amount of research; students frequently encounter difficulties when they recognize that they will never find one article listing all possible solutions. But it is during the first stage that the conflict between the research concepts of the composition teacher and the research strategies espoused by the reference librarian comes to the forefront.

In this first stage of the discovery process, the teacher asks the students to consider the written and substantial context of the community.[2] Teachers could give students certain tasks such as asking them to look at indexes that cover their field and to consider how the subject headings organize the major issues; to ascertain what people in the field write–both in style and subject matter–by looking at several different professional journals to discover the major emphasis of each and the statements they make about the profession; or to review titles of articles written about the profession in popular magazines–by using Infotrac or another general index–rather than journals produced for and by the profession to discern how those writing outside this particular community use different written conventions. A variant on this option consists of asking students to look at titles of articles in their particular field and perform the same analytical task, approaching it from the inside. In addition, the students might examine one professional journal to consider how it defines itself–in terms of organization, structure, substance, writing conventions, format–within the professional community (*Freshman Committee* 1991).[3] Although this list of possible options for understanding a context, as well as for learning about the profession, is only representative, none of these assignments work specifically toward the later formal assignment the students will eventually research and write, even though they all enable students to learn the context of the community about and within which they will eventually be writing.

Although none of these tasks are impossible and many of them are inherently interesting, the transmission of these assignments in the composition classroom and their later dilution in the reference library illustrates the conflict. To offer a possible scenario, the composition teacher in the classroom explains to the students–in a visionary and prophetic

136 *The Reference Librarian and Implications of Mediation*

fashion–how she wishes them to discover their topic within the library, providing a series of tasks that will enable them to begin. The first serious problem results from student anxiety about the nature of these assignments: they contradict the traditional notion of research assignments. The encounter with the reference librarian only reinforces this anxiety. The student walks into the library, turns abruptly toward the reference desk, and announces succinctly: "I need to find some indexes about my profession." The reference librarian, wishing to ascertain which index will be the most appropriate, asks, "What are you looking for in these indexes?" The student, typically, replies, "I don't know, but my composition teacher gave me this assignment." The reference librarian, always mindful of the eventual goal, rephrases the original query: "Well, what are you going to write about?" The student shrugs and states, "I don't know. A problem in my profession, I guess." With that one small statement, the notion of development in research collapses in upon itself. In this instance, the librarian privileges the goal while the composition teacher focuses on the search.[4]

Although this last approach to teaching the research assignment deserves the most detail because it effectively encapsulates a radical shift in the use of library resources, it is probable that all of these methods, ranging from the traditional research assignment to the social constructionist's revisionary techniques, exist in one mutation or another in composition programs, causing a muddle of goals and expectations for any assignment requiring research. The split between theory and practice, the divisive field of composition studies, the individual composition program, and the differences within each classroom all contribute to a confusing array of ideas about teaching the research paper, a confusion that contributes to chaos in the library.

Regardless of the pedagogical shifts informing composition studies, it is impossible to escape the reality that, for many librarians, traditional library research strategy is linear and goal-oriented, beginning from the research topic. Planning an effective research strategy traditionally depends upon identifying the research topic. Indeed, Knapp (1966) has observed that students undertake research expecting to find the answer, and the step-by-step, goal-directed strategy promoted by librarians reinforces this product-oriented objective. Yet composition teachers who promote the notion of discovery or the power of retracing and synthesizing different steps are not insisting on adhering to a plan that fulfills all the "demands of library research" (Wesley, 1991, p. 23). And research, no matter how attractively packaged, is demanding for the students, particularly because of these prescriptive ideas about the research process.

The different approaches espoused by individual composition teachers complicate the encounter between the reference librarian and students who are searching to discover a vague "something" about a loosely-defined area. This encounter is further complicated by some contradictory impulses in the field of bibliographic instruction. The reference librarian's understanding of bibliographic instruction is quite frequently as complicated as the composition teacher's understanding of the pedagogy of teaching research assignments. And those complications can affect the encounter between students and the reference librarian, often dictating the questions that the reference librarian asks students, as well as the various resources that the reference librarian offers students to complete the given tasks. The manner in which the reference librarian theorizes bibliographic instruction changes the contours of a triangle that has become impossibly twisted because of these conflicting methodologies.

A review of the polemics informing instructional practices in the library reveals that bibliographic instruction has increasingly focused on the role of the reference librarian as teacher, despite the fact that many library schools do not offer courses in bibliographic instruction. Smalley (1977) points out that library science is an applied discipline with a practical, technically-oriented educational background; she argues that if librarians "are to be taken seriously as teachers, then we must ourselves take seriously the process of teaching" (1977, p. 282). In response to her influential article, many instructional librarians have abandoned the "how-we-do-it" format that had dominated the literature and have sought to incorporate educational theory into library user instruction. But the lack of a well-defined goal (Oberman, 1982) has led many instructional librarians to accept as their purpose the generalized objective of education for its own sake.

With the growing emphasis on self-directed, life-long learning–an emphasis even more pronounced in the current notion of "information literacy"–the reference librarian's attention has shifted from meeting the students' need for immediate information to enhancing their skills for critical thinking. With education as the expressed objective, the task of the reference librarian expanded beyond providing access to materials and ensuring the ability of the user to locate appropriate sources; the librarian assumed the additional responsibility for instilling in students those cognitive skills necessary to assimilate, assess, and synthesize information (Nelson, 1983). Those cognitive skills encompass logic, problem-solving (Suprenant, 1987; Tuckett & Stoffle, 1984), critical thinking (Madland & Smith, 1988), evaluation of information sources (Nelson, 1983; Dunn, 1988), and the organizational structure of disciplinary litera-

138   *The Reference Librarian and Implications of Mediation*

tures (SantaVicca, 1986). In many ways, these are the very skills that the composition teacher strives to teach her students in the movement away from the traditional research paper. But, within the composition classroom, there is a simultaneous movement towards the process of writing, while the goal in bibliographic instruction is not as clearly defined.

The shift in emphasis from satisfying the students' immediate, course-related needs to ensuring a lifetime of independent learning has fostered the attitude that library instruction is an end in itself rather than one component in the educational process. But the notion of the reference librarian as teacher, working toward a long-term goal, engenders another question: Can educating for a lifetime of independent learning through self-directed information gathering simultaneously satisfy the more immediate, short-term information needs of today's students? This question applies to the plight of composition students caught between the composition teacher's and the reference librarian's ideas of the research process, while struggling, at the same time, to overcome their own conception of library research as drudgery.

In answer to this question, some reference librarians have returned to "those things we do best, such as teaching students library mechanics, helping them to achieve short-term competencies, and developing confidence in using the library, (Feinberg & King, 1988, p. 25). In contrast to those who wish to teach cognitive skills, Feinberg and King emphasize instruction in short-term skills directed at fulfilling the students' immediate needs. Three primary objectives structure their interaction with students: "(1) teach for short-term research competency; (2) raise students' confidence in using the library so they will develop a positive attitude about libraries in general; and (3) demonstrate that librarians are information specialists who can direct users today and, by implication, tomorrow, toward the best approach to research a particular question" (1988, p. 26). Feinberg and King's answer to the question is to focus on the particular assignment rather than attempt to teach skills necessary for a life-time of information gathering.

These approaches to library instruction form a continuum from the concentration on practical, short-term skills at one extreme to the inculcation of cognitive skills at the other. The reference librarian behind the desk is often haunted by both extremes in responding to the student who passively hands her a research task given by the composition teacher. Certainly many library presentations are inescapably informed by this mixed bag of goals. These two conflicting methodologies have left the composition teacher's assignment in a space that those occupying the three points of the triangle cannot reach. The tension that shapes the reference librarian's response–whether she prefers to focus on the cognitive or the practical points–is compounded because the goal of the research, which is the central factor in both theories of bibliographic instruction, is de-emphasized by the composition teacher.

Obviously, there is no one solution to this problem; any commingling between two different disciplines will always be accompanied by a certain amount of tension, misunderstanding, and, at worst, suspicion on the part of all of the participants. In the best of all possible worlds, all of the participants should clearly understand the philosophies that inform their respective practices. But practice necessitates a certain amount of leniency in theoretical formulations; both the composition teacher and the reference librarian work with a variety of different approaches in the attempt to answer one question. Yet the issue of the question is paramount. As a result of the movement away from the traditional research assignment, the questions raised in the composition classroom often deny both the possibility of a definitive answer and the necessity of a positive goal attached to their formulation. For librarians who are accustomed to answering questions, the notion that the question need not be focused toward a particular goal may seem contradictory.

But identifying the question might be an approach that serves to straighten out the battered shape of the triangle to allow for clearer communication. Traditionally, both the composition teacher and the reference librarian have valorized the answer of the question over the question itself; yet the activities in the composition classroom now tend to center on the questions that formulate the process of discovery through research. To insist–as reference librarians frequently do–that research must begin with the term-paper topic–or to be even more specific, the topic sentence–undermines the process of discovery, setting the students on a linear path that serves to dictate and narrow the topic rather than enabling them to review a variety of different options before focusing on a definite goal. Admittedly, the process of honoring the question shifts the role of the reference librarian from mediator to facilitator, yet, at the same time, the librarian does remain a demi-god of information who helps the students formulate the necessary questions.

Although this proposal admittedly contains more idealism than practical solutions, the notion of honoring the question as a process of discovery–a notion alive in the composition classroom–can in the library change the dialogue between the student and the reference librarian.[5] Instead of feeling compelled to point the student toward a specific goal, the librarian can validate the questions informing the student's expressed need to locate certain indexes in the profession. Within that context, the

140   *The Reference Librarian and Implications of Mediation*

student can respond, "I am interested in finding out [read: my teacher wants me to find] what types of titles, and, in those terms, what types of subjects, are being published in my field. Also, I want to discover through the indexes how this profession structures its information needs." The questions hidden within these statements do not work towards one definite goal, yet they do allow the reference librarian to ascertain what indexes or other sources might be the most acceptable for the student to continue that line of question. This approach will not cause students to rush in great excitement toward the reference library from the composition classroom, but they may not immediately classify the interaction that occurs between the two areas as tragically flawed. And a dialogue, based on questions rather than answers can repair the communicative triangle between the composition teacher and the reference librarian.

NOTES

1. Certain universities and colleges will offer bibliographic instruction classes for students, but the studies conducted on the effect of these classes for student performance in utilizing the library (Shapiro & Marcus, 1987) and in writing papers (Kohl & Wilson, 1986) do not demonstrate any correlation between formal classes and student achievement. Also, the availability of these classes is limited and relies on student initiative for enrollment; in consequence, the classes have little, if any, influence in the composition classroom.

2. We are focusing on these series of assignments to illustrate the difficulty of allowing students to find a goal in the research process; another variation of the same difficulty occurs in an assignment sequence designed by Douglas D. Hesse (1988), who asks students to survey several volumes of a trade or professional journal and to find an important issue in that survey.

3. This series of tasks that enable the student to study both the context and the written conventions of a community has taken several years to evolve. Along with a variety of other people, Jim Williams, Erika Lindemann, Glenn Blalock, and Harry Crockett of the English Department at the University of North Carolina at Chapel Hill have helped to initiate, develop, and translate this sequence so that it is workable and effective.

4. To write about problems posits that these problems have occurred; however, despite the farcical dialogue, we have been fortunate to work with many dedicated reference librarians who have attempted to match bibliographic instruction with the methodology of research. In particular, Gary Momenee, Mitch Whichard, and Myrna Schwartz of the Robert H. House Undergraduate Library at the University of North Carolina at Chapel Hill deserve appreciative thanks for both their patience and tireless energy.

5. We are emphasizing the dialogue that occurs in the library; at the same time, composition teachers do have a responsibility to understand the resources

Specialized Mediation

of the library. As a personal attempt to reconcile the different attitudes of the two fields, composition teachers can–and many do–show any assignment requiring research to a reference librarian in order to ensure that the resources of the library and the expectations of the composition teacher do mesh.

REFERENCES

Blalock, G. (1991). *Context and discourse communities: Creating more effective writing assignments.* Unpublished Manuscript, University of North Carolina at Chapel Hill, English Department, Chapel Hill.

Bruffee, K. A. (1986). Social construction, language, and the authority of knowledge: A bibliographical essay. *College English, 48* (8) 773-790.

Coon, A. C. (1989). Using ethical questions to develop autonomy in student researchers. *College Composition and Communication 40* (1), 85-89.

Dunn, E. B. (1988). The challenges of automation and the library instruction program: Content, management, budget. *North Carolina Libraries, 48,* 219-222.

Feinberg, R., & King, C. (1988). Short-term library skill competencies: Arguing for the achievable. *College & Research Libraries, 49,* 24-28.

Ford, J. E., & Perry, D. R. (1982). Research paper instruction in the undergraduate writing program. *College English, 44*(8), 825-831.

Freshman Committee (1991). *Staff manual, 1991-92: U.N.C. writing program, Department of English, University of North Carolina, Chapel Hill.* Unpublished Manuscript.

Hesse, D. D. (1988). Insiders and outsiders: a writing course heuristic. *The Writing Instructor, 7,* 85-95.

Jeske, J. (1987). Borrowing from the sciences: A model for the freshman research paper. *Writing Instructor 6,* 62-67.

Kleine, M. (1987). What is it we do when we write papers like this one–and how can we get students to join us? *The Writing Instructor, 6,* 151-161.

Knapp, P. B. (1966). *The Monteith College library experiment.* New York: Scarecrow.

Kohl, D. F., & Wilson, L. A. (1986). Effectiveness of course-integrated bibliographic instruction in improving coursework. *RQ, 27,* 206-211.

Larson, R. L. (1982). The 'research paper' in the writing course: A non-form of writing. *College English, 44*(8), 811-816.

Lutzker, M. (1988). *Research projects for college students: What to write across the curriculum.* Westport, CT: Greenwood Press.

Macrorie, K. (1984, 1988). *The I-search paper: Revised edition of "searching writing."* Portsmouth, NH: Boynton/Cook Publishers.

Madland, D., & Smith, M.A. (1988). Computer-assisted instruction for teaching conceptual skills to remedial students. *Research Strategies, 6,* 52-64.

Mensching, T. B. (1989). Trends in bibliographic instruction in the 1980s: A comparison of data from two surveys. *Research Strategies, 7,* 4-13.

Nelson, I. (1983). The computer: Cure-all or snake oil? *RQ, 23,* 7-9.

142 The Reference Librarian and Implications of Mediation

Oberman, C. (1982). Why theory? Or, the end of bibliographic instruction. In C.A. Kirkendall (Ed.), *Bibliographic instruction and the learning process: Theory, style and motivation* (pp. 1-14). Ann Arbor: Pierian Press.

Quantic, D. D. (1985). Insights into the research process from student logs. *Journal of Teaching Writing, 5* (2), 211-225.

SantaVicca, E. F. (1986). Teaching research skills in linguistics: An interdisciplinary model for the humanities and the social sciences. *Research Strategies, 4*, 168-176.

Schmersahl, C. B. (1987). Teaching library research: Process, not product. *Journal of Teaching Writing, 6*, 231-238.

Schwegler, R. A. and Shamoon, L. K. (1982). The aims and processes of the research paper. *College English 44*, 812-824.

Shapiro, B. J., & Marcus, P. M. (1987). Library use, library instruction, and user success. *Research Strategies, 5*, 121-125.

Smalley, T. N. (1977). Bibliographic instruction in academic libraries: Questioning some assumptions. *Journal of Academic Librarianship, 3*, 280-283.

Strickland, J. (1986). The research sequence: What to do before the term paper. *College Composition and Communication, 37* (2), 233-236.

Suprenant, T. T. (1987). Learning theory, lecture, and programmed instruction text: An experiment in bibliographic instruction. *College & Research Libraries, 43*, 31-37.

Tuckett, H. W., & Stoffle, C.J. (1984). Learning theory and the self-reliant library user. *RQ, 24*, 58-66.

Tyryzna, T. N. (1986). Research outside the library: Learning a field. *College Composition and Communication, 37*, 217-223.

Wesley, T. (1991). Teaching library research: Are we preparing students for effective information use? *Emergency Librarian, 18*(3), 23-30.

Williams, N. (1988). Research as a process: A transactional approach. *Journal of Teaching Writing, 7*, 193-204.

IV. MEDIATION AND ACCURACY

The Reference Librarian as Mediator:
Predicting Accuracy Scores
from User Impressions

F. W. Lancaster
Kurt M. Joseph
Cheryl Elzy

In 1989, a major evaluation was undertaken of the reference services offered at Milner Library, Illinois State University (ISU). ISU is a multi-purpose university of more than 22,000 students that offers 191 degree programs in 33 academic departments organized into five colleges. Library services are centralized at Milner Library in five subject divisions: Education/Psychology/Teaching Materials Center, General Information and Reference, Social Sciences/Business, Science/Government Publications, and Humanities/Special Collections. The five divisions are staffed by 20 members of the library faculty, 19 classified employees, and student assistants.

The study has been described and discussed in detail elsewhere (Elzy

---

F. W. Lancaster is Professor of Library and Information Science at the Graduate School of Library and Information Science, University of Illinois at Urbana-Champaign. Kurt M. Joseph is a doctoral candidate in the Department of Psychology at Kansas State University in Manhattan, KS. Cheryl Elzy is Assistant Professor and Head of the Education/Psychology/Teaching Materials Center Division of Milner Library at Illinois State University in Normal, IL.

© 1992 by The Haworth Press, Inc. All rights reserved. *143*

et al., 1991, Lancaster et al., 1991). In brief, it was an unobtrusive evaluation of the ability of the professional librarians to answer reference questions. Questions of the type commonly dealt with by academic libraries, and all of which could be answered from materials held by Milner Library, were collected. From several hundred such, 58 were actually chosen for use. Twenty undergraduate students, eighteen from ISU and two from Illinois Wesleyan University, were trained to pose the questions. The students, who were paid for their work and who promised to observe complete confidentiality, were given the reference desk schedules for the various divisions. They were to put their questions to particular librarians, identified by nameplate, so that all librarians could be included in the study. The 58 questions were applied, as appropriate to the subject matter of the various divisions, to 19 librarians. Some questions were put as many as 8 times (to different librarians) and some only once. In all, 190 reference "incidents" (the posing of a question to a librarian) took place.

For each question posed, the student completed an evaluation form (included as an appendix to this paper). Besides identifying the questioner and the librarian, it recorded details of the question, date and time it was posed, time spent on the question by the librarian, the answer obtained, and the source of the answer.

Most of the evaluation form, however, is taken up by a series of 28 "attitudinal" statements designed to collect the student's impressions of the librarian as a person and the way he or she is treated by the librarian. However, it was recognized early in the study that the students were not really qualified to deal with statements 24-27, so the attitudinal data were based on student responses to 24 statements (1-23 and 28).

Since the correct or satisfactory answer to each question was known by the investigators, it was possible to score each incident both for accuracy (correctness of response) and attitude. The accuracy scale adopted is shown in Table 1. Use of this particular scale has been justified by Elzy et al. (1991) and Lancaster et al. (1991). The scale reflects the values of students wanting questions answered as painlessly as possible. Thus, it judges the librarian on ability to *provide answers* rather than ability to *instruct* the student. In retrospect, the investigators are satisfied with the scoring method used, except that they would now assign a zero value to "Librarian did not find answer" and *negative* values to inappropriate actions or incorrect answers.

Table 2 shows the accuracy and attitude scores achieved by each of the 19 librarians, and Table 3 shows the scores as they relate to the performance of the five subject divisions. The accuracy score is the mean

Table 1

Scoring method used

	Points
Student _provided_ with complete and correct answer	15
Student _led to a single source_ that provided complete and correct answer	14
Student _led to several sources_, at least one of which provided complete and correct answer	13
Student _directed to a single source_ that provided complete and correct answer	12
Student _directed to several sources_, at least one of which provided complete and correct answer	11
Student given an _appropriate referral to a specific person or source_ that provide complete and correct answer	10
Student provided with partial answer	9
Student is given an _appropriate referral to the card catalog or another floor_	8
Librarian _did not find an answer_ or suggest an alternative source	5
Student given an _inappropriate referral_ to catalog, floor, source, or librarian unlikely to provide complete and correct answer	3
Student is given _inappropriate sources_	2
Student is given _incorrect answer_	0

146 *The Reference Librarian and Implications of Mediation*

Table 2

Accuracy and attitude scores for each librarian

Librarian	Number of Questions Asked	Attitude	Accuracy	Mean minutes spent
1	10(1)*	8.1900	10.3333	4.35
2	10	7.0000	7.6000	5.45
3	10	7.6300	7.5000	6.975
4	9(1)*	7.6000	7.1250	5.65
5	10(1)*	8.7500	13.8889	7.88
6	10	8.2100	13.0000	4.85
7	10	7.7200	11.8000	6.7
8	10	8.2300	10.8000	6.3
9	10(1)*	8.2900	9.6667	4.3
10	10	7.8000	9.5000	7.6
11	10(1)*	5.7400	7.2222	2.15
12	10(1)*	7.3600	11.8889	3.95
13	10(1)*	7.7800	11.2222	6.95
14	10	7.8700	8.6000	8.05
15	10	8.1800	9.7000	5.85
16	12	7.0750	8.5833	4.75
17	10	8.6900	13.4000	7.30
18	9	8.2444	10.2222	8.05
19	10(1)*	8.6600	9.6667	8.5
Mean	190(8)	7.8342	10.1538	

* Missing data for accuracy scores.

Mediation and Accuracy

of all scores (on the 15-point scale of Table 1) achieved by the librarian or division on all of the questions handled, while the attitude score is the mean of all values recorded for each of the 24 attitudinal statements for these same questions (i.e., the attitude score for a single incident is the mean of the values recorded for each of 24 statements and the attitude score for a librarian/ division is the mean of the values for all statements for all questions handled).

As Table 2 shows, attitude scores for librarians ranged from a high of 8.75 (10-point scale) to a low of 5.74, while accuracy ranged from 13.889 (15-point scale) to 7.125. The librarian who scored highest in attitude also did best on accuracy but the same was not true for the lowest scores in each category. On a division basis (Table 3), division E achieved both the lowest accuracy figure and the lowest attitude score, C achieved highest marks for attitude, and B was most accurate.

A further analysis investigated the rather unsystematic relationship between accuracy and attitude as reported in Elzy et al. (1991). Accuracy was found to be minimally associated with overall attitudinal scores (r (182) = .2482, $p \leq .0001$). That is, answering a question cor-

Table 3

Accuracy and attitude scores by division

Division	Questions	Attitude	Accuracy
A	30(3)*	8.2100	10.4074
B	30	8.2067	12.7333
C	20(2)*	8.5200	11.7778
D	71(2)*	7.7141	9.6377
E	39(1)*	7.1256	8.1053
Mean	190(8)*	7.8342	10.1538

* Missing data for accuracy scores.

148   *The Reference Librarian and Implications of Mediation*

rectly and completely did not reasonably correlate with how well students perceive they are being treated. This low correlation also suggests that librarians who project positive images may not necessarily answer questions with the highest accuracy. Minutes spent with students apparently did affect the attitudinal scores they assigned to the librarians. Librarians who spent four or more minutes with students tended to get assigned a higher attitude score than those who spent less time ($F = 7.592$, $p < .00001$).

The weak correlation between attitude and accuracy may be the result of collapsing 24 attitudinal variables, some of which may not be related to accuracy, into a single attitudinal measure. It is likely that some of these variables are more highly correlated with accuracy than others. For instance, the ability of a librarian to listen attentively to a patron may correlate more with librarian accuracy than a librarian's ability to be tactful and patient. The remainder of this paper undertakes a more rigorous statistical analysis that explores the relationship between attitude and accuracy.

METHODOLOGY

Multiple regression was used in an attempt to identify attitudinal characteristics that could be used to predict librarians' accuracy scores. A stepwise multiple regression seemed most appropriate for our purposes, which were descriptive or exploratory, and not used to test a formal hypothesis. The stepwise procedure is commonly described as a series of part correlations (Hays, 1988). Initially, a regression equation is generated. Then, given any number of variables that could be used as predictors, the one that accounts for the largest proportion of variance, relative to all others, is chosen. After selecting the first variable for inclusion in the equation, the next variable chosen will be that which has the largest squared-part correlation with the dependent variable after adjustment for the first variable. Thus, the second and subsequent variables entered into the equation will have any variance from the first variable removed before they are entered.

Doing this allows for a reasonable estimate of the proportion of variance accounted for by each successive entry into the equation. Suppose we have a group of variables and wish to find which will combine to give the best prediction of performance on some dependent measure. The stepwise procedure would select and enter X_a, the variable that accounts for the most variance, relative to the others in the group. Next, it would select X_b, that variable (remember, the equation has assumed removal of X_a's contribution to the total variance accounted for when selecting X_b) that contributes the most to explaining variance, relative to the remaining variables in the group. This stepwise fashion continues until some criterion is reached (usually when the selected variable is no longer significantly contributing to the explanation of Y's variance given X_n). When this criterion is reached, a subset of the original group of variables has been selected and this subset can be used to predict performance. The use of stepwise regression has ranked the best predictors of performance in a descending order by the proportion of Y variance for which they account. However, when discussing predictors, one can never say for certain that a selected variable X_n is the best predictor of performance: Since the set of all possible predictors has not been sampled, one can only speak with reference to the set that has been.

RESULTS

A stepwise multiple regression was used as an exploratory procedure to attempt to determine the best attitudinal predictor of accuracy scores. The twenty four attitudinal variables were initially collapsed into three categories and entered into the equation. The three categories were labeled *attitude, interview,* and *search*. The first category was based on statements dealing with the student's judgment of the librarian's attitude and physical demeanor (statements 1-11), the interview category represented statements relating to the student's verbal interaction with the librarian (12-21), and the search category represented impressions of the librarian's ability to exploit library resources to answer the question posed (22-24).

Results indicated that the interview category was the best predictor of the accuracy scores assigned to librarians. Collectively, the interview questions accounted for 80.96% of the total accuracy score variance, $R^2 = .809$, $F(1,177) = 752.78$, $p < .00001$. The interview category correlated very highly with the accuracy score, $r = .9053$, $p < .0001$. That is, librarians who had high scores on quality of verbal interaction with patrons also scored well on accuracy of answer. The attitude category was the next best predictor of accuracy score; however, it accounted for less than 16% of the total variance, $R^2 = .159$, $F(2,176) = 2730.95$, $p < .00001$. Like the interview category, it also correlated highly positive with accuracy score, $r = .8659$, $p < .0001$. Thus, accuracy scores are primarily determined by how approachable the librarian is and, to a lesser extent,

150   *The Reference Librarian and Implications of Mediation*

on how friendly the librarian is. These two categories combined to account for nearly 97% of the total accuracy score variance.

The use of the interview and attitude categories to predict accuracy scores involves an instrument that requires a rating on twenty-one of the original twenty-four variables. Such an instrument is rather large. A further regression analysis, with each of the twenty-four variables treated separately, was performed to try to determine which of the variables is the single-best predictor of how accurate a librarian will be. Results of the second stepwise regression indicated that the librarian's accuracy scores were best predicted by user ratings of the librarian's courtesy, $R^2 = .671$, $F(1,71) = 145.07$, $p < .00001$. Librarian courtesy was positively correlated with accuracy, $r = .7453$, $p < .0001$. Two other variables added considerably to the proportion originally accounted for by the librarian's courtesy rating. A librarian's persistence in pursuing a question also contributed significantly as a predictor, although not as much as librarian courtesy, $R^2 = .116$, $F(2,70) = 129.78$, $p < .00001$. Highly persistent librarians were likely to be found more accurate, $r = .7669$, $p < .0001$. Finally, rating of a librarian's ability to refer the patron to a specialist source accounted for the third largest proportion of accuracy score variance, $R^2 = .059$, $F(3,69) = 127.58$, $p < .00001$. A moderately positive correlation suggests that librarians who refer to an appropriate specialist source will likely receive a high accuracy rating, $r = .4378$, $p < .0001$. Note that the combination of these three variables accounted for 84.60% of the total proportion of accuracy variance.

The second analysis proves fruitful when one considers the efficiency gained by using three variables to predict nearly as much accuracy score variance as compared with the twenty-one variables originally used. Thus, of the variables included in the original assessment instrument, four variables combine to account for large proportions of the variance associated with the dependent measure (i.e., accuracy). However, as with any regression analysis, of all possible predictors, these may not be the best. What is important for our purpose is that these variables may be included with a new set of variables to create what might be a better assessment instrument. Moreover, that instrument might be categorized to include certain smaller variable groups which could best predict search performance. For example, it would be very efficient from an assessment viewpoint to have a small number of variables that could account for the search performance of a librarian. In such a case, the process of assessing a librarian's performance is economized and more time can be spent on specific problem areas. Important, too, would be the development of an instrument that could be utilized at different institutions.

CONCLUSIONS

Since not all possible attitudinal variables were examined in the study, it is dangerous to conclude that any one variable is the *best* predictor of librarian accuracy. Nevertheless, the set of twenty-one variables tested in the analysis does seem rather comprehensive. Thus, some tentative conclusions can perhaps be drawn. Results of the multiple regression analysis offer considerable support for the long-held belief that the quality of the interaction between librarian and user, to determine precisely what the user wants, is likely to have a major effect on the completeness and correctness of the answer provided. The effective reference interview would seem to be a courteous one, in which the library user is treated with respect, welcomed rather than regarded as bothersome. The library users involved in this study placed much emphasis on the librarian's ability and willingness to listen to them, and the results reported here indicate that the perceived listening skills of the librarian may be a major factor in determining the user's overall impression of a library and its staff.

REFERENCES

Elzy, C. et al. 1991. Evaluating reference service in a large academic library. *College and Research Libraries*, 52, 454-465.

Hays, William L. 1988. *Statistics*. 4th edition. New York: Holt, Rinehart and Winston, pp. 608-670.

Lancaster, F. W. et al. 1991. The diagnostic evaluation of reference service in an academic library. In: Bryce Allen, ed. *Proceedings of the 32nd Allerton Park Institute held October 28-30, 1990*. Urbana-Champaign: University of Illinois Graduate School of Library and Information Science, pp. 43-59.

APPENDIX

Evaluation Form

Questioner: _____

Librarian/Floor: _____

Question: Number: _____ Short phrase: _____

Time question asked: Date: _____ Hour: _____

Time spent with Librarian in minutes: _____

Answer (actual answer, directions given. Sources or floors
provided by librarian: _____
_____
_____

Source:
    Title: _____
    Date or edition: _____
    Volume: _____
    Page: _____

<u>Attitude and Demeanor</u>

1. Looks approachable

Not at All		Seldom		Some of the time				Mostly		To a large Extent	
1	2	3	4	5	6	7	8	9	10

   Comments:
   _____
   _____
   _____

2. Acknowledges user's approach to desk

Not at All		Seldom		Some of the time				Mostly		To a large Extent	
1	2	3	4	5	6	7	8	9	10

   Comments:
   _____
   _____
   _____

Mediation and Accuracy

3. Friendly attitude

Not at All	Seldom	Some of the time	Mostly	To a large Extent
1	2	3	4	5	6	7	8	9	10

Comments:

_____
_____
_____

4. Appropriate facial expression--Smiles, shows interest

Not at All	Seldom	Some of the time	Mostly	To a large Extent
1	2	3	4	5	6	7	8	9	10

Comments:

_____
_____
_____

5. Appropriate non verbal communication--Eye contact, head nod

Not at All	Seldom	Some of the time	Mostly	To a large Extent
1	2	3	4	5	6	7	8	9	10

Comments:

_____
_____
_____

6. Appropriate tone of voice--Volume

Not at All	Seldom	Some of the time	Mostly	To a large Extent
1	2	3	4	5	6	7	8	9	10

Comments:

_____
_____
_____

154   *The Reference Librarian and Implications of Mediation*

APPENDIX (continued)

7. Listens attentively

Not at All		Seldom		Some of the time			Mostly		To a large Extent
1	2	3	4	5	6	7	8	9	10

Comments:

_____
_____
_____

8. Responses are non-judgemental

Not at All		Seldom		Some of the time			Mostly		To a large Extent
1	2	3	4	5	6	7	8	9	10

Comments:

_____
_____
_____

9. Is tactful, patient

Not at All		Seldom		Some of the time			Mostly		To a large Extent
1	2	3	4	5	6	7	8	9	10

Comments:

_____
_____
_____

10. Responds positively to unusual questions

Not at All		Seldom		Some of the time			Mostly		To a large Extent
1	2	3	4	5	6	7	8	9	10

Comments:

_____
_____
_____

11. Keeps trying to answer questions, be helpful--doesn't give up too easily

Not at All		Seldom		Some of the time			Mostly		To a large Extent
1	2	3	4	5	6	7	8	9	10

Mediation and Accuracy **155**

Comments:

_____

_____

_____

Reference Interview--Librarian-Patron Interaction

12. Treats user with courtesy

Not at All		Seldom		Some of the time			Mostly		To a large Extent
1	2	3	4	5	6	7	8	9	10

Comments:

_____

_____

_____

13. Puts user at ease--doesn't talk down to user, is not condescending

Not at All		Seldom		Some of the time			Mostly		To a large Extent
1	2	3	4	5	6	7	8	9	10

Comments:

_____

_____

_____

14. Determines level of help needed

Not at All		Seldom		Some of the time			Mostly		To a large Extent
1	2	3	4	5	6	7	8	9	10

Comments:

_____

_____

_____

15. Sensitive to user's needs

Not at All		Seldom		Some of the time			Mostly		To a large Extent
1	2	3	4	5	6	7	8	9	10

156   The Reference Librarian and Implications of Mediation

APPENDIX (continued)

Comments:

_____
_____
_____

16. Is easy to understand--does not use library jargon

Not at All		Seldom		Some of the time			Mostly		To a large Extent	
1	2	3	4	5	6	7	8	9	10

Comments:

_____
_____
_____

17. Goes to tools with patrons

Not at All		Seldom		Some of the time			Mostly		To a large Extent	
1	2	3	4	5	6	7	8	9	10

Comments:

_____
_____
_____

18. Explains tools and how to use

Not at All		Seldom		Some of the time			Mostly		To a large Extent	
1	2	3	4	5	6	7	8	9	10

Comments:

_____
_____
_____

19. Refers users to other subject specialist when appropriate

Not at All		Seldom		Some of the time			Mostly		To a large Extent	
1	2	3	4	5	6	7	8	9	10

Comments:

_____
_____
_____

Mediation and Accuracy 157

20. Reminds user to return for more help

Not at All		Seldom		Some of the time			Mostly		To a large Extent	
1	2	3	4	5	6	7	8	9	10

Comments:

_____
_____
_____

21. Suggests alternatives outside the library if appropriate

Not at All		Seldom		Some of the time			Mostly		To a large Extent	
1	2	3	4	5	6	7	8	9	10

Comments:

_____
_____
_____

Search Strategy

22. Evidences good knowledge of own collection

Not at All		Seldom		Some of the time			Mostly		To a large Extent	
1	2	3	4	5	6	7	8	9	10

Comments:

_____
_____

23. Evidences good knowledge of Milner's collection as a whole

Not at All		Seldom		Some of the time			Mostly		To a large Extent	
1	2	3	4	5	6	7	8	9	10

Comments:

_____
_____
_____

158 *The Reference Librarian and Implications of Mediation*

APPENDIX (continued)

24. Finds complete answer

Not at All		Seldom		Some of the time			Mostly		To a large Extent
1	2	3	4	5	6	7	8	9	10

Comments:

_____

_____

_____

25. Answer accurate

Not at All		Seldom		Some of the time			Mostly		To a large Extent
1	2	3	4	5	6	7	8	9	10

Comments:

_____

_____

_____

26. Answer appropriate

Not at All		Seldom		Some of the time			Mostly		To a large Extent
1	2	3	4	5	6	7	8	9	10

Comments:

_____

_____

_____

27. Shows knowledge of Milner's subject specialists

Not at All		Seldom		Some of the time			Mostly		To a large Extent
1	2	3	4	5	6	7	8	9	10

Comments:

_____

_____

_____

Mediation and Accuracy

28. Uses minimum of tools--is efficient

Not at All		Seldom		Some of the time		Mostly		To a large Extent	
1	2	3	4	5	6	7	8	9	10

Comments:

General comments and impressions about this librarian and/or the question (or its answer):

V. THE ECONOMY
AND ITS INFLUENCE

Mediation
in a Shrinking Information Economy

Renee Tjoumas

SUMMARY. The purpose of this article is to outline the current socioeconomic factors present within the United States and explore the effect of these trends on libraries and information services. The resulting portrait depicts a deteriorating information environment where mediation is often hampered or obstructed. The closing segment offers conclusions and a recommendation for professionals seeking to maintain their role as information mediators.

INTRODUCTION

During the closing months of 1990, the country entered into a recessionary period that lingered through the early stages of 1991.[1] With the ending of the Gulf War, expectations were high that the country would make a speedy recovery. Prognosticators reading the economic tea leaves presented three diverse forecasts: (1) the downturn would end quickly;

Dr. Renee Tjoumas is Associate Professor at the Queens College Graduate School of Library and Information Studies in Flushing, NY. Queens College is a part of the City University of New York.

© 1992 by The Haworth Press, Inc. All rights reserved. *161*

162   *The Reference Librarian and Implications of Mediation*

(2) the economy would flounder before fully restoring itself by early Fall; and (3) the recession would deepen well and last until the end of the year.[2] At this point, it is difficult to state which of these predictions will become a reality. It is clear, however, that the recovery, if it does exist, has been a bumpy and uneven one.

The measure of this recession is the government's acknowledgement of the country's deteriorating economic health. Citizens have also had to peek under the mask of well-being and confront an America with not only serious economic problems but with a startling array of social ills as well. The purpose of this essay is to first relay a snapshot view of current socioeconomic conditions in the United States. The effect of these trends on libraries and information services will then be highlighted. The final portion of this article will present conclusions and a recommendation for professionals seeking to maintain their roles as information mediators.

ECONOMIC FACTORS

A review of just a few economic indicators recorded during the first six months of 1991 reveals a somewhat negative picture. During the first quarter, the real per capita disposable personal income fell by 2.7 percent continuing a downward trend established in the last three quarters of 1990.[3] Corporate profits for the first quarter were estimated to have declined by 21.4 billion pre-tax dollars.[4] Industrial production fell 0.8 percent in February 1991 after declines of 1.1 percent (December 1990) and 0.5 percent (January 1991).[5] In March 1991, trade and manufacturing sales fell 1.0 percent and inventories fell by $6.9 billion.[6] The producer price index for all finished goods rose 0.2 percent in April 1991.[7] For that month, the consumer price index for all urban consumers also rose 0.2 percent, an index 4.9 percent above its year earlier level.[8] On a more upbeat note, the merchandise trade deficit fell to $18.4 billion from $27.7 billion in the fourth quarter of 1990,[9] but this is still a substantial deficit.

The unemployment statistics for 1991 are not overly encouraging. The unemployment rate for civilian workers steadily rose from 6.2 percent (January) to 6.8 percent (March). It dipped downward in April to 6.6 percent[10] only to rise in May to 6.9 percent as another 370,000 individuals were added to the jobless roster.[11] Workers without jobs for protracted periods of time also rose. For fifteen to twenty-six weeks, it jumped from 12.7 percent (January) to 14.8 percent (April) and for twenty-six weeks and over, it climbed from 11.0 percent (January) to 12.1 percent (April).[12]

The Economy and Its Influence

163

To a great extent, these statistics reflect the all but complete cycle of downsizing in the manufacturing sector with millions of blue-collar jobs eliminated. On the other hand, cutbacks in the service sector, which constitutes 75 percent of the total employment in the country have just begun. One example of this trend is that American companies have started to move routine office operations overseas to lower wage areas. By 1995, it is estimated that 25 percent of the "major non-government service sector employers" will transfer clerical processes abroad.[13] "For high school graduates unable or unwilling to go to college or university, it will mean a reduction by as much as one-third of the job opportunities available to today's teenagers hoping for a white-collar career."[14]

These figures illustrate the recessionary struggles of the country, but these economic difficulties have only served to amplify pre-existing problems which were prevalent prior to the downturn. The recession did little to lighten the load of unsold real estate, shaky banks, and heavy debt.

The real estate boom of the 1980's has begun to turn downward. The United States currently has approximately a ten year supply of office space. Los Angeles vacancy rates, for example, are expected to reach 25 percent by 1992.[15] Many developers have begun to default which in turn has weakened the profit margin of many lending and banking institutions. Some homeowners have also had to face the decline of their property values in such areas as the Northeast and California. Confronted with the erosion of home property values, the middle class citizen has often reacted by restricting personal spending.[16]

Slipping real estate values have not been the only factor contributing to the loss of profits in the banking industry. Loans to Third World nations and leveraged buyouts have also proven risky business. In terms of corporate clients, their treasurers shift surplus cash quickly rather than letting it lie in bank coffers for long periods. When money is needed, companies find it cheaper to sell commercial paper, short-term I.O.U.s, on Wall Street instead of turning to banks for loans. It should be noted that nearly 90 percent of American banks made money in 1990, but the level of profit has dropped. During the 1970's, banks earned about eighty cents annually for each $100 of investments and loans. Analysts estimate the industry earned less than fifty cents on each $100 during 1990, a pattern repeated a third time in four years.[17]

America's debt load from consumer, corporate, and governmental sectors has reached $10 trillion which is double the country's 5 trillion gross national product (GNP).[18] The indebtedness of U.S. households, according to some governmental sources, rose from $1.3 trillion at the end of 1980 to a bit under $3.4 trillion ten years later which averaged a

164 **The Reference Librarian and Implications of Mediation**

10 percent increase annually.[19] The two major factors examined for comprising the 1990 statistic for household debt were home mortgage debt (2.6 trillion) and consumer debt ($800 billion).[20] Corporate debt during the period between 1980-1989 climbed 30 to 40 percent of GNP while the U.S. governmental debt also rose from 27 to 45 percent of GNP for the same ten-year period.[21]

The fiscal resources of state and local governments have also deteriorated. Areas particularly hard hit are New England, New York, and New Jersey as a consequence of slumping real estate sales and contractions within the finance, defense, and high-technology industries. Resources have also dwindled because of federal cut-backs, and state governments have, in turn, diminished their assistance to local levels. Both state and local governments have attempted to compensate for the loss of funding by altering tax policies, but collections have been lower than expected in 1988 and 1990. The deficit of state and local governments grew from $3 billion (1986) to $30 billion (1990).[22] The shortfalls began in the 80's as state and local budgets climbed to meet educational, Medicare, and prison expenses. Many budgets were in trouble prior to the recession, but once it hit, the deficits deepened.

Budget shortfalls are not uncommon in American government. But in contrast to the federal government, all the states except Vermont are constitutionally required to balance their budgets. Deficits of this magnitude have occurred in the past (during the 1950s and 1960s) when tremendous outlays were directed for construction of roads, schools, and other infrastructure. In contrast, the current deficits do not represent disproportionate spending for construction programs. Outlays for building activities during the mid-1980s amounted to approximately 10 percent of all expenditures.[23]

Governors and mayors are proposing dire measures to compensate for these shortfalls. Most are making severe cutbacks in spending for services related to education, fire fighting, and police protection. Outlays may also contract in areas important to the public infrastructure. Spending within this sector did rise in the 1980s by 50 percent from its lowest levels in 1983.[24] However, these outlays were not sufficient to combat the deterioration of the public infrastructure that embraces such diverse elements as water treatment facilities, roads, prisons, schools, and hospitals. Trends indicate that additional pressures will be exerted in these areas in the future. After a reduction of 3.4 percent in the 1980s,[25] the number of school-age children will grow by 3.2 million. Medical inflation and the increasing number of poor youngsters eligible for health care benefits guarantee that medical costs will increase. State governments have been

The Economy and Its Influence   165

forced to expand their correctional facilities to accommodate a growing population. The nation's 43,000 mile interstate highway system is crumbling, with an estimated $750 billion needed for repairs.[26] Government leaders on all levels disagree on who should pay for repairing the nation's roads and bridges.

Despite these indicators, the United States remains a worldwide economic power. For example, it is still the world leader in productivity and its gross national product is twice that of Japan's.[27] But the rest of the world is catching up with us. As one author so aptly observes, "The issue for America isn't whether it remains out front in the global race but whether it can restore to its citizens a sense of well being and the promise of better times."[28] Much of the future will depend on the level of investment provided for developing the country's best resource–the human one.

Human Resources and Social Trends

This segment of the essay is devoted to furnishing a quick overview of two related questions. First, what investment is America making in developing human resources? Secondly, what are some of the trends regarding education, health, nutrition, and housing? The overriding motif will be the nation's children, based on the assumption that the manner in which a country cares for its young is an indicator of the value that is placed upon the well being of its citizens and a gauge of its commitment to future generations.

Allan Carlson, a member of the National Commission on Children, insists that "Americans on average, simply do not like or value children as much as they used to."[29] Among the reasons he cited for this opinion were the country's low birth rates and the high demand for abortions. In 1960, the total fertility rate was approximately 3.7 children per woman but by 1975, the figure had dropped to an average of 1.8, a statistic that has remained constant throughout the 1980s.[30] The number of abortions rose from 586 thousand (1972) to approximately 1.5 million annually.[31] Another trend that Carlson points out is the concentration of poverty among our nation's children. For persons under the age of eighteen, the number in poverty dropped between 1959 (18 million) and 1969 (10 million) while the official poverty rate declined from 27 percent to 14 percent. During the 1970's, the number of children within this economic group hovered at 10 million or 16 percent for the population below eighteen. After 1978, the number of children in poverty rose to almost 14 million by 1983 but then the numbers began to decline. In 1989,

166   The Reference Librarian and Implications of Mediation

12.6 million children (20 percent) lived below the poverty line, one quarter more than the number during the 1970s[32]

Part of the reason for these figures is the increasing number of children in single-parent families. These children have a 50 percent chance of being in poverty in contrast with children with both parents where the odds are less than one in ten. Even though the poverty rates for families maintained by women have declined, the number of children living in these families are growing.[33] Divorce and out-of-wedlock births are the largest contributors to the creation of these one-parent households. In 1988, 38 percent of our children lived with a divorced parent, an increase from the 23 percent reported in 1960.[34] The statistics regarding illegitimate births are even more dramatic. Daniel Patrick Moynihan, the senior United States Senator from New York, reported the following figures:

> In 1963, three percent of white births in the nation were illegitimate but 24 percent of black births were out of wedlock. By 1987, these ratios had increased to 16 percent for whites and 63 percent for blacks. In 1987, in New York City, 30 percent of white births were illegitimate and 63 percent of black births were illegitimate.[35]

Another part of the explanation for the growing poverty of children is the increase of two-parent families experiencing poverty. The major factor contributing to this trend is the stagnation of the father's wages. Poverty rates might have been higher for these families if not compensated for by three trends: (1) increased incomes provided by working mothers; (2) smaller families, and (3) delayed childbearing. Most of these families are called the "working poor" and they often do not qualify for public assistance except food stamps or are not covered by health insurance.[36] Even though the United States has spent as much as 11 percent (1986) of its gross domestic product on health, which exceeds Sweden (8.5 percent), Germany (8 percent), and Japan (7 percent),[37] 33 million Americans, two-thirds of whom are in families where the head of household has full-time employment, have no health insurance.[38]

Other factors contributing to the number of children in poverty include the recessions of the 1980s and federal cutbacks in eligibility definitions and benefit levels for Aid to Families with Dependent Children (AFDC).[39] Compounding the problem is the removal of cheap housing through gentrification, rising rents, and mounting costs of home ownership. Between 1981 and 1989, federal government support for subsidized housing declined from $32 billion to $6 billion.[40] The sum result is that homeless families with children comprise approximately 34 percent of the

The Economy and Its Influence 167

entire homeless population. Many of these families are black or Hispanic.[41] Along with poverty and homelessness, malnutrition is on the increase. One estimate predicts that 20 million Americans will be hungry some time during each month.[42]

Statistics collected by international organizations detail the plight of many American children:

- The United States lags far behind most industrial nations in preventing childhood disease and injury. A quarter of preschoolers and a third of poor children under 5 are not immunized.
- Reports of child abuse in the United States have increased steadily in the past decade. The majority concern cases of neglect where children are denied adequate medical care.
- In the United States, three-fifths of the households that receive food stamps contain children. The average amount received, in constant dollars, has not changed since 1980.[43]

The lack of health insurance and prenatal care for many expectant mothers have contributed to some other distressing figures:

- A child born in Japan, Finland, Hong Kong, Ireland, Australia, Canada, Singapore, or any of 12 other industrialized nations has a better chance of surviving his or her first year than a child born in the United States.
- A child born in Czechoslovakia or Bulgaria has a better chance of celebrating its first birthday than a black child born in America's urban areas or the rural South. From now until the end of this century, 520,000 infants will die if the U.S. infant mortality rate continues unchecked. This is more than the total number of all battlefield deaths of American forces in World War I and II, Korea, and Vietnam.[44]

In terms of numbers, 1986 calculations indicated that 10.4 deaths occurred per 1,000 live births with the black infant mortality rate (18 percent) twice as high as white infant deaths (8.9 percent).[45] Low birth weight is the factor most closely linked to infant mortality. Those who survive are likely to suffer one or more handicaps. On an annual basis, it is estimated that 11,000 low birth babies born in the United States will experience long term disabilities.[46]

If children survive the birth process, the characteristics of their daily reality are very different from those of previous generations. Increases in

168   *The Reference Librarian and Implications of Mediation*

the percentage of children living in poverty, growth in the numbers of those living in single parent homes, the rise of children born to unwed mothers, and the decreased presence of mothers in the home due to outside employment are trends that present major challenges to them, their families, and the country's educational system.

Not only do these social trends add great pressures to the education sector, but the expectations and needs of a competitive America entering the 21st Century are also contributing factors. Jobs in the future will require more technical and literacy skills than in the past. Employment opportunities for high school dropouts in the 1990s will decrease from 18 to 13 percent while demand for college graduates will increase from 22 to 30 percent for the same period.[47]

Other variables that will exert tremendous influence are demographic in nature. Even though the number of births per woman has decreased, the total number of births has increased as the Baby Boomers have reached their child-bearing years. For example, thirty percent of all births between July 1986 and June 1987 were to women 30 to 39 years old.[48] As a consequence, the demand for elementary education has increased after declining between 1970 and 1985.[49] High school enrollments are projected to grow from 13.2 million (1990) to 14.5 million (1995).[50] Because of immigration and higher minority birth rates, the number of minority children is growing. Between 1980 and 1985, the Hispanic population has grown by approximately 5 million, an increase of 34 percent while the Black population grew by 12.7 percent for the same period.[51] These demographic trends indicate the make-up of future school age populations will change, with a decrease of white non-Hispanics from 73 percent (1985) to 66 percent (2000).[52] Such changes in racial and ethnic composition will demand a restructuring of curricula and require additional ESL (English as a Second Language) instruction to meet the needs of a redefined school age population.

Many minority children are susceptible to educational failure because of unstable family lives and poverty. Statistics gathered in 1989 illustrate this crises. Of the young people under 18 years of age living in poverty, 14.8 percent were white, 36.2 percent were Hispanic, and 43.7 percent were black.[53] The economic displacement of these children will increasingly tax the resources of the educational system to offset the disintegration of an entire generation.

What investments have been made for our children's education? Public expenditure for education in the United States was 5.7 percent of the gross national product in 1987. This ratio was higher than those of Italy (4.0 percent), Japan (5.0 percent) and the United Kingdom (5.0 percent),

The Economy and Its Influence   *169*

but considerably lower than that of Canada (7.2 percent), Norway (6.8 percent), Sweden (7.4 percent), and the U.S.S.R. (7.3 percent).[54] Nationally, expenditures for elementary and secondary education increased 21 percent between 1978-79 and 1988-89.[55] The financial responsibility for educating the nation's children falls primarily on the shoulders of state and local governments. In 1986, these government expenditures for primary and secondary schools amounted to 20 percent of total spending.[56] Forecasters are concerned that tax support for education will begin to evaporate. Homeowners who are childless, non-minorities, and older and wealthier people may not want to fund a public school system striving to educate a growing black and Hispanic population. This problem is compounded by the recent budget shortfalls on state and local levels.

How well are our schools succeeding in educating the nation's young? Real gains have occurred in a variety of areas. For example, the number of public school teachers has increased at a faster rate than the number of students. The pupil-teacher ratio has consequently improved from 19 to 1 (1979) to 17 to 2 (1989). Teacher salaries have also improved by approximately 20 percent between 1980-81 and 1989-90.[57] Increases have also been noted in the amount of education completed by Americans: "In 1989, 77 percent of the population 25 years old and over had completed high school and 21 percent had completed 4 or more years of college. This represents an increase from 1980, when 69 percent had completed high school and 17 percent had 4 years of college."[58]

For minority children, the diagnosis is mixed. Significant progress has occurred in reducing the gap between blacks and whites in terms of achievement test scores, but black and Hispanic scores are still well below those of whites. Enrollments in kindergarten have accelerated for minorities, but the black and Hispanic enrollments in pre-kindergarten have declined throughout the 1980s.[59] Black male dropout rates have fallen from 11 percent (1969) to 6.2 percent (1987); however, Hispanic dropout rates have not declined and are at higher levels than black and white rates.[60] Since 1980, all groups have experienced substantial increases of individuals below model grade level, but the group with the highest average of individuals within this category were 13-year-old black males.[61]

In terms of student performance, international comparisons present a revealing if not troubling picture. American 13-year-olds participated in the 1988 International Assessment of Educational Progress involving five other countries–Canada, Korea, Spain, the United Kingdom, and Ireland. The students from the United States ranked last in mathematics, and second to last in science. To illustrate these results, 40 percent of the

Korean students were able to comprehend complex mathematical concepts compared with 9 percent of the Americans.[62]

Students' abilities to read, write, and think are evaluated by the National Assessment of Educational Progress (NAEP), a congressionally mandated project. Results from 1988 indicated that 40 percent of the 13-year olds in the 7th and 8th grades had difficulty in reading their textbooks.[63] Students on all grade levels had problems in successfully defending their opinions based upon the materials they had read. Of the 11th graders tested, 22 percent wrote "elaborated" responses while 36 percent wrote "inadequate" or "minimal" responses.[64] As a point of comparison, only one percent of the seventeen-year olds are illiterate in Germany and Japan in contrast with 13 percent of their American counterparts.[65] These factors contribute significantly to America's high rate of functional illiteracy which by some estimates is as high as 23 million adults with an estimated growth of 2.3 million annually.[66]

This thumbnail sketch of social trends seems to indicate that large pockets of our society are encountering at best, benign neglect and at worse, an unspoken acceptance that only the fittest will survive. The gap between the rich and poor is widening because many lack the necessary skills to advance economically. The top fifth of the population earns 43.7 percent of all income in contrast with to the bottom fifth's 4.6 percent.[67] The lack of hope for a bright future among our young, especially for those in poverty, is manifested by the number of youngsters packing guns in their school lunch boxes and annihilating each other in the streets. Homicide is the leading cause of death for black males between 15 and 24 years of age.[68] The suicide rate, another indicator, has tripled since 1950 for all individuals between the ages of 15 and 24.[69] The effect of long term poverty for some individuals has generated some shattering results. An African-American male born in Harlem is more likely to die before the age of forty than an impoverished peasant from Bangladesh.[70]

The decline in academic proficiency and the disintegration of social structures have had an economic impact. Poor academic skills have been linked to shortfalls in the GNP, where calculations are estimated to reach $3 trillion by 2010 if present conditions prevail.[71] The price tag for functional illiteracy is $6 billion dollars annually in welfare programs and unemployment compensation. On a yearly basis, $257 billion are forfeited in unrealized earnings by individuals insufficiently prepared to function in the work environment. Corporate America spends millions on remedial courses to compensate for their employees' educational inadequacies. Unemployment and poverty are also linked to crime. It is estimated that $6.6 billion is spent annually to incarcerate 750,000 illiterates.[72]

The cumulative effect of these socio-economic trends is the deterioration of America's ability to compete in the global marketplace. A report by the Council on Competitiveness indicated that U.S. industries have dramatically fallen behind their foreign counterparts in a number of technological areas perceived as essential to the nation's commercial and economic well-being.[73] The summary of social and economic indicators presented here reveals a disturbing portrait of a deteriorating America and in some instances, many of our fellow citizens lead lives that are often associated with Third World realities.

LIBRARIES AND LIBRARIANS

Economic constrictions and governmental deficits of the past decade have affected libraries, their personnel, and the services they provide. An overview of the funding arena reveals that many libraries have a serious case of fiscal hiccups. Monies disappear or budgets are drastically curtailed, but at the brink of disaster, funds are partially if not fully restored. In other situations, cutbacks, entrenchment, and downsizing characterize a demoralizing downward cycle with no relief in sight.

An early warning signal of things to come occurred in 1985 when the Gramm-Rudman-Hollings Act was enacted as a strategy to eliminate the federal deficit. The Library of Congress was one of the first casualties. Its 1986 fiscal budget had already been cut by $8.4 million through normal appropriation procedures, but the Gramm-Rudman-Hollings reductions amounted to an additional 4.3 percent which totaled an $18.3 million decrease from the previous year. The Library of Congress reacted by cutting hours of service; there were also severe reductions in preservation, acquisitions, and personnel. More than $1 million was reduced from the budgets of the National Library Service to the Blind and Physically Handicapped and the Congressional Research Service. It should be noted that the Library of Congress did receive some budget relief in the form of an appropriations amendment in July 1986. The National Library of Medicine and the National Agricultural Library were also affected by the reductions enforced by the Gramm-Rudman-Hollings Act. For example, the National Agricultural Library's budget was reduced 5.9 percent below its fiscal 1985 level.[74]

Deficit reduction efforts also affected the quality, quantity, and accessibility of government information. The Government Printing Office received $3 million dollars less in appropriations in 1986 and with the subsequent 4.3 percent cut brought by Gramm-Rudman-Hollings, overall funding decreased by 14 percent below 1985 levels. Federal agencies

172   *The Reference Librarian and Implications of Mediation*

struggling to survive their budget shortfalls dramatically increased their prices or began charging for materials that previously had been free. For example, during the period between 1981 and 1984, the American Library Association's Washington office reported that the subscription price of the *Federal Register* jumped from $75 to $300.[75]

State librarians have also had to contend with declining budgets. In an overview of fiscal forecasts for FY 1991, some bright spots existed with budget increases reported in, for example, Georgia, Hawaii, Iowa, Nebraska, and Washington. On the other hand, other state librarians disclosed a series of shortfalls, reductions, cuts, and freezes. Most consistently, they expressed concern for the future of library funding because of voter reluctance to support tax increases for library activities. These attitudes are not surprising considering the fiscal gaps experienced by local and state governments, but the projections are troubling because 90 percent of all library funding is derived from these sources.[76]

Academic libraries and librarians have not been unscathed by recent events. "Is the Library a Place?" was the 1991 conference theme of the Association of Research Libraries. Intended as a focal point regarding library design, it metamorphosed to the focal concerns held by participants about the questionable fate of their institutions. Tight budgets were forecast from a report presented at the meeting based upon a 1991 survey of ARL libraries. Of the eighty respondents, 52.5 percent reported fiscal reductions in FY 1991 and 61.2 percent projected shortfalls in FY 1992. Thirty-three individuals were able to describe their cutbacks for FY 1991 in the following terms:

> . . . 9.7 percent were facing cuts of over $1 million;
> 6.5 percent were facing cuts of $600,001-$1 million;
> 6.5 percent were facing cuts of $400,001-$600,000;
> 38.7 percent were facing cuts of $200,001-$400,000;
> 22.6 percent were facing cuts of $100,001-$200,000;
> and 16.1 percent were facing cuts of $20,000-$100,000.[77]

A number of prestigious institutions have had to make serious adjustments to compensate for these fiscal shortfalls. Stanford University libraries had to confront severe budget cuts for both FY 1991 and FY 1992. The entire campus community experienced a process of "repositioning" as a strategy to consolidate and reduce costs. Consequently, Stanford's libraries were merged with the school's Office of Information Resources in September 1990.[78]

Not only have many prominent institutions been impaired by budget difficulties, but a whole range of lesser known publicly supported schools are experiencing budget cuts that have not been imposed since the Depression. A survey of the American Association of State Colleges and Universities revealed that twenty-six financially strapped statehouses made mid-term budget reductions in 1991 with more cutbacks expected in FY 1992. These trends translate to long term problems for the nation's higher education system, when one considers that state supported schools accommodate 77 percent of all collegiate enrollments nationwide.[79]

Consequently, librarians in many of these publicly supported institutions have had to deal with a shrinking fiscal base and a deteriorating information environment. The author's conversations with some academic librarians working within this context in the New York metropolitan area revealed a disturbing state of affairs. Strategic collection development is virtually impossible because funding vacillates between nonexistent levels and unforeseen downpours. Subject bibliographers debate the merits of spending meager funds on multiple copies of reserve materials because an increasing number of students cannot afford to purchase their textbooks. Collections have become obsolescent because new titles, editions, and technological formats cannot be acquired. Online services are no longer available to students and professors must pay for any searches they request; in previous years, both faculty and students could make such inquiries without paying any fees. Personnel shortages are endemic because of hiring freezes and the lack of funds to replace retiring members. Few people are therefore available to staff serials, acquisitions, and reference sectors resulting in reduced hours of service for users. These conditions resemble the library environments of many Third World countries where shortages of all types jeopardize the mediation of information.

The fiscal health of state and local coffers as well as the level of community support have had tremendous impact upon school and public libraries. On a positive note, some examples exist of libraries flourishing throughout the nation. The following cases are samples of noteworthy events: Voters in Fairfax, Virginia approved a $39.1 million bid for construction of seven new branches. A bond issue was also passed in Corvallis, Oregon by 69 percent of the voters for a $6.8 million renovation project of the county library. Birmingham Public Library in Alabama was the recipient of $3 million from a $75 million bond issue to replace two branches and remodel two others.[80] The City Council of Huntington Beach, California unanimously approved an $8 million expansion program for its Central Library. The added facilities will house a theater, a computer and technology center, and study areas.[81] In terms of school

174   *The Reference Librarian and Implications of Mediation*

libraries, the community of Norman, Oklahoma continued to provide support to these programs despite a lingering economic downturn produced by the 1983 oil crises. The residents' commitment was rewarded when the Norman Public School District won a 1989 National School Media Program of the Year Award. Sponsored by ALA's Association of School Librarians and the Britannica Companies, the award applauded the strong ties created between library media programs and the curricula.[82]

Further perusal of recent news reported by the professional press reveals that many more areas across the country are experiencing a very different reality. Declarations of budget shortfalls, hiring freezes, curtailment of services, and closings abound. A pastiche of several headlines conveys the tenor of current trends: "Closed Libraries Dramatize Gaps in Service to Native Americans"; "Chartered By George III: 225-Year-Old N.J. Library to Close Due to Funding Woes"; "NYPL Gets Budget Cut For Third Year in a Row"; "Library Life Goes On Despite Philly Fiscal Crises"; "Economic Woes Stall Growth of De Kalb County PL," and "Worcester PL Faces Budget Crises."[83]

Going beyond the headlines, one recognizes that the plight of libraries has often been dramatic. The declining fiscal scene in California is a case in point. Most librarians throughout the state were scrambling to counteract the governor's proposed FY 1992 budget. If his proposal passed, California libraries would lose 50 percent of their state funds, amounting to a decrease of $20 million (FY 1990) and $10 million (FY 1992). Economic stagnation had already affected local libraries and this proposal added to a series of other setbacks. For example, the Los Angeles Public Library had begun to contemplate reducing its hours of service. The system had already experienced a ten percent staff shortage due to a city-wide hiring freeze. One third ($87,246) of the Santa Cruz City-County Library System's funding had been cut as an attempt by the county government to recover losses in collecting property taxes. In response to the governor's budget proposal, school districts reacted by initiating a class action suit against the state as a strategy to offset financial calamity.[84] This example exemplifies the extent to which library institutions hang by their thumbs as state and local officials decide their fate.

On the federal level, a recent publication discloses a revealing attitude about the role of public and school libraries in American society. President Bush outlined a long range plan for improving the nation's education system in a document entitled, *America 2000: An Education Strategy.* The goals itemized by the President as targets were listed in the following terms:

The Economy and Its Influence

1. All children in America will start school ready to learn.
2. The high school graduation rate will increase by at least 90 percent.
3. American students will leave grades four, eight, and twelve having demonstrated competency in challenging subject matter including english, mathematics, science, history, and geography; and every school in America will ensure all students learn to use their minds well, so they may be prepared for responsible citizenship, further learning, and productive employment in our modern economy.
4. U.S. students will be first in the world in science and mathematics achievement.
5. Every adult American will be literate and will possess the knowledge and skills necessary to compete in a global economy and exercise the rights and responsibilities of citizenship.
6. Every school in America will be free of drugs and violence and will offer a disciplined environment conducive to learning.[85]

These objectives offer some hope that steps will be implemented to rectify existing problems, but not much has changed since the appearance of other key documents. *A Nation At Risk* is a prime example and only the future will reveal if *America 2000* will be a case of "sound and fury signifying nothing." The prominent feature in both of these publications is the exclusion of libraries.[86] These omissions can be interpreted as strong indicators of the unimportance attributed to libraries. Information centers and "people places" are not favorably regarded in the prevailing climate of apathy and egocentrism.

As illustrated in this essay, libraries and librarians in many parts of the country are confronting severe funding problems which in turn, reflect the nation's shrinking economic base. On a more profound level, the condition of our information centers mirrors the collapse of our social structures and values. Information is no longer esteemed as a vital component to enhance citizens' talents nor an essential ingredient to preserve a democratic state. At best, it is perceived as a product primarily available to those who can afford it. An essential function of the profession, the mediation of information, is unraveling as accessibility becomes more constricted. Due to inadequate funding and spiraling information costs, librarians have fewer options in providing complete and up-to-date services to their patrons. What is most disturbing is the awareness that American society and its libraries are beginning to acquire attributes associated with the Third World.

176 *The Reference Librarian and Implications of Mediation*

RECOMMENDATIONS AND CONCLUSIONS

Librarians have not been known as innovators and they often accept the status quo. If this attitude were embraced by professionals after viewing these trends, they would consent to the theory that the healthiest and the heartiest have the right to survive. In such a conceptual framework, no action nor strategy for change would be undertaken. Communities or organizations that possess the desire and the means would invest in strengthening their information resources. The remaining libraries could either perish or survive with a mediocre pool of materials to serve their clientele. Once the institutions with the most extensive collections realize they have become the net lenders for the nation without benefit or profit, the entire interlibrary loan system could deteriorate. The information infrastructure could devolve into a desert with isolated oases to serve the needs of the select few. Librarians would become the information mediators for the elite.

Are any options open to professionals striving to counteract these trends? Our history may furnish us with important insights. During the 1950s, 1960s and 1970s, the American information infrastructure was the envy of the world. Consultants flew to the four corners of the earth and shared their expertise. In some instances, these missions were absolute failures but more frequently, dynamic cross-cultural communication occurred and the development of information structures was facilitated.

Today's reality is somewhat different. As the economic environment shrinks, the information network is becoming frayed and the interlocking threads broken. Professionals in a variety a of institutions are coping with a deteriorating set of circumstances which hampers their role as information mediators. The point of juncture has arrived when Third World consultants need to be invited to the United States. Their insights could be very instructive as they share their strategies for maximizing mediation in an underdeveloped information environment. Such an exchange could provide a fresh opportunity to reprioritize goals and generate creative solutions. New conceptual strategies could be formulated about information management and the delivery of services to the widest user community possible despite the shrinking economic base.

In closing, the rate of deterioration may have reached such a level that the United States will never regain its former power. This dark vision does not remove our responsibility for striving to improve the information infrastructure. The assistance of Third World consultants could stimulate fundamental changes which in turn would offset some apocalyptic disaster. But at the very least, if further disintegration of the na-

The Economy and Its Influence 177

tion's information network were to occur, the profession's self-respect would be intact, comforted by the knowledge that it struggled to maintain its role as mediator despite the pressures and constraints it encountered.

NOTES

1. "Monetary Policy Report to Congress–Report submitted to the Congress on February 20, 1991, pursuant to the Full Employment and Balanced Growth Act of 1978," *Federal Reserve Bulletin*, 77, 33 (March 1991), 149.

2. James C. Cooper and Kathleen Madigan, "Is the Economy Back on Track? Which Paper Do You Read?" *Business Week*, No. 3219 (June 24, 1991), p. 37.

3. Prepared for the Joint Economic Committee by the Council of Economic Indicators (102d Congress, 1st Session), *Economic Indicators*, No. 5 (May, 1991), p.6.

4. Ibid., p. 8.

5. "Industrial Production and Capacity Utilization," *Federal Reserve Bulletin*, 77, 5 (May, 1991), 297.

6. *Economic Indicators*, No. 5 (May, 1991), p. 20.

7. Ibid., p. 22.

8. Ibid., p. 23.

9. Ibid., p. 36.

10. Ibid., p. 12.

11. Eva Pomice and Diana Hawkins, "The Misery Continues," *U.S. News & World Report*, 110, 23 (June 17, 1991), 50.

12. Ibid.

13. Robert D. Metzer, "The Ominous Exporting of U.S. Clerical Jobs," *USA Today*, 117, 2526 (March, 1989), 30.

14. Ibid., p. 31.

15. Karen Pennar, Mike McNamee, Michael J. Mandel, Eric Schine, and Geoffry Smith, "The New Face of the Recession: Fallout From the Financial Excesses of the 80's Colors This Downturn," *Business Week*, No. 3193 (December 24, 1990), 60.

16. Ibid., pp. 60-61.

17. Marc Levinson and Carolyn Friday, "Why Our Banks Are Hurting." *Newsweek* 117, 3 (January 21, 1991), 43.

18. Robert F. Black, Don L. Boroughs, Sara Collins, and Kenneth Sheets, "Heavy Lifting: How America's Debt Burden Threatens the Economic Recovery," *U.S. News & World Report*, 110, 17 (May 6, 1991), 53.

19. Glenn B. Canner and Charles A. Luckett, "Payment of Household Debts," *Federal Reserve Bulletin*, 77, 4 (April, 1991) 218.

20. Ibid.

21. Robert F. Black, Don L. Boroughs, Sara Collins and Kenneth Sheets,

178   *The Reference Librarian and Implications of Mediation*

"Heavy Lifting: How America's Debt Burden Threatens the Economic Recovery," p. 53.

22. Laura S. Rubin, "The Current Fiscal Situation in State and Local Governments," *Federal Reserve Bulletin*, 76, 12 (December, 1990), 1009.

23. Ibid., pp. 1009-1010.

24. Ibid., p. 1015.

25. Michael J. Mandel, Christopher Farrell, Debra Fowler, and Sandra Atchison, "The Sad State of the States," *Business Week*, No. 2310 (April 22, 1991).

26. Kirk Victor, "Paying for the Roads," *National Journal*, 23, 7 (February 16, 1991), 374.

27. Karen Pennar, "Yes We're Down. No, We're Not Out," *Business Week* No. 3192 (December 17, 1990), p. 62.

28. Ibid.

29. Allan Carlson, "Family Questions," *Society*, 27, 5 (July/August, 1990), 5.

30. U.S. Bureau of the Census, "Changes in American Life," *Current Population Reports*, Special Studies, Series P-23, No. 163 (Washington, D.C.:1989), 8.

31. U.S. Bureau of the Census, *Statistical Abstract of the United States 1989*. 109th Edition (Washington, D.C. : 1989) Table 103.

32. Suzanne M. Bianchi, "America's Children: Mixed Prospects," *Population Bulletin*, 45, 1 (June, 1990), 13-14; U.S. Bureau of the Census, "Poverty in the United States: 1988-1989," *Current Population Reports*, Series P-60, No. 171, Washington, D.C.: June 1991), Table 2

33. Suzanne M. Bianchi, "America's Children: Mixed Prospects," p. 15.

34. U.S. Bureau of the Census, "Changes in American Life," p. 15.

35. Daniel Patrick Moynihan, "Families Falling Apart," *Society*, 27, 5 (July/August, 1990), 22.

36. Suzanne M. Bianchi, "Americas Children: Mixed Prospects," p. 16.

37. U.S. Department of Health and Human Services, *Health United States 1988*, DHHS Pub. No. (PHS) 89-1232 (Washington, D.C.: March 1989), p. 3.

38. Christopher Farrell, Joseph Weber, and Michael Schroeder, "Why We Should Invest in Human Capital," *Business Week*, No. 3192 (December 17, 1990), p. 39.

39. Kay Young McChesney, "Family Homelessness: A Systematic Problem," *Journal of Social Issues*, 46, 4 (1990), 192.

40. Richard P. Appelbaum, "The Affordability Gap," *Society* 26, 4 (May/June, 1989), 6.

41. Mickey Leland, "The Politics of Hunger Among Blacks," *The Black Scholar: Journal of Black Studies and Research*, 21, 4 (January-February-March, 1990), 4.

42. Physician Task Force on Hunger in America, *Hunger in America: The Growing Epidemic,* (Boston, MA: Harvard University School of Public Health, 1985) as *cited in* Agnes W. Hinton, Jerianne Heimindinger, and Susan B. Foerster "Position of the Dietetic Association: Domestic Hunger and Inadequate Access to Food," *Journal of the American Dietetic Association*, 90, 10 (October, 1990), 1437.

43. "Children's Crusade," *Time*, 116, 15 (October 8, 1990), 48.

44. Patricia Rowe, "Preventing Infant Mortality: An Investment in the Nation's Future," *Children Today* 18, 1 (January-February 1989), 17.

45. U.S. Department of Health and Human Services, *Health United States 1988*, p. 2; Table 2.

46. Patricia Rowe, "Preventing Infant Mortality: An Investment in the Nation's Future," p. 18.

47. Jeanne E. Griffith, Mary J. Frase, and John H. Ralph," American Education: The Challenge of Change," *Population Bulletin*, 44, 4 (December, 1989), 4.

48. U.S. Bureau of the Census, "Population Profile of the United States 1989," *Current Population Reports* Special Studies Series p. 23, No. 159 (Washington, D.C.: 1989), p. 1.

49. Ibid.

50. Ibid., p. 20.

51. Ibid., pp. 36-38.

52. Based on U.S. Bureau of the Census, "Projections of the Hispanic Population 1983 to 2080," *Current Population Reports*, Series P-25, No. 995 (Washington, D.C.: November 1986) and "Projections of the Population of the United States by Age, Sex, and Race 1988 to 2000;" *Current Population Reports*, Series P-25, No. 1018 (Washington, D.C.: January 1989) as *cited in* Jeanne E. Griffith, Mary J. Frase, and John H. Ralph, "American Education: The Challenge of Change," p. 10.

53. U.S. Bureau of the Census, "Money Income and Poverty Status in the United States 1989," *Current Population Reports*, Series P-60, No. 168 (Washington, D.C.: September 1990), Table 20.

54. United Nations Educational, Scientific, and Cultural Organization, *Statistical Yearbook 1988* as *cited in* National Center for Education Statistics, *Digest of Education Statistics 1990*, (Washington, D.C.: February 1991), p. 357.

55. Jeanne E. Griffith, Mary J. Frase, and John H. Ralph, "American Education: The Challenge of Change," p. 17

56. U.S. Bureau of the Census. *Statistical Abstract of the United States 1989*, p. 268.

57. National Center for Education Statistics, *Digest of Education Statistics 1990*, p. 1.

58. Ibid., p. 6.

59. National Center for Education Statistics, *The Condition of Education 1990*, Vol. 1, Elementary and Secondary Education (Washington, D.C.: 1989), p. 11.

60. Ibid., p. 20.

61. Ibid., p. 18.

62. Ibid., pp. 7-8; 30-31.

63. Gregory R. Arrig and Archie E. Lapointe, "What We Know About What Students Don't Know," *Educational Leadership*, 47, 3 (November, 1989), 5.

64. National Center for Education Statistics, *1989 Education Indicators*, (Washington, D.C.: nd), p. 8.

180   *The Reference Librarian and Implications of Mediation*

65. Christopher Farrell, Joseph Weber, and Michael Shroeder, "Why Should We Invest in Human Capital," p. 90.

66. Library of Congress. *Books in Our Future: A Report From the Librarian of Congress to Congress*, (Washington, D.C. U.S. Government Printing Office, 1984), p. 10.

67. Charles G. Burck, "Toward Two Societies," *Fortune*, 118, 8 (October 10, 1988), 48.

68. Wiley M. Woodard, "Warning: Being Black May Be Hazardous To Your Health," *Black Enterprise* 20, 10 (May 1990), 13.

69. U.S. Department of Health and Human Services, *Health United States 1988*, p. 22.

70. Wiley M. Woodward, "Warning: Being Black May Be Hazardous To Your Health," p. 13.

71. Christopher Farrell, Joseph Weber, Michael Schroeder, "Why We Should Invest in Human Capital," p. 89.

72. Stanley N. Wellborn, "Ahead: A Nation of Illiterates?" *U.S. News and World Report* 92, 19 (May , 1982), 53-54.

73. Susan Dentzer, "Staying Ahead of High Tech," *U.S. News and World Report* 110, 12 (April 1, 1991), 53.

74. Susan Randolf, "Reducing the Federal Deficit: The Impact on Libraries," *Special Libraries* 78, 1 (Winter, 1987), 7-10.

75. Ibid., pp. 12-13.

76. Judy Quinn and Michael Rogers, "Special *LJ* Roundup: The Fiscal Fate of the States," *Library Journal* 116, 1 (January, 1991), 16-33.

77. Judy Quinn and Michael Rogers, "ARL Libraries Fight for Their Place on Campus," *Library Journal* 116, 11 (June 15, 1991), 16.

78. Thomas M. Gaughan, "Stanford 'Prepositions', Library Faces Major Cuts," *American Libraries* 21, 5 (May, 1990), 391, 397; Thomas M. Gaughan, "Budget-struck Stanford Library Merged with Computer Center," *American Libraries* 21, 9 (October, 1990), 830.

79. Connie Leslie, Mark Starr, Pat Wingert, Karen Springen, and Patricia King, "The Public Ivy is Withering," *Time* 117, 17 (April 29, 1991), 84-85.

80. "Referenda Roundup: Four Wins, One Defeat," *American Libraries*, 21, 1 (January, 1990), 11.

81. Judy Quinn and Michael Rogers, "Huntington Beach Library to Expand," *Library Journal*, 118, 9 (May 15, 1991), 18.

82. "Well-oiled Oklahoma Program Among School Library Winners," *American Libraries*, 20, 6 (June, 1989), 485.

83. "Closed Libraries Dramatize Gaps in Service to Native Americans," *American Libraries, 20*, 3 (March, 1989), 188; Thomas M. Gaughan, "Chartered by George III: 225-Year Old N.J. Library To Close Due To Funding Woes," *American Libraries*, 21, 6 (July-August, 1990), 627; Gordon Flagg, "NYPL Gets Budget Cut For Third Year in a Row," *American Libraries*, 21, 6 (July-August, 1990), 628; "Library Life Goes On Despite Philly Fiscal Crisis," *American Libraries*, 22, 2 (February, 1991) 122; Beverly Goldberg, "Economic Woes Stall

The Economy and Its Influence   *181*

Growth of DeKalb County PL," *American Libraries*, 21, 11 (December, 1990), 1014; Judy Quinn and Michael Rodgers, "Worcester PL Faces Budget Crises," *Library Journal*, 118, 9 (May 15, 1991), 16.

84. Beverly Goldberg, "California Libraries Dig in During Fiscal Retrenchment," *American Libraries*, 22, 3 (March, 1991), 195.

85. U.S. Department of Education, *America 2000: An Education Strategy*, (Washington, D.C.: 1991), p. 19.

86. Leonard Kniffel, " Ed. Notes: A Standing Ovation for the Omission of Libraries," *American Libraries*, 22, 8 (September, 1991), 692.

VI. THE MEDIATOR AS GUARDIAN

Academic Librarians and Mediation in Controversial Scholarly Communication

Gordon Moran

The terms "mediator" and "intermediary" imply the bringing together, or working with, at least two persons or groups, but they can have different aspects. The terms can apply to situations in which the mediator/intermediary helps persons seeking goods or services to find them. On the other hand, the terms can apply to situations in which the mediator/intermediary acts within an adversarial setting, attempting to accommodate, balance out, explain, and elucidate opposing positions. Librarians can be involved in both aspects.

By nature, libraries are meeting places for persons seeking information and for the products of the producers of information. And librarians try to make the specific searches for information as easy and efficient a possible. In this sense, problems of mediation might be administrative in nature (budget, space, personnel, etc.), but there should be no problem in terms of desire and commitment to try to help patrons find the information they are seeking.

Adversarial situations occur when persons or groups try to restrict, in one way or another, patrons from having access to information. Censorship thus sets up a potential adversarial mediator situation. In *Bookbanning in America*, William Noble lists four categories of censorship,

---

Gordon Moran is an independent scholar at Via delle Terme, 3, Firenze, Italy.

© 1992 by The Haworth Press, Inc. All rights reserved.   *183*

184   *The Reference Librarian and Implications of Mediation*

or bookbanning: political, religious, sexual, and social issues.[1] In principle, librarians are opposed to censorship, but sometimes they also mediate directly with those who wish to censor. For example, in *Surveillance in the Stacks*, Herbert Foerstel describes how the American Library Association met with the Internal Revenue Service (which, according to ALA, had been involved in censorious activities): "On August 5, 1970, representatives of ALA and the IRS met in Washington, D.C., and issued a joint statement agreeing to develop guidelines acceptable to both organizations. The statement concluded . . .'an attempt will be made to identify areas of reconciliation. . . .'"[2] The end purpose of such mediation on the part of librarians, to be sure, is to obtain, for the library user, the greatest possible access to material that the user requests or needs. In effect, the librarian does not give a blank check to religious leaders or political leaders as authorities on moral virtue or political virtue, and does not recognize their authority in these fields to determine which material shall be included on, or excluded from, the library shelves.

Although Noble lists four categories of censorship, there is, in effect, another one, namely, peer review censorship in academia. This category leads to an adversarial mediator situation in academic libraries. Such situations often grow out of scholarly controversies, and the task of the academic librarian, as mediator, is to try to give the interested scholarly community access to as much pertinent information as possible, that is, to present all sides of the questions involved in the controversy.

In such cases, however, from the very outset the academic librarian might display deference and subordination–rather than resistance–to the would-be censors (peer review authorities). In fact, in selection of academic library materials, there is a rather widespread tendency, for one reason or another, to trust and cater to the opinions and judgments of the alleged academic experts and authorities.

A recent controversy in the field of biomedical science, known as the *Cell*-Baltimore controversy (or scandal, as the case may be), helps illustrate both censorship and deference in such cases. The controversy revolves around an article published in a major scholarly journal, in which one of the authors is a famous Nobel Prize scientist, the discovery of alleged serious defects and errors in the article (discovered by a junior scientist), attempts to have the errors corrected, attempts to have a rebuttal article published, censorship of the dissenting material, closing of ranks behind the famous scientist, Congressional investigations (since the scientific research was carried out with United States government funds), the finding of serious error (if not fraud) in the research and conclusions, and the eventual "retraction" of the article by the authors.

The Mediator as Guardian

From the standpoint of deference, the ideas of Bernard Davis (a Harvard professor who became involved in the controversy) are revealing. Davis is quoted as follows: "Whose judgment am I to take more seriously? I have to look at the fantastically productive record of Dr. Baltimore, not only before, but since he won the Nobel Prize [vs.] a postdoc [Ms. O'Toole]. You can call that a ganging up, or covering up, but whose judgment am I to take more seriously? . . . I felt with so many experts close to the field going over it, it would be presumptuous of me to think that I could shed any new light." [3]

Although not directly related to the specific Baltimore case, similar deference to the authoritativeness of peer review authorities can be found in library literature. In a recent article, Michael Koenig gives emphasis to the "authoritativeness" of material: "Increasingly, patrons will expect from librarians and information systems advice about the authoritativeness, or intellectual worth, of material. . . . Library patrons want authoritative information. . . . Pertinent and relevant as authoritativeness is to library users. . . . A student at Rosary College may well want to know whether a title is frequently used and often put on reserve at Yale University." [4] Charles Osburn, an academic librarian who is also a specialist in the field of scholarly communication, goes even further, by suggesting that academic librarians should select material that the peer review authorities have already selected. He implies that the other material (including that which the peer review authorities have rejected?) is "noise" that overloads an overburdened scholarly communication system. His justification for such a selection process is found in one of his recent works: "The relative importance of a given output of scholarly communication is determined through its acceptance or rejection by peer review authority. . . ." [5]

Osburn was questioned on this point, and specifically on whether errors made by the peer review authorities should be corrected. In his courteous reply to this inquiry (via a letter dated October 31, 1989), Osburn stated that errors should be corrected, but only by the peer review authorities themselves. But such a situation seems heavily involved in potential conflict of interest. In fact, in an article entitled "Confronting Scientific Fraud," Eugene Dong observes how correction of error has been impeded in a number of cases in past years due to conflict of interest tendencies and pressures: "The universities and institutes that make up the scientific community have an obvious conflict of interest in investigating allegations concerning their own faculty members. Their record indicates no zeal for the task. . . . Scientists typically assume that published data are accurate. . . . They are not accustomed to analyzing

186   The Reference Librarian and Implications of Mediation

published results with a view to uncovering intentional misrepresentation. . . . Even assuming total integrity, faculty members within the same institutions should be disqualified from reviewing the work of their fellow professional colleagues, on grounds of conflict of interest. . . . The recent history of scientific fraud starts with the infamous 1973 'patchwork mouse' experiments. . . . Since then, the number of reports of falsified research data has increased gradually, with allegations of investigative incompetence and/or cover-up by the administrations of the universities involved accompanying virtually every claim. This is documented in a 1989 report by Rep. Ted Weiss's Subcommittee on Human Resources and Intergovernmental Relations."[6]

In terms of correction of error in academia, conflict of interest is aligned with the concept of "closing ranks" behind authoritative scholars who control, to a large degree, the so-called peer review "core" literature. From the time of Semmelweis (with his theories about childbirth fever) more than a century ago to the present day, there has been an undeniable tendency among academic peer review authorities to deny that they have made serious errors in the referred scholarly literature whose contents they control. The aforementioned *Cell*-Baltimore case is just one more example, and some excerpts from Serge Lang's *Baltimore File* reveal and document how it all works: "The discrepancy between the rhetoric and the reality is partly documented by scientific journals refusing to publish an article critical of the Baltimore paper, and is further documented in the way Maddox now describes first hand Baltimore's reaction. . . . '[He was] . . . an angrily defensive person, most offended that work with which he had been associated should be challenged. . . . He angrily rejected suggestions . . . that he should publicly allow the possibility of error'. . . . Scientific journals such as *Cell, Science,* and *Nature* turned down a paper by Stewart-Feder, analyzing the article by Baltimore et al. which had been questioned by Margot O'Toole. They were thus closing off what should have been the natural channels of scientific criticism. . . . The National Academy of Sciences *Issues in Science and Technology* published only Baltimore's tendentious point of view. . . .They did not publish an opposite point of view. . . . In the *New York Times* editorial of 26 March 1991 . . . the editors state: . . . 'Dr. Baltimore . . . orchestrated a chorus of support from sympathetic colleagues by sending a letter to 400 scientists warning that Congressional intervention could cripple American science.' What the *New York Times* does not say is that it itself helped the orchestration. . . . Throughout the Baltimore case, one could not rely on the establishment press for systematic and correct information. One had to look elsewhere."[7]

The Mediator as Guardian

But where is "elsewhere" in such a situation? In a pamphlet published by the ARL Task Force on Scholarly Communication (Charles Osburn, Chair), entitled *The Changing System of Scholarly Communication*, there is reference to ". . . the role of the librarian as mediator between the scholar and the information system," and it is observed that the "exchange of ideas is fundamental to the nature of scholarship."[8] In the *Cell*-Baltimore case, however, it seems that real scholarly exchange was prevented in the peer reviewed core literature as well as in the so-called establishment press. In such a situation, the librarian, as a mediator, must look beyond the normal channels of information in order to give access to a true "exchange of ideas" among the protagonists in the scholarly controversy. In a somewhat similar academic dispute–the so-called Guido Riccio controversy in the field of art history*–Sanford Berman suggested the following action on the part of art librarians: "*Good* library procedure would dictate–with respect to a major intellectual and academic dispute like that surrounding Guido Riccio–that extra measures be taken to IDENTIFY AND MAKE AVAILABLE THE ENTIRE SPECTRUM OF VIEWPOINTS AND DOCUMENTATION. Such measures would require, at minimum, the cataloging or indexing by author–and, ideally, also by title and subject–*all* relevant material on the controversy, including periodical literature, pamphlets, and monographs. Further, such cataloging/indexing data should appear in a convenient and readily accessible place so that *any* library user can locate the references easily. Beyond that, given the unquestionable interest in this particular matter, a proactive, truly helpful and alert librarian would also prepare–and possibly duplicate for broad distribution–a special bibliography on the case. Such a resource-list should be posted prominently in the library and updated frequently. In addition, it should be published in an appropriate art journal, in order that all interested scholars, historians, and others have the opportunity to fully and dispassionately investigate the dispute and reach their own, informed conclusions."[9]

I think it is interesting and revealing to compare Berman's suggestions for academic librarians in their handling of academic controversies with the specific reactions of the Director of the National Library of Medicine, Donald Lindberg, in the *Cell*-Baltimore case. In 1986, Margot O'Toole, Walter Stewart, and Ned Feder compiled and analyzed data concerning the *Cell* article in question, concluded that the article contained serious

---

* in which the present author plays a prominent role.

188   The Reference Librarian and Implications of Mediation

error, and reported their conclusions to officials at the National Institutes of Health (the government agency that subsidized the research for the *Cell* article). In 1987, Stewart wrote, " . . . we believe that many research groups are now relying on this inaccurate paper. . . . I wince when I think of how many scientists have been relying on the article (to their detriment). . . ." But as mentioned above, there was a determined and successful effort to prevent correction of error or rebuttal of any kind to the *Cell* article from being published in the core scholarly literature. During 1986 and 1987, officials at the National Institutes of Health were asked about their policies about correction of error in general regarding published research in which NIH funds were used, and about corrections of error specifically in the *Cell* article. In direct reply to inquiries made from scholars (outside of NIH) to officials at NIH relating to the *Cell*-Baltimore case, the Director of the National Library of Medicine intervened. In fact, in a letter of October 19, 1987, Robert B. Mehnert, an official of NIH, writes as follows: ". . . the National Library of Medicine indexes retractions for its bibliographic publications and its computerized databases. Dr. Donald A.B. Lindberg, director of NLM, has asked me to send you two items he has recently published on this subject. . . ."

It immediately became evident, however, that Lindberg was talking about only those cases in which scholars or authors had admitted errors and had already made formal written "retractions." But in the *Cell* case (which specifically prompted Lindberg's intervention, as noted above), the authors–and high NIH officials–would not admit any errors were made, and furthermore, the authors, NIH officials, and peer review authorities were not allowing rebuttals and correction of errors to be published in the scholarly literature. How, then, could a scholar find the dissenting point of view, in all its detail, in the National Library of Medicine?

As a result of this situation, Lindberg was asked, in a letter of November 2, 1987, how the National Library of Medicine could, or would, keep scholars informed concerning the ongoing controversy. Excerpts of the letter include the following remarks: " . . . considerable damage might be currently being done, insofar as your MEDLINE, *Index Medicus*, etc., might be indexing erroneous information contained in a *Cell* article published by Prof. David Baltimore, among others. Is there any way that you can alert readers of medical literature that there might be a problem here? How much erroneous information might be piling up and spreading within the literature . . .?. . . . Despite the NIH rhetoric and your assuring words, however, it seems to me that the reality of the situation is quite different. . . .'. . . Every scholar who is interested in the field of study should have the opportunity to read and analyze the evidence on both sides of the debate, without having a chosen few decide that only one side of the debate can be published . . . . ' . . . Now, what is your role in this, Mr. Lindberg, as Director of the National Library of Medicine? Or, what do you feel your role should be at this point? Should you hope that Stewart and Feder are wrong, or should you alert users of *Index Medicus* and MEDLINE, in the meantime (before the Feder-Stewart article is published; if it ever is published) that there might be errors in the *Cell* article? If there are errors in the *Cell* article, will you continue to allow, at this point, these errors to be extended and expanded further throughout the medical literature, piling error on top of error . . . ? . . . . I ask you these specific questions, (and I hope you will reply to them) based on your own following published ideas: 'The publication of research results is the foundation of all subsequent investigation. . . .We must do what we can to limit the damage of errors in the literature. . . . '" (Moran, letter of November 2, 1987).

A couple of months later, in a letter of January 4, 1988, further inquiries were made, this time involving indexing policies at the National Library of Medicine: "It seems to me in this case that it is possible that if an article contains material that corrects error of another article previously indexed, you might include it among a list that is not selected for indexing, and thus the error will remain uncorrected. Could you please let me know what your criteria are for selecting and not selecting articles to be indexed? Is it the 'importance' of the material, or the 'reputations' of the authors or their institutions, collegial professional ties, or some other bases?" (Moran letter of January 4, 1988).

More than a month later, another letter was written to the Director of the National Library of Medicine, reminding him that no reply, nor even an acknowledgement, had been received for the previous two letters. This letter included the following remark: "Since my last letters to you were written, other comments about the peer review system have come to my attention which would further indicate the misleading nature of the ideas you published about peer review. . . . At any rate, I hope that you will reply to the inquiries I made in my previous letters to you. . . . Thank you for your consideration, and I look forward to your courteous reply." (Moran letter of February 18, 1988).

Several *years* have passed by now, and still no replies, nor even acknowledgements, have been received for the letters of November 2, 1987, January 4, 1988, and February 18, 1988. Who knows if Donald Lindberg will ever reply to them, and who knows if any successor to Lindberg as Director of the National Library of Medicine will ever reply? And who

190   *The Reference Librarian and Implications of Mediation*

knows if similar stonewalling in the handling of the *Cell*-Baltimore case at NLM was instrumental in delaying the resolution of the case? Or to view the situation from the other side of the coin, it seems possible that the *Cell*-Baltimore case might have been resolved sooner—and with less bitterness and embarrassment—if Lindberg and the National Library of Medicine had treated the case in the way Berman suggested that art librarians should treat the Guido Riccio affair. In terms of the librarian as mediator, such an approach in the *Cell*-Baltimore case would include giving scholars access to the unpublished text by Stewart and Feder that was being suppressed and censored by NIH officials and peer review authorities, and providing extensive testimony from the scholar O'Toole, who, according to John Swan, "first spotted the faked data and then lost her job and her house."[10] It would also include accessibility to *The Baltimore File*, compiled by Professor Serge Lang (with additions and updates to Lang's compilation).

It is interesting to note that while the three letters of 1987-1988, discussed above, apparently were being stonewalled by Lindberg, others at the National Library of Medicine were trying to demonstrate to the scholarly community how NLM alerts scholars to errors in the literature of science. For example, the following was presented by NLM librarians as part of the program of The First International Congress on Peer Review in Biomedical Publication (Organized by the American Medical Association, and held in Chicago, May 1989): "In 1987, the National Library of Medicine (NLM) implemented a procedure that identifies substantive errors to the text, abstract, or descriptive parts of an article introduced during the publication process that were corrected in subsequently published errata notices. . . . While the NLM alerts users to the existence of errors, usually this occurs several months after the original citations appeared."[11] A few months later, in September 1989, a "Workshop on the Responsible Conduct of Research in the Health Sciences," organized by the Institute of Medicine, was held in Washington, D.C. The report of this workshop includes the following: "The National Library of Medicine has developed a system for tagging references in MEDLINE to alert bibliographic searchers to notices of fraud or scientific error."[12] What the librarians did not report in their peer review congress paper, and what the authors of the Institute of Medicine report did not reveal, is that the very organizers and protagonists of the AMA Chicago congress and of the Institute of Medicine Washington workshop included persons who were among the most ruthless and powerful suppressors and censors of work that "identifies substantive errors," and of "notices" of "scientific error" in the *Cell*-Baltimore case. And if the NLM librarians did not

The Mediator as Guardian 191

know about this specific suppression and censorship, one reason might be that the Director of their library did not inform them of the undeniable, documented evidence for such censorship and suppression.

Furthermore, neither the Chicago peer review congress nor the Washington workshop reveal that, because of such academic censorship and suppression as has been taking place in the *Cell*-Baltimore case, it often takes several years–if not longer–for knowledge of "scientific error" to come out into the open and for official published "retractions" to be made. What vast sums of money might be being wanted, and what amount of human suffering and numbers of deaths might be taking place, because of such delay in the correction of error? For example, an article published on September 15, 1991, entitled "U.S. probe cites lies, errors in AIDS article," discusses serious errors in a widely-acclaimed piece published in *Science* in 1984: "Dr. Robert Gallo's landmark 1984 article reporting the isolation of the AIDS virus is riddled with fabrication, falsification, misleading statements and errors, an 18-month investigation of Gallo's research has concluded . . . . Responsibility for the fraudulent portions of the article, which contributed substantially to Gallo's status as a scientific superstar, was attributed by investigators to Dr. Mikulas Popovic, a Czechoslovak refugee who was then Gallo's chief virologist. . . . In less than a decade, Gallo rose from an obscure government scientist to become the world's most prominent AIDS researcher and a frequently mentioned candidate for a Nobel Prize. Now it seems likely the scientific article that arguably did the most to enhance his reputation will have to be retracted." [13]

In terms of wasted research money, human suffering and death, it seems that the "retraction" of scientific error years or decades–or even longer–after the error was published, as well as the academic librarian's "tagging" of such retractions for the benefit of scholars, are somewhat similar to the proverbial concept of closing the barn door after the horses have already run away. Even though, in this sense, the NLM "tagging" system is late, it is nevertheless important that the library, and other libraries, identify and bring attention to published research results that turn out to be erroneous and/or fraudulent. Why not try to accomplish this sooner, however, through the role of mediator, by identifying the academic controversies and bringing them to the attention of interested scholars an soon as there is evidence that peer review authorities are attempting to censor and suppress uncomfortable and unsettling findings and theories?

It seems quite possible that there might be some very important, vital, and significant theories and findings that are currently being suppressed

192 *The Reference Librarian and Implications of Mediation*

in the scholarly literature. For now, reference to and brief descriptions of two situations will be made: Prof. Harold Hillman's views about current research involving the human cell and Louis Pascal's ideas on the origin of AIDS.

In light of the strenuous resistance to critical thinking, and determined attempts at suppression, on the part of some scholars in the Guido Riccio case, the idea came to mind that if such behavior can occur over an issue as innocuous as the attribution and dating of the Guido Riccio fresco, perhaps there might be a basic flaw in cancer research–given the many billions of dollars and countless hours being poured into it–which is impeding progress. Then, in the course of studies of peer review and academic suppression, the situation of Prof. Hillman's research came up, including this passage: ". . . he [Hillman] suggested that the problems with techniques used to study cells were one major cause of slow progress in understanding such diseases as cancer, multiple sclerosis, and Alzheimer's disease. . . . Flawed cell pictures are only part of the problem inherent in these studies, says Hillman. He also feels that a string of other hypotheses, crucial to his research–the existence of receptors that no one has ever seen, for example–are unproven yet accepted as gospel. In the article he likened medical orthodoxy to a religion, with its priesthood and theology." Professional retaliation–somewhat similar to that against Margot O'Toole–has apparently been taken against Hillman, since he has lost his job (or was forced into early retirement, after a long fight); and as far as can be determined, his findings and ideas are still being suppressed in the specialized scholarly literature.[14]

Based on mass media headlines and coverage, there is little question that the AIDS problem is one of the most crucial subjects of current academic research. It also seems that the problem is made much more intricate and complicated by the implications of the statement, "I am the only person who knows what I meant," made by Robert Gallo in relation to a key part of the famous *Science* article.[15] In terms of scholarly communication, this statement would imply that in some aspects of AIDS research, the world's most famous researcher has been unable to get ideas clearly across to other scholars, or else he has, for one reason or another, obfuscated to such a degree that the meaning is ambiguous to all those trying to make clear sense out of it. Within the highly elusive nature of the AIDS problem, Louis Pascal claims that ideas and evidence about the "origin of AIDS" are being suppressed in the specialized academic community. He also states, ". . . I am claiming the material is so straightforward as to be understandable regardless of background." This quotation is taken from an item described as "Short Form. Issue IC4," an unpublished account from the International Committee for Academic

Freedom (an organization being formed in England). Other information on this "Short Form" includes, "Contamination is rampant in all phases of tissue culture, and attempts to expose and combat the problem have been heavily suppressed. . . . Other animal viruses will likely become serious human diseases, as AIDS has now done, if these vaccine procedures continue. . . . No attempt is made to refute the evidence, but no journal will publish it. Letters to AIDS researchers almost always go unanswered. . . . The idea has been suppressed since July 1985 when an expert panel assembled by WHO whitewashed the problem. . . . Journals . . . involved in suppression: NATURE, LANCET, NEW SCIENTIST. . . . 'There is just no way that I can publish a 19,000 word paper (even if I thought it was going to save millions of lives . . .)'. . . ." (See Appendix.)

Without attempting to judge the merits of the ideas, evidence, or findings in question, the cases that have been cited in this article have been chosen to bring to the attention of librarians that academic peer review authorities do suppress and censor, that the censorship and suppression can become determined, mean, and vicious, and that academic censorship can extend into areas as vital as research in cancer and AIDS. In their role as "mediator between the scholar and the information system," academic librarians should stand up to, and challenge the censorship and suppression that takes place during academic controversy, rather than closing their eyes to it or pretending it does not exist or merely going along with the expert peer review judgment in specific cases. Perhaps this is easier said than done. It does not seem, however, that such a challenge to academic censors would require more than the ringing rhetoric and fervent activity that librarians have been engaging in against Moral Majority preachers, Reagan, Bush, the FBI, the IRS, conservative concerned parents (or other groups), whenever they (or similar groups or persons) are perceived to be attempting censorious and suppressive policies regarding the accessibility of reading materials.

REFERENCES

1. William Noble. *Bookbanning in America*. (Middlebury, VT: Paul S. Eriksson Publisher, 1990), pp. 269, 271.

2. Herbert N. Foerstel. *Surveillance in the Stacks*. (Westport, CT: Greenwood Press, 1991), p.6.

3. As reported in *The Baltimore File*, April 3-10, 1991, p.4 (Unpublished manuscript, compiled by Prof. Serge Lang, Yale University, Mathematics Dept.). Lang apparently took the quote from an account in the *Washington Times*. Lang comments on Davis's ideas in this manner: "Here we behold a scientist going

194 *The Reference Librarian and Implications of Mediation*

against one of the basic tenets of science by relying on authority and big time certifications such as the Nobel prize, thinking it 'presumptuous' to engage in his own independent analysis.'' Lang submitted this part of *The Baltimore File*, entitled "Aftermath of the NIH Draft Report on the Baltimore Case," for publication in *Issues in Science and Technology*, a journal of the National Academy of Sciences, which published Baltimore's point of view ("Baltimore's travels") in the Summer 1989 issue. Lang's article, critical of Baltimore's views and critical of the views of scholars who supported Baltimore in this case, was rejected.

4. Michael E.D. Koenig. "Linking library users: A culture change in librarianship." *American Libraries*, October 1990: pp. 844, 845, 847, 849.

5. Charles Osburn, "The Structuring of the Scholarly Communication System." *College aid Research Libraries*, May 1989; pp. 281, 285.

6. Eugene Dong, "Confronting Scientific Fraud." *The Chronicle of Higher Education*, October 9, 1991: p. A52.

7. Serge Lang. *The Baltimore File* (unpublished). April 3-10, 1991: pp .1-3.

8. *The Changing System of Scholarly Communication.* (Association of Research Libraries: Task Force on Scholarly Communication, 1986).

9. Letter of September 12, 1986, written by Sanford Berman to Irene Hueck (an official of the Kunsthistorisches Institut, Firenze, Italy).

10. John Swan. In review of *Intellectual Suppression: Australian Case Histories, Analyses and Responses*, Brian Martin et al. (North Ryde, Australia: Angus and Robertson, 1986), *Intellectual Freedom Newsletter* September 1991: p. 149.

11. Lois Ann Colainni, Sheldon Kotzin, Nancy Selinger, "Online Identification of Published Errata Notices." In *Guarding the Guardians: Research on Peer Review* (Program of "The First International Congress on Peer Review in Biomedical Publications, Chicago, IL, May 10-12, 1989): p. 23.

12. Committee on the Responsible Conduct of Research, Institute of Medicine. *The Responsible Conduct of Research in the Health Sciences*, (Washington, DC.: National Academy Press, 1989): p. 96.

13. John Crewdson, "U.S. probe cites lies, errors in AIDS article." *Chicago Tribune*, September 15, 1991: Section 1, p. 1.

14. Richard Stevenson. "Good Scientists, Bad Science? Clinging to a 'Dubious' Position Can Destroy a Career." *The Scientist* July 25, 1988: p. 20.

15. John Crewdson, "U.S. probe cites lies, errors in AIDS article." *Chicago Tribune*, September 15, 1991: Section 1, pp. 18-19.

APPENDIX

International Committee for Academic Freedom (ICAF). Short Form. Issue IC 4.

1. Name of suppressee(s): Louis Pascal.
Address: 51 MacDougal St., apt 146, New York, NY 10012, U.S.A.
Tel no. Unavailable. Nationality: U.S.

The Mediator as Guardian   195

2. Personal: professional credentials: I have no particular relevant background and no advanced degrees; however, two pieces I wrote were published in a professional philosophical journal, and one of these was reprinted in a collection of the best work ever done in the field of applied ethics and was published by Oxford University Press (APPLIED ETHICS, ed. Peter Singer, 1986), and I have no formal philosophical credentials either. My background is unimportant in any event because I am claiming the material is so straightforward as to be understandable regardless of background.

3. Nature of invention/discovery: The origin of AIDS. Summary: Contamination is rampant in all phases of tissue culture, and attempts to expose and combat the problem have been heavily suppressed (see Michael Gold, A CONSPIRACY OF CELLS, State University of New York Press, 1986). Viral contamination of the monkey kidney cultures used for vaccine manufacture is common and acknowledged, and when the vaccines are live, no means exist for killing the contaminating virus. Attempts are made to find and eliminate contaminated batches, but these frequently fail, and many batches of live oral polio vaccine are known and acknowledged to have been contaminated with monkey viruses, such as SV-40, and to have infected millions of people. AIDS' closest relatives, the simian immunodeficiency viruses, or SIVs, have been found in all 3 monkey species used to produce oral polio vaccine. Tests for contamination would not have detected SIV, at least in earlier years. The first batch of oral polio vaccine ever used was given to Belgian colonial subjects in Central Africa in 1957-58, exactly where AIDS is now striking hardest, and exactly when and where it is believed to have begun. The same batch was used in 1958 in the city where the earliest definitely confirmed HIV-positive blood sample was taken in 1959. This same batch, made by Koprowski, was later found by Sabin to be contaminated with an unidentified virus. SIV is not very infectious when given orally, and few of those vaccinated would have become infected. Today's AIDS victims were not infected by vaccine but rather via person-to-person spread originating from those few unlucky people infected by this vaccine batch used in what are today Rwanda, Burundi, eastern Zaire, and the city of Kinshasa. All objections I have seen are easily answered. Other animal viruses will likely become serious human diseases, as AIDS has now done, if these vaccine procedures continue. Even if my particular claims about AIDS' origin were disproven the danger from other monkey viruses would remain.

4. Nature of suppression: (including whether historical or continuing today): No attempt is made to refute the evidence, but no journal will

publish it. Letters to AIDS researchers almost always go unanswered, and the few exceptions are mere perfunctory acknowledgements.

5. Duration of suppression: The idea has been suppressed since July 1985 when an expert panel assembled by WHO whitewashed the problem. I found out about it much later and wrote my first piece in late 1987.

6. Journals/Institutions/individuals responsible for/involved in suppression: NATURE, LANCET, NEW SCIENTIST, INSTITUTE OF MEDICAL ETHICS (NORWAY). All AIDS researchers have heard the idea by now, as it is "in the air," but they have ignored it.

7. End of suppression. It continues, though AFRICAN COMMENTARY agreed to publish a simplified version after Alice Walker sent them my work. Unfortunately that periodical ceased publication before my article came out.

8. References. The only published piece by researchers to accept this position is a letter by G Lecatsas and JJ Alexander, SOUTH AFRICAN MEDICAL JOURNAL, 76: 451 (but also see 452), 21 Oct 1989. They were unaware of the location of the first polio campaign, which is described in G Courtois, BRITISH MEDICAL JOURNAL, 26 July 1958: 187-90. The contamination of this batch is in AB Sabin, BRITISH MEDICAL JOURNAL, 14 Mar 1959: 678. SV-40 contamination is in BH Sweet, MR Hilleman, PROCEEDINGS OF THE SOCIETY FOR EXPERIMENTAL BIOLOGY AND MEDICINE, 105: 425-6, 1960.

9. Source(s) and price incl p&p (in advance) of five pages of further information: None available.

10. Source(s) and price of more lengthy information: (This can be itemised by class, 1 thru 8): All available from ICAF; (c) Recommended by Ivor Catt as first reading, £12 or $18, 17 April 1991; WHAT HAPPENS WHEN SCIENCE GOES BAD. The 64-page double-spaced version requested by JOURNAL OF MEDICAL ETHICS and rejected because it is very much longer than the piece asked for. "You have a potentially very important thesis . . certainly prima facie it seems a highly plausible thesis . . . There is just no way that I can publish a 19,000 word paper (even if I thought it was going to save millions of lives . . .)," Raanan Gillon, editor, 27 May 1991. (a), (b), (d), (e), further literature, information from ICAF to those who send £1 or buy (c). [N.B. If (c) has been compressed before receipt of your order, some of your payment will be returned.]

ICAF, c/o Catt, 121 Westfields, St. Albans, England.
End of short form. Date August 1991.